The Psychology of Freedom

The Psychology of Freedom

Liberty and Love
as a Way of Life

Peter R. Breggin, M.D.

Ю *Prometheus Books*
1203 Kensington Avenue
Buffalo, New York 14215

Published 1980 by Prometheus Books
1203 Kensington Avenue, Buffalo, New York 14215

Copyright © 1980 by Peter R. Breggin
All Rights Reserved

Library of Congress Catalog Number: 80-7459
ISBN 0-87975-132-0

Printed in the United States of America

Previous Books by the Author

Fiction:
> *The Crazy from the Sane*
> *After the Good War: A Love Story*

Nonfiction:
> *College Students in a Mental Hospital* (jointly authored)
> *Electroshock: Its Brain-Disabling Effects*

For Sharon Jane Breggin
and
Linda Karen Breggin
with joy in their progress
from childhood to womanhood

Table of Contents

	Page
Preface	1
Chapter One: Liberty and Love	3
Chapter Two: The Person as a Sovereign Moral Agent	6
Free Will	6
Self-determination	7
Personal Sovereignty	8
Awareness of Self as a Moral Agent	10
Awareness of Self as Separate from Others	11
Awareness of Self as Separate from One's Own Body	13
Personal Freedom Compared to Personal Sovereignty	18
Chapter Three: Self-love, Self-esteem, and Self-interest	19
Self-esteem	19
Self-love	20
Self-love and Self-interest	21
Does Self-love Lead to License?	23
Self-love and Natural Rights	23
The Self and Selfishness	24
Self-interest and Personal Happiness	25
Happiness versus Rational Self-interest	27
Self-interest versus Survival	28
Do People Always Pursue Self-interest and Personal Happiness?	29
Chapter Four: Love and Esteem for Others	31
Love and Esteem	31

Love versus Esteem 32
Love for Babies and Animals 34
Love and Mutual Interests 35
Love for Humankind versus Love for Liberty 36
Reformers and Do-gooders 36
The Equality of Selves... 38
Love Is Created, Not Learned 38
The Love Wavelength 39
Unconditional Love 40

Chapter Five: The Supremacy of Reason over Emotion 43
Emotions as Reactions 43
Emotions as Signals.. 45
Emotion versus Free Will 46
Emotion versus Reason 47
Resentment over Controlling One's Emotions 50
Is Life Fair? 51

Chapter Six: Libertarian Ideals to Live By 53
Voluntary Exchange 53
Libertarianism 56
Unconditional Ethics 57
The Unconditional Right to Self-defense 59
Self-interest and Self-defense.................................... 61
Civil Disobedience in Personal Life............................... 61
Limits on Self-defense.. 62
The Captive's Rights 63
No Assaults on Personal Sovereignty 64
When to Stand and Fight 64
The Oppressor's Fear of Self-defense 66

Chapter Seven: Self-oppression — How People Choose to Fail 68
Personal Failure... 68
Personal Failure versus "Mental Illness"......................... 69
Personal Responsibility 70
The Unconscious 70
Dreams 72
The Unconscious and Creativity 73
Attitudes toward Time 75
Oppression 76
Loss of Liberty Hurts 78
Self-oppression 78
Obsessions, Compulsions, and Phobias 80

Chapter Eight: Three Basic Lifestyles of Self-oppression —
  Paranoia, Depression, and Anxiety 83
  Blaming Others as a Lifestyle (Paranoia) 83
  Blaming Oneself as a Lifestyle (Depression)..................... 86
  Blaming No One as a Lifestyle (Anxiety) 87
  Helplessness: The Common Denominator 90
  Ed, the Maniac.. 92
  Craziness as a Failure of Nerve 96
  A Dismaying Fact of Life 97
  Courage 97

Chapter Nine: The Emotions of Self-oppression and Personal Failure —
  Guilt, Shame, and Anxiety 99
  Blaming Others and Shame 99
  Self-esteem versus Paranoid Pride............................. 101
  Differences between Shame and Guilt.......................... 102
  Blaming No One and Anxiety 104
  Fear as the Root of Guilt, Shame, and Anxiety 104
  The Fear of Death 105
  Existential Anguish 106

Chapter Ten: Guilt Is an Unethical Emotion 110
  Guilt Fails as a Deterrent 110
  Sharing Pain as a Form of Guilt 112
  The Fear of Hurting Others 115
  Jealousy and Resentment as Personal Failure 117
  Martyrdom and Resentment toward Others..................... 118
  Love, Hate, and Anger: The Differences Are Real 119
  Violence and Hate 120
  When Should You Feel Guilty, Ashamed, or Anxious? 123
  Criteria for Determining the Irrationality of Guilt, Shame, and Anxiety .. 125

Chapter Eleven: The Oppression of Children 129
  The Totalitarian Situation of the Child......................... 129
  The Severity of Childhood Oppression 131
  Techniques of Parental Oppression............................ 134
  Natural Rights and Parental Control 137
  The Very Disturbed Child..................................... 138
  Parental Rationalizations 140
  Why Parents Abuse Their Children............................ 142

Chapter Twelve: More Subtle Aspects of the Oppression of Children 144
  Childhood Oppression through Systematic Reward 144
  Conditioning Boys versus Conditioning Girls 147
  Adolescent Rebellion 148

x Table of Contents

    The Loneliness of Children 149
    The Titanic Complex... 150
    Overcompensation 153
    The Submissiveness of Children to Parents 154

Chapter Thirteen: Parenthood with Minimal Use of Force 156
    How It Might Have Been for You as a Child 156
    Children Have Free Will and Personal Sovereignty................. 158
    The Development of Ethics in the Child 162
    The Noncoercive Parent 163
    What Punishments Are Legitimate 168
    Good Reasons to Coerce Children.................................. 169

Chapter Fourteen: How Parents Can Live with Free and Happy Children . 171
    Permissiveness and Parental Self-defense......................... 171
    Compulsory Education and Other Coercive Institutions 174
    Teaching Good Habits 177
    Protecting the Child 178
    Honesty Is Not Always Your Child's Best Policy 180
    What Children Owe Their Parents 182
    What Parents Owe Their Children 184
    Terminating the Parent-Child Relationship 185
    Unconditional Love for Children 186
    No Utopian Solutions 187

Chapter Fifteen: How to Love Freely and Happily 189
    Love and Self-sacrifice 189
    Giving Love Outweighs Getting Love 191
    Desperate Need and Love Are Not the Same 193
    Nondependence and the Fear of Needing Too Much 195
    Needing People 196
    Love Can Be Painful... 197
    Love Can't Make You Crazy 198

Chapter Sixteen: Love and Sexuality.................................. 200
    An Affirmation of Sexual Possessiveness.......................... 200
    Romantic Love and Bodily Sex 202
    Men and Sex... 203
    Women and Sex.. 205
    Children and Sex 207
    Masturbation 209
    Homosexuality... 210
    Sexual Appearance 211
    Sex as Loving Communication 211
    Manipulative versus Honest Communication 214

    Keeping Lost Love Alive.. 215
    The Paradox of Liberty and Love 218

Chapter Seventeen: The Individual in the World......................220
    Confronting One's Parents 220
    Confronting Oneself as a Child 226
    Choosing a Career You Love 228
    Romantic Love and Rebellion against Authority..................230
    Knowing Human Reality 231
    Freedom from Authority 232
    The Personal and the Political 235

Epilogue: You Own Yourself..237

Selected Bibliography of the Author.................................240

Preface

I have taken the precaution of disguising the identity of everyone mentioned in this book. Anyone who thinks he or she can identify himself, herself, or a friend is mistaken, for each person has been fictionalized beyond recognition.

Yet I hope that many readers will be able to say, "I have exactly the same problem. It's as if he's talking about me." I have rarely found any personal conflict within a client that was not already familiar to me from within myself or my friends. Our uniqueness is not expressed through our problems and our failures, but through our self-directed successes.

It has taken me years to give up the temptation to create false importance by means of a complex language and a technical vocabulary. Once the most difficult ideas are reduced to simple English, the author must face whether or not he has said anything of value. I have tried to apply the stern test of plain English to the psychology of self-determination.

I also believe that any thoughtful person should be able to make sense out of himself or herself and out of life, regardless of how little he or she has read or studied great books. Each individual has one source of knowledge about life that overrides all others in importance — his or her own personal experience. This experience is available to all to be used or misused as they choose.

Because I have always absorbed what I read into my own particular viewpoint, it is impossible to footnote the various influences on my thinking. For those who might be interested, my intellectual roots lie most deeply in a tradition of personality theory and clinical observation that needs to be revived in modern psychiatry and psychology: Freud and the neo-Freudians, Carl Jung, Alfred Adler, the early Wilhelm Reich, Harry Stack Sullivan, Karen

Horney, Frieda Fromm-Reichmann, Erik Erikson, Erich Fromm, Carl Rogers, and a number of other theorists and clinicians with existential and humanistic leanings. In more recent years, my thinking has received direction from Thomas Szasz's advocacy of individual liberty and personal responsibility, and Nathaniel Branden's analysis of the rational pursuit of self-interest. In the process I have moved ethically and politically from what might be called a collectivist, altruistic position to a more libertarian, individualistic stance. What ethics and politics have to do with psychology and personal life is the subject of this book.

By more than anyone else, I have been influenced for the better by my wife and closest friend, Phyllis Lundy Breggin, without whom I may never have experienced, let alone described, unconditional romantic love. She is the bravest and most honest woman I have ever met and in the last ten years has done more to help me learn about liberty and love in my personal life than the combined influence of all the books and all the people I have encountered in my forty-plus years.

I cannot say enough about how much I value the support given my work by my literary agent, Shirley Fisher. I also want to thank Paul Kurtz, who published my first paper on the psychology of freedom when he was editor of the *Humanist* and who as the president of Prometheus Books is responsible for the publication of this book.

Most of my clients and friends have already read a private printing of this book, and many have found it useful as an adjunct to therapy or as an aid in self-development. Their suggestions and enthusiasm continue to mean a great deal to me.

Finally, I want to thank my daughters, Sharon and Linda, aged fifteen and seventeen, to whom this book is dedicated. My feelings for them first made me aware that love is enduring and filled with joy. Their gift of love to me has been one of the happiest rewards in my life.

Since this book is about individual freedom, it seemed especially important to avoid the exclusive use of male pronouns. If this has resulted in awkwardness of language, I hope that the end in this case has justified the means.

Peter Roger Breggin
Bethesda, Maryland

Chapter One

Liberty and Love

Everyone wants to be more free and everyone wants to give and receive more love. Yet few people think they can fulfill their innermost hopes for more liberty and love in their everyday lives. Most people have little hope for living their lives to the fullest.

As I begin to write this book, my son, Benjamin, is four months old. It is obvious that he wants to have everything his own way in life; and as far as I can tell, he usually does. He is rarely bothered by an upset stomach, and only twice has he endured even a minor fever — once from an inoculation and once from a cold. But most of the time he is happily involved in nursing, wide-eyed observation of the world, and playing with his mother, his father, his sisters, and anyone else who happens to want to give him attention. When he wants more nourishment or more attention, he cries aloud for it and is taken care of right away. If anyone tries to restrain him in any way, even with a hug that seems too firm or too sustained for him, he makes his complaint immediately known and is quickly held in a manner more suitable to him. He shows frustration only on such rare occasions when he seems to realize that he cannot move his hands with sufficient coordination to touch the objects that now seem so nearly within his reach. Naturally he smiles a great deal. Who wouldn't with so much loving care and attention.

How many adults have their lives so made to order? Very few. Sometimes there are objective reasons for this: physical illness; being born in abject poverty; famine; war; the loss of loved ones through accidents and illness. But in most of the Western world where this book will be read, objective conditions are not the main reasons that people suffer and sometimes kill themselves or that they fail to have more complete and self-satisfying control over their personal lives. Most people have literally *created* their unhappy lives because of attitudes within themselves.

Many people feel helpless, confused, or uncertain about how to go about living. Others doubt that anyone ever achieves happiness for any sustained period of time. Some dream of liberty and love but feel too vulnerable and afraid to pursue it. Others feel too guilty or ashamed of their aspirations.

Still others believe that liberty and love are incompatible. This is a very common idea. Love is seen as a form of enslavement, and liberty is seen as freedom from attachment. Others believe that liberty is a myth and that love is a mirage.

Often individuals do not believe that they can have any choice in what they think, feel, or do. Taught that they are the product of heredity and environment, they believe there is little or nothing they can do to overcome these influences.

Frequently nowadays, people languish while complaining about the state of the world, racism, sexism, political oppression, and social alienation, as if these have not been the common lot of humankind since the beginning of recorded history. They do little to improve their own lives or the lives of those around them, and, ironically, they also lack the courage to pursue their own political ideals for the betterment of the world.

How does this come about? My son Benjamin's sense of liberty seems to spring spontaneously from his very nature. He reaches out to seek everything he wants, and he does his very best to get it. Similarly, love comes very naturally to him. He evokes love in nearly everyone who takes the time to glance into his face. He also smiles easily and his eyes fill with adoration when he looks at his mother.

He is lucky, you may say. I have no doubt that he is. He has been born into relative material ease and comfort. He has good health. His parents love him and, for the time being at least, have been able to protect and care for him with little difficulty.

Luck is important. But I want to repeat that, for most people reading this book, chance circumstances will not at this moment be the main determinants of their happiness or unhappiness. Chance will not be the limiting factor in how much personal freedom or how much love they have in their lives.

More important, even Benjamin will soon enough find himself doubting liberty and love as ideals by which to conduct his life. Even Benjamin, I must sadly predict, will at times become his own worst enemy and refuse to make the most out of his life. This will be because of something within himself, a response of his own to the inevitable frustrations, threats, and oppressions that he will encounter in his childhood and adulthood.

How does this self-destructiveness come about? Why do people refuse to make the most of their lives? What is the human being all about? And, especially, how can he or she get the most out of life? How can any person exercise choice to the maximum in the pursuit of self-interest and in the fulfillment of personally chosen ideals? This is the subject of the psychology of self-determination.

Chapter Two

The Person as a Sovereign Moral Agent

You and I differ from inanimate objects or things, and to a great degree we differ from all other living creatures, because we have free will. We can exercise some measure of control over our lives. We can pick and choose our values and ideals and decide how rigorously, honestly, and bravely to pursue them.

On the grandest scale, we must determine whether or not we want to live and what we want to do with our lives. We must also decide whether or not we wish to strive for awareness and intelligence in our lives. We must decide to love or not to love, to take care of our children or not to take care of our children, and to work at meaningful jobs or not to work at meaningful jobs. We must decide whether to run from the first sign of tension, conflict, or danger, or whether to fight, and possibly die, for what we believe in.

Free Will

Decision making is so much a part of our existence that it is no exaggeration to describe ourselves as beings who must daily reaffirm or modify our own lives and lifestyles. We determine the style and the goals of our lives in our every thought and action. This means that the unhappy among us, as well as the happy, have created their own lifestyles and pursued their own ends and that the quality of this happiness is often determined precisely by the style and the ends that have been chosen.

Freedom to exert our will in one direction or another is the most distinguishing characteristic or attribute of the human being. To some degree, animals share this quality, but none are as free of heredity and environment as the human being. Correspondingly, no animal has anywhere near the human being's capacity to modify its environment — internal as well as external.

In common usage, free will is:

(1) the power or capacity to choose or to make decisions;
(2) the belief that choices are, or can be, voluntary and not wholly, or ultimately, governed by predetermined internal factors or external causes.

It is basic to the psychology of self-determination that free will operates whether or not the individual acknowledges it or admits awareness of it. Regardless of external pressures or internal forces, the individual makes decisions and chooses among alternatives, however limited they may be. If nothing else, the individual chooses how to relate mentally or spiritually to a situation almost wholly lacking in external alternatives. Even people who are about to die or who are physically paralyzed nonetheless decide how to relate to their physical catastrophe within the privacy of their own minds. Similarly, people who have had great emotional pain inflicted upon them must ultimately decide how to relate to that pain — with dignity and strength, or with helplessness.

Self-determination

The conscious exercise of free will by the individual is the starting point for self-determination. Self-determination is:

> the determination of one's own course of action; freedom to think and to act without restraint or coercion; self-direction.

Self-determination as an *ideal* has at least three related components: (1) the conscious, rational exercise of decision making; (2) freedom from inhibition or internal restraint, as reflected in guilt, shame, and anxiety; (3) regard for the equal rights of others to determine their own lives in their own way.

Every time I have examined someone's troubles in sufficient depth, I have been able to trace them back to decisions or actions in which the individual denied a personal role in determining his or her life. People sometimes misuse therapy, for example, by using it to find excuses for their failures in life. They use psychology and psychiatry to blame their adult problems on their childhood experiences — in effect, to prove their lives are determined by others. The more they see what their families have done to them, the less they face what they do to themselves. These people become chronic patients and remain personal failures because they do not intend to become self-determining.

In dealing with yourself or with anyone else, nothing positive can be accomplished until you decide to be as fully self-determining as possible.

Nearly all people want to become self-determining, but most people are also overcome by doubts about its feasibility, rationality, or morality. Self-liberation is a matter of learning to live by the principles of self-determination.

Beyond self-determination, there is the choice of specific ideals and goals to pursue. A person can determine the course of his or her own life and yet pursue goals that turn out to be destructive to himself or herself and to others.

Personal Sovereignty

The individual will always meet great difficulty in self-determining his or her life within the external, objective world, but one has considerably more liberty in self-determining the subjective, internal world.

By personal sovereignty I mean the capacity and the right to be in charge of one's inner, subjective world of feelings, thoughts, and decisions.

Everything of importance to the human being begins with the ownership and control of one's own feelings, thoughts, and judgments.

Personal sovereignty means more than autonomy — or the capacity to make independent choices — it means the ability to experience the full range of both the passionate and the abstract potential within oneself. The individual who is personally sovereign experiences and tests within himself or herself all human possibilities that lie within his or her potential. This sovereign person is unafraid of any thought or feeling and is willing to contemplate, for however long is necessary, any eventualities in the external world, any emotion within the internal world, and any choices that he or she may wish to make.

The sovereign man or woman is the supreme judge of the importance, validity, and value of everything in his or her personal life. This person may pause to listen to the judgment of others, if he or she wishes; but when the moment of decision comes, the self-determining person makes up his or her own mind.

It is not easy for any of us to be personally sovereign. In the process of learning more about ourselves — our thoughts, feelings, capacities, and desires — we must regularly confront and overcome new barriers to internal freedom. But we must never be led from this realization to an acceptance of limits upon personal sovereignty. From the viewpoint of the liberated individual, personal sovereignty must be treated as an absolute right and as an infinite potential. No one can know what, if any, limits are set upon the human being's capacity to think, feel, imagine, and choose. Just when it seems that these limits have been found or redefined, a new creative mind bursts out of the old confines.

Everything human — our highest potential and our finest aspirations —

requires personal sovereignty. Compared with personal sovereignty, even personal freedom must take second place. Women and men have been known to endure severe compromises of their personal freedom, including seemingly endless imprisonment, and even torture and brainwashing, without giving up their personal sovereignty. Upon release from confinement, their ethics have remained intact or improved. Other people have died for their beliefs, making clear that their personal sovereignty during life remained a priority above survival itself.

But the converse is not true. Without personal sovereignty, personal freedom loses all meaning. Of what consequence is physical freedom or opportunity when the person is unable to bring himself or herself into the experience? For the person lacking in personal sovereignty, personal freedom is a hollow possession. Sham freedom is often mistaken for true freedom as individuals wholly unable to think for themselves try to experience freedom through empty actions in their allegedly free lives.

The high priority placed on personal sovereignty by children is apparent to anyone who has been close to them or who is in touch with his or her own childhood. Many a child in conflict with a parent will prefer severe punishment, such as rejection or a beating, to confessing wrongdoing, if the child believes that he or she has done no wrong. Many children are beaten and tortured because they refuse to choose robotlike subservience to parental demands. Many adult readers may recall key moments in childhood when they decided that, no matter what cruelty befell them, they would never let it touch their inner sense of right and wrong or their stubbornly held sense of self.

Some of my clients and friends can remember deciding to endure punishment and injustice without allowing anyone to dampen their sense of justice. They decided to hide their feelings from others — accepting loss of freedom — while swearing to themselves never to forget their true aspirations. The brave child or adult under stress will attempt to maintain subjective inner freedom in relation to himself or herself, no matter what has happened to his or her personal freedom in relation to others.

When people feel compelled to compromise personal freedom, they compound their problems if they compromise personal sovereignty as well. It is bad enough to decide that you must suppress a certain type of conduct in order to survive in an oppressive environment; it is far worse to suppress your inner feelings, including your resentment of oppression and your desire to become free again. When you compromise personal sovereignty, you become a self-oppressor and are on the way to chronic personal failure; you will lose track of yourself as a person and will not be able to respond to changing circumstances. This self-oppression is the key to every personal failure.

Awareness of Self as a Moral Agent

Personal sovereignty is compromised within individuals who find it difficult or impossible to conceive of themselves as separate from their psychological processes. The person who declares "I can't control what goes on in my mind" has surrendered to a most self-defeating lifestyle.

Each person can to some degree transcend environmental experiences and the impressions these experiences have made upon his or her mind. But we have been taught to believe that we are the same as our thoughts, feelings, fantasies, defense mechanisms, mental associations, and so on. Since we know that our thoughts and feelings are in part the product of educational and social pressures put upon us, we come to the conclusion that we are ourselves inseparable from our educational, social, political, and economic experiences. We lose track of the self within us who makes decisions and selects ideals.

In our everyday lives, we continually verify self-determination in regard to our mental processes. We change our minds, we try to stop thinking certain things, and we dissociate ourselves from thoughts and feelings that we consider self-destructive or evil. We are persons who can transcend and in part determine our subjective experience of ourselves and of life.

We are moral agents, initiators, innovators, who can choose to change or not to change our minds, much as we choose to change or not to change our environment. But, unlike our relationship to our environment, our relationship to ourselves has no known or prescribed limits. We alone set the standards for our own mental, moral, and spiritual development. In the arena of personal sovereignty, we are artists working with a medium that has no known finite limitations. It is up to us to create ourselves in our own image.

Typically, the person who denies moral agency and personal sovereignty has many rationalizations about this personal failure. It would seem unspontaneous or fake to modify one's own thinking processes. It would seem dishonest to declare certain ideas rejectable or unworthy. Behind this lies a helplessness over life and an unwillingness to face the enormous and exacting task of modifying one's own inner experience.

Mental action or conduct is as real as physical action or conduct. The work, practice, and concentration required to control one's mind are at least as great as the athlete's in improving physical control of his body or as the artist's in transforming inanimate materials into an expression of life. Mental action takes time, effort, and patience. It takes courage and endurance. It requires a commitment to self-discipline and training. It requires daring.

Each person confronts or fails to confront responsibility for enlarging personal sovereignty or self-determination of the subjective inner world. If successful, he or she becomes increasingly more self-aware in deciding the quality of his or her inner experience.

Anyone who pursues self-liberation — homemaker, business person, artist, or child — must increase this control throughout his or her lifetime. Successful living requires sufficient awareness of oneself as a moral agent to remain ethical despite threats and worldly temptations. This personal supremacy means that the individual can no longer be corrupted by bribery, extortion, or other real or imagined pressures. He or she thinks and feels independently, despite the prevailing political, religious, or moral standards and despite pressures from friends and family.

The major goal of all therapies and self-help programs should be this moral supremacy of the individual within his or her own personal world.

Awareness of Self as Separate from Others

A person who is unhappy enough to seek help invariably has great difficulty governing himself or herself and often cannot separate himself or herself from others. In the first few sessions of therapy, this client may ask the therapist* questions that only the client can answer, such as "What do you think is the most important thing in my life?" or "How hard should I work in therapy?" or even "What am I feeling?"

If the client is an intelligent thirty-year-old woman who has vague, unhappy complaints about her marriage, the therapist may press her about her wishes and desires in marriage; but she may refuse to respond in terms of herself. If asked a general question, such as "What do you want to do with your life in the next few years?" she is likely to be stuck for an answer. If the therapist becomes more specific — "If you could choose any way you want to spend the coming week, what would you want to do?" — the client may still have considerable difficulty coming up with any kind of personal answer. If asked what she wants to do with her entire life, she may be dumbfounded.

If the client is a young boy, when asked about himself he may talk about what his parents want or what the other kids want. If he is older he will talk about his wife, the needs of his children, or the debilitating limits of old age. How ironic it is to hear old people justify their self-defeating patterns on the basis of age while young people do it on the basis of inexperience! Usually the person is merely repeating moralistic homilies, the childhood source of which he or she has forgotten. Individuals can become so spiritually enmeshed with these influences that they will not recognize that they fail to answer the question in terms of personal desires.

---

*The terms *therapist* and *therapy* have medical and psychiatric connotations that are incompatible with my view in "Psychotherapy as Applied Ethics" (1971; see bibliography). Alternative terms designating ethical re-education would be more appropriate, but none have gained any general acceptance. Although I am a psychiatrist, I prefer the term *client* to *patient*. It has more dignity. Besides, the people who consult me have problems to solve, not illnesses to be cured.

When such a self-oppressed person at last tries to speak about personal feelings, he or she may again end up talking about the wishes of others, now disguised more subtly as wishes of his or her own. Several women I know, when feeling particularly unhappy with themselves, will attempt to speak about their own aspirations, but their tone of voice will be identical to the one they use to mimic their mothers. They are still speaking for their mothers, but masquerading as themselves. One male client, when he tries to lift himself above the level of mouthpiece for his parents, will shift into the second person. He will say, "You want this" or "You feel that" when he means himself. Another client, although a successful businessman, cannot keep his attention focused on the question, "What do *you* want?" even when repeated time and again. His mind wanders, and he discusses vague family problems or business difficulties.

Individuals who oppress themselves not only have trouble separating their aspirations from those of others but also try not to feel any aspiration that would call up real or imagined blocks to its fulfillment. They are unable to experiment within their imaginations with any wish that at first seems beyond fulfillment. When asked "Would you want to get married again if a woman would love and respect you as an individual?" this person may answer, "There is no such woman." Or if asked, "Have you ever thought that you might have the capacity to love?" he is likely to respond, "Love is a meaningless idea." Or, when asked if he wants more sexual freedom, he will answer, "I have no experience, so how am I supposed to know?"

Alienation from self commonly becomes extreme enough for the individual to allocate his or her most personal aspirations to made-up characters who resemble the individual to one degree or another. The individual becomes master over these fictitious lives, but not over his or her own. As a child, a close friend of mine changed her given name, Stephanie, to Steven. Whenever she played games, Steven had all the fun. She had a real friend named Leah who took the boy's name Lee, and for many years of childhood Steven and Lee had all their fun in these fantasies.

In more extreme examples of self-alienation, the individual may make up a character with a wholly new name who has no apparent relationship to its author. This manufactured person then develops an independent existence filled with glory and success within the daydreams of his or her creator, who always remains on the sidelines describing and observing the successes of the fantasy character.

Such self-alienated fantasies may be harbored with embarrassment well into adulthood. Only a trusted friend or therapist may eventually be made privy to their existence. One may be tempted to denigrate such fantasies as signs of craziness, but they are best viewed as life-enhancing aspirations for power and happiness within a bleak existence. Give me a person who dreams dreams, however unreal they seem. I have more hope for this individual than for a person who accepts "mundane reality." Needless to say, the real life of an individual who sustains these fantasies into adulthood is likely to be joyless and depressed, much as that person's real life must have been in childhood, when the fantasy characters were first created.

Instead of treating such fantasies as immature and ridiculous forms of escapism, the individual should take them very seriously. They appear childish because they probably date all the way back to childhood. Their continuation into adulthood signals that the individual still feels helpless and frustrated enough to relegate personal or private wishes to the realm of fantasy. He or she has little or no hope for enjoyment and success in life. Fantasy friends are the companions of a frustrated self who must learn to confront his or her true desires with a dedication to their fulfillment. It may be entirely possible for this person to gain enough personal freedom to more than fulfill his or her fondest dreams.

Awareness of Self as Separate from One's Own Body

Nowadays, it is a very commonly held belief that "self" is identical to "mind" and that mind is identical to "brain." Here I am merely restating the modern belief that a person is his or her body and, especially, his or her brain.

This is an age-old discussion: mind versus body, the spiritual versus the material. Within certain limits, I believe that experience teaches us that there is a difference between self and brain or between the human being as a moral agent and the brain as a machine.

As moral agents, we decide what we will do with whatever body function we have at our command, including our brain function. When one man is intoxicated with alcohol, he uses it as an excuse to beat his wife. But another man may use it as an opportunity to overcome his fears of expressing more love to his wife. In each case, the person experiences emotional blunting and intellectual dysfunction but continues to make moral decisions. An intoxicated automobile driver may decide to pull over to the side of the road, or he may decide to drive his car in a dangerous fashion, risking his own life and the lives of others. Even within the decision to risk driving, he may drive in such a way as to risk his own life by staying on the outside of his lane near the guard rail, or he may decide to risk the lives of others by driving down the middle of the road.

Before I became a psychiatrist, I worked extensively in state mental hospitals where many inmates had been long ago discarded as "vegetables" into the back wards. Some of these people had very severe organic brain diseases. I learned that none of these people were "vegetables" and that nearly all could be reached on a human level, however minimal that level might be.

More recently, I have had considerable experience with individuals who have suffered the most extreme damage to their highest intellectual centers. While it is clear they have little ability to reason abstractly, to speculate, or to create, it is still possible to get in touch with the "person inside." I am thinking of one man who had been lobotomized on three separate occasions, as well as subjected to a variety of other brain-damaging psychiatric treatments. He did not become a nonperson. Instead he became a "deeply hidden" person. He could communicate, though very slowly and with great effort, and he could express warmth and affection as well as moral judgment, all within the limits of his badly damaged intellectual function.

As a physician, I have seen people die in hospitals while under the debilitating influence of both cancer and toxic anticancer drugs. To their deaths, these individuals display moral agency. Some die while maintaining their respect and love for themselves and others, while some die creating pain and havoc for themselves and others, much as they did during their lifetimes.

There is of course a degree of brain damage that makes it impossible for us to determine whether or not a moral agent is at work within the person. In my own experience, however, this occurs only at the very borderlines of complete physical unconsciousness or death. In a person who has any degree of consciousness remaining, the moral agent can be perceived at work. To return to my original example, some "drunks" pass out amid attempts to punch their friends, while others pass out peacefully in the arms of their wives or husbands.

Over the centuries, determinists have tried to link any number of physical ailments of the brain to specific kinds of conduct. Epilepsy for many hundreds of years has been said to cause various kinds of good and bad moral conduct, but actual research has failed to come up with any evidence confirming this linkage. Similarly, "minimal brain disease" has become our most recent alleged connection between mechanical brain dysfunction and specific conduct. Most commonly, minimal brain disease is said to cause a child to be "hyperactive" — that is, restless, upset, angry, and generally rebellious. Not only is there no sound evidence to support this viewpoint, but observations of children and adults with *known* brain damage show no correlation between brain damage and any specific conduct. Brain damage causes objective mental dysfunction, such as impaired abstract reasoning, but the individual can respond to that damage in a variety of ways.

The same point can be made in regard to mental retardation in children and mental deterioration in old age. Some retarded persons do have actual brain disease. But these people do not necessarily become "crazy" or otherwise helpless or unethical. As is true in the lives of most people, there is an increased likelihood that they may choose destructive lifestyles if they are rejected by their families or thrown into horrible institutions. But given a loving and responsible home, they have as good a chance as anyone to become loving and responsible. Their brain equipment is defective, but not their moral agency.

Retarded people can become very good people, and they can be both loving and loved. The same is true in regard to elderly individuals with known deterioration of the brain. They too range in their responses from being nasty old people to being sweet old people. There is nothing inherent in their loss of brain function that determines a specific moral attitude.

Many people believe there is scientific evidence that a specific genetic, hormonal, or brain defect can produce violence. This subject has generated great political controversy, especially since some of these alleged scientific opinions have been rooted in racism.* Objective reviews of the subject have found no connection between any form of genetic, hormonal, or brain dysfunction and violence. I believe no such evidence will be forthcoming, for the reason that the research is based on a false premise: moral or immoral conduct is not produced by biologic dysfunction but by free will or volition.

Our bodies do not determine our morality. An overflow of male sex hormones does not make a rapist. Hormones may increase a youthful male's sexual drive, but the person must then decide whether to become a rapist or a more ardent lover. He may even decide upon abstinence until he learns to manage his increased drive. Similarly, if there is such a thing as a genetic disposition to "aggressivity," such a disposition cannot bring with it a prescribed morality. One person may use aggressivity to become a great athlete, while another becomes a great bully. Still another may become a powerful but gentle person. As moral agents, we decide what to do with the biological drives and energies with which we are endowed. This is an obvious truth with which every adolescent male and female must daily struggle.

The effect of hallucinogenic drugs upon the individual and the supposed production of schizophrenic-like symptoms has been used as evidence for the allegedly biological origin of so-called "mental illness." Even when the individual ingests substances that have a marked effect upon perception and other aspects of mental function, the moral agent determines the quality of the experience for better or worse. One person responds to LSD by sitting happily alone within his or her distorted perceptual world, while another becomes frightened, helpless, and "crazy." Even when succumbing to panic in response to hallucinogenic effects, one person may end up harming himself or herself, while another person takes it out on others. Still another person, who senses the oncoming panic, will seek out helpful companionship. Thus, even within the phantasmagoria of a nightmarish "drug trip," the moral agent determines the moral style that the individual imposes upon the experience. Molecules do not contain morality; they cannot dictate specific actions.

---

*See Peter Breggin,"The Politics of Psychosurgery" (1975) and "Psychosurgery for the Control of Violence" (1975) in the bibliography.

Just as drug molecules or physical changes in the brain cannot create bad or unethical conduct, so too they cannot improve upon ethical conduct. Psychiatrists have confused this issue, as well as harmed a great many people, by alleging to improve ethical conduct through the use of drugs and other physical interventions into the brain and into mental function.* Tranquilizers cannot make a "better person," they can only make a more sluggish, dull, or listless person. In the case of the so-called minor tranquilizers, which many people take voluntarily in order to "relax," the drug acts somewhat like alcohol in taking the edge off mental and emotional function. Many people find this state advantageous. They use it to stave off emotional pain (as well as pleasure), but it cannot by itself improve their conduct.

In the case of the so-called major tranquilizers used in mental hospitals, the drugs make the person sluggish and immobile and can cause permanent brain damage. By "defusing the brain" or suppressing the activating system of the brain, these drugs make the patient physically and mentally unable to carry out difficult and complex tasks. The alleged "cure" is nothing more than the creation of artificial docility. But even when such drugs are poured into mental patients, some individuals decide to rebel until they are knocked into complete unconsciousness by massive injections of these substances.

In this modern technological age, in which science and the pseudo-science of psychiatry have replaced religion and philosophy, it is not surprising that "patients" and "doctors" alike seek out biological and mechanical explanations for human failure. In previous centuries when religious philosophies dominated the society, disruptive, disagreeable, and rebellious people were accused of harboring the devil within themselves; and some especially self-destructive people accused *themselves* of harboring the devil. Nowadays the same process goes on, but the philosophy is scientific rather than religious. Disruptive, disagreeable, and rebellious individuals are accused of suffering from "mental illness" or "brain disease," and sometimes they accuse themselves of the same thing. In extreme cases, some doctors attribute unethical conduct, such as violence, to misfiring brain cells, much as some patients attribute their helplessness to being controlled by "magnetic waves" and other pseudoscientific forces. Often, the views of doctors and patients dovetail, with both parties attributing the patient's irresponsible conduct to everything from vitamin deficiency to excessive exposure to fluorescent lighting. Not only is scientific evidence lacking for any of these viewpoints, but the viewpoints themselves are irrational. They confuse unethical conduct with physically impaired conduct.

---

*See Peter Breggin, *Electroshock: Its Brain-Disabling Effects* (1979), and "Brain-Disabling Therapies" (1980), in the bibliography.

Let us consider the possibility that we may someday discover ways to improve the machinery of the brain. Let us suppose that new pharmacological agents will improve everything from our hearing to our intelligence. Since children raised in starvation conditions may have reduced mental abilities, and since vitamin deficiencies can vastly impair mental functioning, there is always the possibility that new and better pharmacological agents will enhance what we now call normal brain function. While I doubt such an outcome, I do not consider it logically impossible.

But even if we can at some future date improve the machinery of the brain, we cannot in the same manner improve the morality or ethics with which the individual will use that machinery. Exactly as a better computer may be used for good or evil purposes, so too an improved brain can be used for good or evil purposes. This is another way of restating the reality that human beings create or choose their *purposes,* and that these purposes have ethical or moral aims and implications. Different people will use their brains, however impaired or improved, for different moral purposes.

The self as a moral agent will reappear throughout my presentation in such words as self-esteem, self-love, and self-determination. The self plays the traditional role of the "soul," shorn of its mystical and religious connotations. It designates the individual as a moral actor. I do not know if this self is eternal or limited to the physical existence of the body. I do not know if the self reflects a state of existence that transcends the material world or whether it is merely a refinement of the physical brain. My bias has already been expressed; I do not think that any combination of molecules adds up to a moral being. When we love each other, we are not experiencing a "uniquely harmonious oscillation of molecules"; we are experiencing one self reaching out toward another with recognition and understanding.

But the reader need not go all the way with me in this regard in order to accept the basic principles of the psychology of self-determination. Even if the reader wishes to see the self as part and parcel of the material brain, he or she can still verify the experience that the ethical capacity of the brain can work to overcome its own imperfections and disabilities and that this capacity of the brain is one of its most enduring and overriding qualities as long as a shred of consciousness remains. Go along this far with me and you have gone far enough to love and to respect yourself, to love and to respect others, and to insist upon and to recognize moral responsibility even in the face of brain damage and disease.

The realization of yourself as a moral agent, separable from the function of your brain, will be a great advantage to you. We all confront on a daily basis physical illnesses and fatigue that compromise our mental function. Most of us will experience old age with its special physical and mental disabilities. Some of us may die lingering deaths with prolonged compromises of our physical and mental function. If we maintain conscious awareness of our moral sovereignty throughout such experiences, we can continue to "be ourselves" and to live life by the ethics we deem best. This is not only a more hopeful view of life, it is a more real view. As moral agents we continue to decide what to do with our ailing bodies, brains, and minds.

Personal Freedom Compared to Personal Sovereignty

Personal freedom springs from personal sovereignty. The self-liberating individual aspires to express his or her thoughts and feelings as completely as possible and, furthermore, to implement or to act upon these choices as fully as possible. The individual desires to implement personal sovereignty to its fullest with other people and within the world. This is the aspiration for personal freedom.

Personal freedom has objective limitations, such as political circumstance, the confines of our bodies, resistance from others, and death.

Personal freedom also has ethical limitations, for no philosophical or moral system advocates total freedom, such as the freedom to commit rape or murder. The aim of the psychology of self-determination is to maximize human freedom by establishing principles of conduct consistent with the right of each individual to make the most of his or her own life.

We can now define personal sovereignty and personal freedom more exactly. In the psychology of self-determination, personal sovereignty involves:

(1) recognition and exercise of oneself as a moral agent; (2) free will and self-determination at work within the subjective, internal world; (3) the right and the capacity of the individual to be independent and self-governing within the sanctity or privacy of his or her own mind; (4) individual conscience.

Personal sovereignty is the manifestation of the person as an active force through self-awareness, self-love, alertness, honesty with oneself, clarity and rationality of thought, spontaneity of feeling, and all other activities that take place inside the person.

Personal freedom in the psychology of self-determination is:

(1) fulfillment of oneself in the external world as a moral agent; (2) free will, personal sovereignty, and self-determination, expressed or carried out in the external world; (3) the right and the capacity of the individual to conduct himself or herself as he or she pleases, free of restraint or coercion; (4) political freedom.

Personal freedom and ultimately political freedom provide the most advantageous context for expressing free will and for the development of love, creativity, and productivity of all kinds.

Chapter Three

Self-love, Self-esteem, and Self-interest

Emotions such as love, hate, self-esteem, and guilt result from our actions. They are not mysterious, magical forces that rise up to dominate our lives; they are reflections of the ways in which we choose to govern our lives. The kind of emotions that we feel follow directly from the kind of choices that we make. Choices that enhance our lives and fulfill our ideals produce high self-esteem and self-love; choices that defeat our lives and destroy our values produce low self-esteem, usually in the form of guilt, shame, or anxiety. Feelings do not determine us; we determine our feelings. We determine them for the better by the rationality of our chosen values and by the ardor and honesty with which we pursue them.

Self-esteem

As in common usage, self-esteem is respect for oneself. It is a by-product of successful living.

In the psychology of self-determination, self-esteem is defined as:

the good feeling generated by placing high value on the conscious, ethical, and rational exercise of free will, personal sovereignty, personal freedom, and self-determination.

Self-esteem rises and falls like a barometer of one's ethical life. It reflects the actual state of functioning of the individual. It is conditional: If a person's conduct is self-oppressive or other-determined, self-esteem deteriorates into guilt, shame, and anxiety.

Dictionary definitions and common usage sometimes imply that self-esteem can be inflated due to a false or exaggerated opinion of oneself. This is euphoria rather than self-esteem. It is self-destructive and typically short-lived.

Self-esteem must be distinguished from happiness associated with factors other than ethical functioning. Self-esteem is *earned* happiness, not happiness over a good meal, good health, or even professional success, except as this happiness is related to satisfaction over one's own personal contribution to these outcomes. Conversely, personal misery produced by catastrophes outside of one's control can reduce one's overall objective happiness but not one's subjective self-esteem.

As the person grows in ability to control life, self-esteem more nearly approximates overall happiness. But the two can never become identical, for we must rely for overall happiness upon the health of our bodies, the good will of other people, and the conditions of our environments. We must be prepared to suffer unhappiness from the chance loss of bodily health, loved ones, or safety.

Self-esteem cannot be sought directly or by any shortcuts through spiritual exercises or drugs; instead, self-esteem is achieved by learning to think and to live ethically or in a self-determined, self-fulfilling manner. Once ethical living is approximated or achieved, the individual discovers that he or she has self-esteem.

When I say that self-esteem is a barometer of one's ethical life, I do not mean to imply that low self-esteem is rooted in rationality, reality, or sound ethics. Nor do I mean that low self-esteem reflects a failure to live by conventional moral standards. To the contrary, low self-esteem is typically based on irrational, unrealistic principles, and often results from attempts to pursue self-destructive forms of conventional morality. Many people, for example, feel guilty, ashamed, and anxious about their initial attempts to resist arbitrary authority or to become self-determining.

What are my standards of rationality, reality, or sound ethics? This must obviously be answered in the process of describing how and why guilt, shame, and anxiety are typically self-destructive, irrational, unrealistic, or unethical in their origins. Much of this book will deal with these questions, which will be reapproached more specificially in chapter ten, "Guilt Is an Unethical Emotion."

Self-love

As a conditional viewpoint of oneself, self-esteem rises and falls according to our success and failure in self-determination. If this were our primary relationship to ourselves — if self-esteem were indistinguishable from self-love — our positive feelings toward ourselves would collapse every time we brought a serious failure upon ourselves. Because the bottom would fall out of our feelings toward ourselves, we would lose our motivation to take care of ourselves or to pursue our own self-interest and would spiral downward after every failure. Every personal failure would become a personal tragedy. Unhappily, many of us live on such a roller coaster.

Instead, we must believe in our right to pursue self-interest even after making a failure of our past and present life. We as individuals must have the capacity to generate good feelings toward ourselves simply because we value ourselves as human beings.

In the psychology of self-determination, self-love is defined as:

> the good feeling generated by placing high value upon one's own existence, human nature, life force, or self and by recognizing or understanding one's own humanity or inherent worth; joy or happiness in the presence of oneself.

Self-love and Self-interest

Self-love reflects a choice to pursue self-interest, or to seek one's own well-being, welfare, or happiness. Self-love is love of the life within oneself. It is truly love of life itself, in this case directed at one's own life.

Like the emotion of self-esteem, the fire of self-love cannot be artificially fanned. It results directly from conducting one's life according to specific principles — in this instance, the pursuit of self-interest and personal happiness.

There are so many anti-life forces in the world that living things can survive only if they vigorously *pursue* their own survival. Life may be defined as that process that seeks its own growth and survival. Human life has many purposes — as many as the individual is willing and able to postulate — but few purposes can be fulfilled without survival and without careful attention to self-interest.

Egoism is the ethical doctrine that holds self-interest to be the valid end of all actions. I have refrained from labeling the psychology of self-determination as egoistic because my concept of love extends self-interest to include the interests of others in a manner beyond what is ordinarily called egoism and because I do not believe that self-interest is the only or even the most fundamental value in life. First and foremost, I uphold the libertarian value of each person's right to pursue self-interest — a concept that will be elaborated in chapter six, "Libertarian Ideals to Live By." I believe in the *ethical* pursuit of self-interest as a valid goal.

Nor do I believe that the ethical pursuit of self-interest is necessarily the *only* valid goal. Again, the pursuit of libertarian ideals may come first, even if this pursuit does not necessarily suit one's own immediate or even long-term interests. For example, I do not believe in the use of force or fraud to achieve one's ends, even if it vastly serves one's own self-interest. While the psychology of self-determination is libertarian to the core, it is not necessarily egoistic in every aspect. However, for most practical purposes in everyday life, the pursuit of self-interest and personal happiness remains a valid and adequate standard for conduct. In my psychotherapy practice among relatively ethical persons, most of my effort goes into encouraging people to pursue their own self-interest with only occasional injunctions against interfering with the rights of others to carry on the same pursuit.

Self-love is the motivator of self-interest. Dictionary definitions of self-love are sterile by comparison to those of love, which ascribe to love an affectionate, fond, or warm attachment to others, or a devotedness, loyalty, or enthusiasm for others. The lexicologists are accurate in recognizing that we do not generally associate self-love with that same quality of warmth or enthusiasm. Instead, self-love is seen as a malignant regard for one's own most crass advantage. These dictionary definitions are useful in underscoring the direct relationship between self-love and the pursuit of self-interest; but when I speak of self-love, I also mean a warm, fond, or affectionate attachment to oneself, a devotion and loyalty to oneself, and an enthusiastic dedication to one's own advantage, well-being, welfare, or happiness. I literally mean love for oneself, with all the glowing warmth produced by love. Self-love is devotion or dedication to one's self as a source of life or to the life force as it manifests itself through oneself. It is a very spiritual attitude — a worship of oneself as an expression of life.

Self-love is not a negative or destructive force. Self-love is the assignment of value to oneself and in no way excludes the attachment of value to others. Instead, self-love suggests the capacity to love others as well as oneself. Because value is placed on one's own existence rather than upon one's accomplishments or activities, self-love implies that all people deserve to love themselves, regardless of their achievements. Self-love, therefore, leads logically to affirmation of each individual's right to life, liberty, and the pursuit of happiness.

Self-love is directly proportional to the degree to which we feel close to ourselves or familiar with ourselves. Anything that encourages us to know ourselves will encourage us to love ourselves. In therapy or in life, as we learn more about our own thoughts and feelings — as we become more self-aware — we grow in love for ourselves. This is especially true as we choose to identify ourselves as persons with all other persons and with humanity.

But as we learn more about ourselves, we will not necessarily gain greater esteem or respect for ourselves. If we have been very unethical or very crazy, we will discover many reasons to hold ourselves in low esteem. We may be critical of ourselves without languishing in guilt, shame, or anxiety. Familiarity with ourselves can breed a certain amount of disrespect for our conduct, but it cannot breed self-hate, unless we believe in the essential loathsomeness of human life and human nature. As our self-knowledge grows, we will grow to love ourselves enough to pursue our own happiness, regardless of the judgment that we must make on our past conduct. This is because life is worth loving and knowledge of life evokes love in us.

Does Self-love Lead to License?

Personal sovereignty and personal freedom do not lead to murderous, hateful impulses, precisely because they encourage self-love. Murder and hate are the expressions of a thwarted being; love, including self-love, is the expression of a being in possession of himself or herself and able to share this self-possession.

Sometimes, in the question period after one of my talks, a person will tell me that, if people were truly free to pursue their own self-interest, they would unleash murderous hatred upon each other. This is also an occasional fear among clients early in therapy. Frustrated in nearly all their aspirations, and prevented by guilt from taking even the minimally necessary measures of self-defense, individuals feel pent-up, enraged, and prepared to murder. Murder, in this context, is a last futile act to destroy those who have subjected the person to such severe oppression. In every single instance in my experience, such murderous rage results from helpless dependency: an unwillingness to encourage a change in the other person's conduct or to leave the oppressor for good. Unable to leave because of guilt and fear, murder becomes a pseudopotent solution; but once free of his or her modifiers and their effects, the individual can find better methods of self-protection without futile, misdirected murderous outbursts. He or she no longer hates.

The press and even sophisticated literature take the worst expressions of society — the haters and the destroyers — as models of human nature. Having misidentified himself or herself, and all people, with the helpless reactions of the frustrated and the unfree, the individual becomes afraid of self-knowledge. This monstrous self-image makes the person leery and even terrified of encountering still worse aspects of himself or herself. Self-exploration comes to a halt, much as explorers might turn back on reaching the alleged borders of hell itself.

Self-love and Natural Rights

Self-love is recognition of the *inherent* value of the self; hence, it implies recognition of the value of all selves. This confirms the universal quality of natural rights, or the right of each individual to life, liberty, and the pursuit of happiness. Self-love suggests commitment to all life because it affirms that each person, oneself included, deserves all that can be gotten out of life and, in particular, everything good that can be achieved for oneself.

To ensure survival, self-love must be unconditional — a self-generated, independent devotion to one's own well-being or natural rights. The individual who has been a moral failure in the past must be able to affirm: "I am a human being, however fallible, however wrong, however evil in my worst intentions and actions; I am a person, a self, a part of life, and I have the potential to exercise free will, to create, and to love — however badly I have thus far acted. I love myself, knowing myself to contain the moral capacity to transcend my past. Regardless of what I have done, I have the right to build a better life for myself."

An analogy to the critical importance of self-love in personal survival can be found in the love of a mothering parent for a small child who is as yet unable to generate independent self-love. When the parent responsible for mothering withdraws love from an infant, the infant may become robotlike and unresponsive. The baby may refuse food and die. So, too, we live in a life-and-death relationship to ourselves: when we stop loving ourselves, we stop pursuing our own self-interest, even our own survival. In extreme circumstances of lovelessness and moral chaos, people have withdrawn from themselves to such a degree that they have died without apparent physical cause.

Love for oneself must be even more constant in its attachment than love for others. We cannot reject ourselves and yet survive. We cannot say to ourselves "I quit myself," or "I'm fed up with me and plan to take a long vacation from me." People do try to withdraw from themselves in this manner, often through frantic activities, drugs, or other artificial distractions, and even, sometimes, through quiet apathy. This is a desperate condition.

The Self and Selfishness

Most people believe the mass propaganda put out against the ideal of self-interest. We have been so corrupted in this regard that many dictionaries wholly equate self-interest with petty selfishness, greed, and other destructive intentions.

Anyone who discourages you from pursuing your self-interest is really in favor of your pursuing someone else's self-interest, usually his or her own. This person wants you to devote yourself to himself or herself or to his or her ideological commitments.

Do the principles of self-love, self-interest, and the pursuit of personal happiness add up to a "selfish" and even a "hedonistic" or pleasure-seeking philosophy?

It is rarely in our self-interest to conduct our lives in a selfish manner, if by selfishness we mean "without regard to others" or "a petty preoccupation with personal gains."

Any philosophy or psychology that places so much emphasis on *each person's right* to pursue self-interest is hardly selfish in the negative sense of disregarding others. Selfishness as disregard for the rights of others runs directly counter to the principles of self-determination, which stress respecting the rights of others to pursue their own self-interest.

Selfishness can be a childish or petty attitude, and it is the individual's right to act in this manner, but it is usually not in his or her best interest. The person who is preoccupied with getting the advantage in any situation, no matter how trivial, probably feels very frightened and easily cheated. By being preoccupied with minor details, he or she is also overlooking more important long-range interests.

But the pursuit of self-interest is *intended* to be selfish in a much larger sense of the word. To understand this larger concept we must examine the meaning of "self."

When I speak of self, I designate an individual source of human action, an agent or actor, a being able to exercise free will, personal sovereignty, and self-determination. *Self*, as used in words such as self-determination, self-interest, or self-love, is the essence of the individual human being — an essence manifested in its own way in every person. It is the unique moral agent who can create or pursue personally chosen values and ideals.

On one level or another, we are each aware of this "self" and link it closely to our essential identity. We love ourselves to the extent that we are "in touch" with this self, and we esteem ourselves to the extent that we have the courage to express this self in our lives. In my own opinion, this self *is* our identity. It is not something that is "in us" or something which we "have." It is our essential being. It is exactly who we are in the most real sense of identity.

If by "selfish" we mean a person who forfeits or betrays his or her own ideals in the pursuit of petty gain, then selfishness is indeed a bad trait. But if by selfish we mean a person who pursues personally chosen values and ideals at all times and in every possible way, then selfishness is the highest form of ethics. If a selfish person is a person who recognizes the right of every self on earth to pursue self-interest and personal happiness, then the psychology of self-determination is the most selfish of all psychologies, for it advocates exactly that — the right of each person to pursue and maximize his or her own life, liberty, and happiness.

Self-interest and Personal Happiness

The pursuit of self-interest is nearly identical to the pursuit of personal happiness. More specifically, happiness is the emotion generated by the successful pursuit of self-interest in an ethical manner. Such a conclusion has two important implications.

First, it means that each person has the *right* to pursue self-interest and personal happiness as nearly one and the same goal.

Second, it means that weighing your own personal happiness is an extremely important part of self-determination. The person who determines his own life and pursues his own interests will be aware of every factor that enhances or detracts from personal happiness. If a woman, for example, finds herself increasingly unhappy in a marriage, she will not dismiss her feeling as irrelevant or unimportant. She will take a hard look at herself and her married life to find out how she is failing in the pursuit of self-interest.

It has taken me a long time to reach these conclusions, and I know they will conflict with what many of my readers believe. In our world, and in the world since recorded history, self-sacrifice has been a higher ideal than the pursuit of self-interest and personal happiness. Perhaps it will help if I describe how I arrived at the conclusion that the pursuit of self-interest and the pursuit of happiness are nearly one in the same and that these pursuits are the right of each individual.

As a child, and even as late as in high school, I had believed in each person's right to pursue his or her own happiness. But my viewpoint had been attacked on all sides, and I gave in all too easily. My convictions were then rekindled with the birth and the growth of my first two children, Linda and Sharon. At the time I was considerably involved in self-sacrifice as a way of life, and I expected it of others as well. But I noticed a wholly different attitude toward my children. I wanted *them* to be happy, and I wanted them actively to pursue their own happiness. I found myself doing everything in my power to encourage their happiness and help them to learn to seek it on their own. It became obvious to me that I loved them and wanted them to love themselves; this led me to want them to make as happy lives as they could for themselves.

Later on, I met and began to love my future wife, Phyllis. I found myself having the same attitude toward her. Though I still imposed certain "sacrifices of happiness" on myself, I never wanted to encourage sacrifice on her part. I loved her and wanted her to get everything she could out of life for herself.

Then a most remarkable turn of events took place. I began to notice that my children and my wife, Phyllis, loved me and wanted *me* to be happy. Whenever I would take an action or accept "an obligation" that made me unhappy, they did not like it. They wanted to see me happy, and they wanted me to make sure that my life went along as happily as possible. I discovered the truth that people who love each other want each other to be happy. It was an extraordinary discovery.

These revelations led me to realize that I acted as if I loved my wife and my children more than I loved myself. This made no sense at all, and even put me at odds with my loved ones, who did not want me to sacrifice for them. In effect, I had two sets of rules for living: one for those people I loved, and another for myself. It dawned on me that I owed it to myself to pursue my own happiness, just as I wanted my loved ones to pursue theirs.

I have found the same principle at work in my private practice. At earlier times when I failed to apply the right to personal happiness to myself, I found myself nonetheless promoting the happiness of my clients as individuals. With the limited exceptions I will describe — the injunction against abandoning children or interfering with anyone else's equal right to pursue self-interest — I found myself encouraging my clients to seek their own self-interest and their own happiness. Whenever I found myself discouraging a client from the pursuit of happiness, I discovered that I was acting out of perverted motives of my own, such as jealousy or guilt, and that I was betraying my client's trust in me.

Similarly, I noticed that my clients responded to my advocacy of their personal happiness by advocating mine as well. On occasions when I obviously failed to pursue my own self-interest, some of my clients would notice it and encourage me to be more devoted to myself. Part of this reflected fondness for me. Out of love, their interests had begun to approximate mine. But part of it stemmed from their realization that the happier I became, the more I would tend to encourage their happiness. Also, it is not very enjoyable to be around someone who is not happy, even if it's only an hour a day or an hour a week with your downhearted therapist.

Happiness versus Rational Self-interest

While happiness is an important gauge of whether a person is indeed pursuing self-interest, it is often an unreliable one, because happiness is an emotion, and emotions are not necessarily rational in their origin. This is a subject that will require a further analysis of emotion and reason (chapter five). Here it is important to recognize that happiness as a feeling may not necessarily reflect whether a person is truly pursuing his or her overall or even momentary self-interest. For example, a professional man may be frustrated and upset about a work-related problem he is having difficulty solving, but at the same time he may be pursuing a long-range goal that is in his overall best interests for happiness; or a woman may be pursuing a new career outside the home that is in her own self-interest and will ultimately increase her overall happiness, but at the same time she may suffer from an irrational feeling of guilt or shame about what she is doing. Conversely, a person may be delighted with a momentary pleasure that nonetheless leads toward disastrous consequences. Therefore, I prefer the concept of rationally determined self-interest to the emotion of happiness as the final gauge in setting goals.

The term *happiness* is also misleading because it is often identified with euphoric and evanescent experiences rather than with substantial and enduring ones. The satisfactions involved in ethical living and in love for oneself and for life lend a profound sense of happiness to one's existence. They are abiding and make the most firm base for happiness. But these conclusions can only be drawn from contemplation, experience, and reason, and not from hedonistic measurements of one's momentary happiness.

Happiness, as an emotion, is generated by thoughts and by actions. It is a signal of how things are going, and as a signal closely related to the pursuit of self-interest it is an important one. But it must be considered from a rational perspective.

Self-interest versus Survival

The pursuit of self-interest is often confused with the pursuit of physical survival. People do not promote their physical survival as much as they promote the survival of their values. Even very sophisticated psychologists often miss this point; but I have rarely met an individual, even the most malicious sort of individual, who put physical survival above the survival of his or her most cherished values. This is true even if those cherished values are very base, such as revenge or a desire to "get even."

Adolf Hitler is a classic example. As many others have observed, Hitler was an idealist, albeit a malicious and hateful one. Instead of placing all his resources into the survival of himself and his Third Reich, until the war's end he continued to divert important resources to other purposes, such as the extermination of the Jews. Petty criminals as well will often, out of pride, vengeance, or hate, take actions that lead to their personal injury or death.

On the other hand, people whom I respect have taken risks in order to maintain their devotion to love and liberty. Many such women and men would risk death rather than kill an innocent person or betray a loved one.

Does this contradict the concept that individuals pursue their own personal happiness? In my own life, and in the lives of others I have come to know well, happiness is not *possible* without devotion to a set of ideals beyond personal survival. If anything, the more an individual focuses upon physical survival rather than the active promotion of his or her values, the more the person becomes frightened, helpless, and overly preoccupied with failure and death. The surest way to demoralize and render a person helpless under stress is to make the person doubt his or her ideals and focus instead on physical survival.

The pursuit of happiness itself often involves risk-taking that threatens survival. Athletes risk breaking their necks because they love perfecting their abilities and because they love competition and victory as well as financial remuneration. I have taken risks fishing in Chesapeake Bay because I love the sport, because I enjoy perfecting my seamanship, and because I enjoy taking risks. I take these risks in a calculated manner. I don't "throw my life away." Nor do I cut down risk-taking to the point where I cannot enjoy life. Again, it is a matter of one's values. I value an interesting and exciting life more than I value personal survival. Put another way, I get more joy out of a life of interest and excitement than out of a life of safety. So do all happy people.

Respect for the lives of others as well as devotion to a variety of values almost always takes precedence over survival in every individual's life and in every society. Very few persons will turn to murder and cannibalism when confronted with starvation. Few will even turn to lesser crimes in the interest of their own survival. Their values are more important to them.

Despite this, some psychologists have attempted to lay down a hierarchy of values based on the conviction that the individual's first concerns are such things as "bread" and "physical survival." These psychologists believe that the individual turns to the fulfillment of higher values such as "self-actualization" and "love" only when the other necessities have been taken care of. This is untrue. Every individual, every society, and nearly every enduring value system I have come across has placed one or another value above that of the survival of the individual or the survival of the group. So does the psychology of self-determination. It places *self-ownership* or the *equal right to life of each individual* above the personal survival of any one individual. Thus, you do not have the right to interfere with my freedom or my survival, even if your freedom or survival depends on it; and conversely, I do not have the right to interfere with your life, even if my life depends upon it.

By putting the promotion and pursuit of values above physical survival, I do not endorse those philosophies that preach love for others ahead of love for self, or self-sacrifice rather than the pursuit of self-interest. I recognize the individual's *right* to sacrifice himself or herself, if he or she so chooses, but I do not *advocate* it. I advocate a set of values and ideals that promote, above all else, each person's right to pursue a full and happy life for himself or herself, as well as for loved ones and anyone else of his or her choosing.

Do People Always Pursue Self-interest and Personal Happiness?

Whether or not people always pursue self-interest is, in part, a semantic problem. A major theme of the psychology of self-determination is the manner in which individuals defeat themselves and bring misery on themselves as a direct result of their own actions. As the saying goes, the individual is often his or her own worst enemy. From this perspective, not everyone consistently pursues self-interest.

From another perspective, it is possible to argue that individuals do pursue their own self-interest and happiness, regardless of their stated intentions or their obviously self-defeating conduct. In evolving the theory of self-oppression, I will show how children turn on themselves in order to placate their oppressive, destructive parents. In acting against their apparent interests, these children are in reality attempting to make the most of a bad situation. Similarly, people who turn to suicide have reasons for doing so, and these reasons involve a weighing of self-interest. They may find the prospect of death less terrifying than the prospect of going on with their wretched lives; or they may believe that in killing themselves they take revenge on hated parents. Such decisions are almost always irrational; they are almost always self-oppressive actions that overlook real possibilities for living a better life. Similarly, altruistic self-sacrifice is almost always motivated by a desire to allay terrible guilt feelings. But these sacrifices result from decisions, and the pursuit of self-interest, however twisted, can usually be found motivating the decision-making process.

For most purposes, however, we do not need to know whether or not people always attempt to act in their own self-interest. We need only determine our own *right* to pursue self-interest.

The psychology of self-determination advocates the pursuit of self-interest, but in a manner that succeeds and at the same time respects the rights of others to pursue their own interests as well. By itself, this might make for a philosophy in which individuals live in wholly competitive relationships to each other. This is in part true; most of us live in a competitive relationship with most of the people in our lives. Love is the value that changes competition with others into a search for mutual satisfactions. Love turns self-interest into mutual interest as loving individuals become almost as concerned with each other's welfare as with their own. Voluntary exchange, which we have yet to examine, also establishes limits on competition that provide the opportunity for each individual to get the most out of any relationship without abusing his or her partners.

Chapter Four

Love and Esteem for Others

When I speak of love, I mean assigning such high value to a life or to an aspect of life that knowledge or awareness of its existence brings joy and meaning into one's own life.

Love toward whom or what?

Love toward any expression of life or toward any principles or ideals that enhance life.

It can be love for life itself or for human liberty; it can be love for oneself and one's personal creativity; it can be love for a child or for an adult or for an animal or a plant; it can be romantic love with its desired sexual union with another person. Love is the placement of a high value on any aspect of life and existence.

Love is self-generated from within the individual and does not require a response from the loved person or object. Love recognizes and accepts the nature of that which is loved. Love is the emotion associated with full awareness of life.

Love and Esteem

Self-love was defined as the placement of a high value upon oneself and, ultimately, as joy in the presence of oneself. It was described as the source of our natural right to pursue self-interest, personal happiness, and self-determined ideals.

Love for others is exactly parallel. In the psychology of self-determination, love for others is:

the good feeling generated by placing high value upon another person's existence, human nature, life force, or self and by recognizing or understanding another's humanity or inherent worth. Joy or happiness in the presence of another person.

Love for others is the source from which we grant rights to others. Through love, we recognize the common humanity of all people, and we assign to them the rights inherent in being human. Love for others as an abstraction becomes love for liberty or the right of each person to express his or her human nature freely and in his or her own way. The concept of love implies that life itself is good and that people can and should respond happily to all expressions of aliveness and vitality in themselves and others.

Esteem, as we discovered in examining self-esteem, depends upon the degree to which we respect functioning or accomplishment. In the psychology of self-determination, esteem for another person is:

> the good feeling generated by placing high value upon another person's conscious, ethical, and rational exercise of free will, personal sovereignty, personal freedom, and self-determination.

Esteem can grow with familiarity, but it can also decline. It depends upon our evaluation of the other person's conduct or accomplishments.

Much of the confusion we feel in our personal relationships results from the failure to distinguish between love and esteem for other people. Much of the confusion within the various philosophies of individualism stems from the failure to realize that human beings yearn to love each other, regardless of whether they hold each other in esteem, and that love can grow even in the absence of esteem.

The overall value we place upon another person will reflect a combination of love and esteem.

I am also aware that love and esteem cannot always be distinguished, and that the definitions are somewhat arbitrary and perhaps not complete or perfect. In particular, certain attitudes that we esteem in a person also make it more possible to love that person. Individuals who are open, trusting, and able to communicate — all estimable traits — will also make their humanity more visible to us and, hence, make themselves more lovable. Similarly, individuals who respect our rights, again an estimable quality, will also seem less threatening to us and enable us to love them more easily. Overall, we can esteem people who make themselves more lovable. However, despite areas of overlap, love and esteem are often separable.

Love versus Esteem

It is entirely possible to love a person whom you do not hold in very high esteem. A man who is very much afraid of aggressive women might choose to fall in love with very passive women whom he cannot hold in high esteem. A woman who is very afraid of her own aggressiveness may love very powerful men, regardless of whether she esteems them. A parent may love a child who has become viciously unethical.

Conversely, a person may hold considerable esteem for a number of people without being able to get close enough to them to feel love for them. The person may also esteem their work from a distance, while he or she might find them too difficult to relate to on a personal level.

Conflicts between love and esteem can be very frustrating. We desire to love those whom we esteem, and we desire to esteem those whom we love. Humans thrive on feeling love and esteem for others. But the pursuit of self-interest depends upon our rationally distinguishing between the two.

The nature of love brings an astonishing phenomenon into understanding: if we know and value another person's humanity or self better than we know ourselves, we will love the other person more than ourselves, and we will pursue his or her self-interest more than we pursue our own. It is not unheard of for an individual to care more for a lover than for himself, or for a parent to love her children more than herself. In the extreme, individuals worship the leaders of religions, cults, and political parties, and sacrifice their own needs and even their lives for these leaders.

But while it is possible to love another more than oneself, by any standard of self-interest it is a form of personal failure. That many people love others more than they love themselves indicates that many people deny their own existence. This is a major source of self-sacrifice — the actual failure to know oneself as a representative of humanity.

Because love is a matter of getting in touch with the universal quality of self, it becomes logically absurd to love others more than we love ourselves. We cannot love them more than ourselves without being out of touch with ourselves as human beings.

It is more rationally plausible to hold another in higher esteem than oneself. People who are failing in their own lives can hold successful individuals in greater esteem than they hold themselves and can improve their own lives by practicing the principles they learn from these more successful people. But they should not love these people more than they love themselves; they should not pursue anyone else's self-interest at the expense of their own.

People who have been closely connected tend to care about each other's fates, even when esteem has fallen. This is because love is generated by knowledge of common humanity. Far too often, however, this alleged love is nothing more than guilt. The individual who claims to love his spouse on the basis of years of contact often turns out to experience little or no joy in her presence. Remember that joy in another's presence is the emotional expression of love; and, if it is absent, one should cast a cynical eye on any claims of loving. Be especially skeptical if you find someone claiming to feel love for others when his or her primary experience is not joy in their presence. Prolonged relationships in the absence of joy are inevitably bound together not by love but by the sticky glue of fear and guilt.

Love for Babies and Animals

The impossibility of equating love and esteem is most obvious in a mother's or father's love for an infant. When my own son, Benjamin, was born, my wife's love for him did not depend upon how smart, ethical, brave, or self-determining he was at birth. It did not even depend upon his "cuteness" or his ability to respond to her, neither of which were wholly apparent in the first minutes after his birth. Her love blossomed and made her as bright as a new morning sun on the first instant that she beheld him at the moment of his birth. It radiated still more the first time she held him to her breast. My own response was a little slower in coming. I was glad he was around and felt fondness for him in the first few weeks. But when he first smiled at me, I too fell in love with him. At four months he could recognize me, and he gave a special smile that was obviously reserved for me, and my own smile beaming back at him was filled with love.

Some of these feelings may be "pride" in fatherhood or motherhood — something akin to self-esteem. But it is a grave mistake to equate such feelings with this profound joy that parents can feel in the presence of a young human being. This is the response of one life to another. It is pure love. It is akin to the love that lovers experience on meeting each other, long before they have any inkling of their individual accomplishments. It is an experience of life recognizing life and taking great joy in that recognition.

Parents who have retarded children and people who work with retarded children confirm this experience. These adults reach out toward their retarded loved ones with the same strength of attachment of any parent who has more reason to take pride in the abilities or accomplishments of his or her children. True, retarded people have accomplishments, but, more important, they can be especially human in their openness and honesty.

For people who do not have such experiences with children, I can often make the point in regard to their feelings for animals. Often an otherwise loveless childhood has been saved by a child's love for a pet. Was the pet esteemed? Hardly. Or, if so, it was but a minor issue. What mattered was the pet's willingness to give and to receive love, and the pet's willingness or ability to make its own "human qualities" apparent to the child. It is no wonder that some people love animals far more than they do people — it is often easier to recognize and share their essential "humanity."

I believe that these simple observations are among the most important in living a happy life. We must be able to love others — babies and grownups alike — for their humanity. More important still, we must be able to love ourselves in the same manner with an unconditional joy in our own existence.

Love and Mutual Interests

Self-love as the granting of high value to oneself is the source of our devotion to self-interest and personal happiness. In the same fashion, love for others as the placement of a high value on others is the source of our devotion to their interests and happiness.

As love for another person grows, that other person's interests increasingly become identical to one's own. If one person fully loves another, interests often become identical. Loving partners may seldom find any need to distinguish between their individual interests. They find such joy in each other and such trust in each other that they often find themselves thinking of the other's interests. There is no sacrifice in this; there is cooperation or mutuality. The two people become a team serving a shared interest.

A loving twosome can add to each other's lives and to their overall welfare more effectively than a person solely devoted to his or her own interest. Every human being grows up with a certain amount of guilt, shame, or anxiety about the pursuit of self-interest. I may find myself turning against myself and my own happiness but may try to rationalize it. My wife, on the other hand, may be more objective about my problem and point out to me that I am treating myself in a way in which I would never treat her or anyone else whom I love.

Parents, therapists, and anyone who has a contractual agreement to serve the best interests of another should obviously function in the same manner as a loving friend. The therapist is motivated by professional ethics and a contractual agreement, as well as by affection. But the outcome should be the same — careful, scrupulous dedication to the self-interest of the person whom he or she serves. Unhappily, parents and therapists alike often fail by encouraging self-sacrifice in those with whose interests they are entrusted.

When both esteem and love are present, a relationship can become as rich as possible. A mutual trust can develop based on both a knowledge of the other person as a person and a respect for that person's ethics and conduct. When such a person is chosen as a partner in friendship or in marriage, most barriers can break down, including the barrier between one's own interests and the interests of the other. A close friend is one with whom there is such a degree of trust and understanding that distinctions between individual interests rarely need to be made; instead, both partners are on the lookout for each other's interest.

Earlier I implied that anyone who urges you to think of the interests of others is making himself into your enemy. Similarly, anyone who urges you to look out for your own interest is becoming a friend. The people whom I wish to be my intimates are people whom I value so much that I find little or no distinction between their interests and mine at any given moment or they are people whom I trust never to take advantage of our intimacy to the detriment of my own interests.

Love for Humankind versus Love for Liberty

A person who loves life itself may choose to do things that foster the good of the human race. He or she may write books with which to communicate truth or beauty to the world, or he or she may donate time or money to people or causes. Love for people may in part determine these activities, while other motives are also at work, especially an inherent interest in the activities themselves.

But I hasten to add that love is an experience, not a fantasy. I have never met anyone who seemed to me to conduct much of his or her life out of a genuine love for humanity. I have met people who claim to love humanity, but usually they seem motivated by guilt or by a desire to use "love" as a lever for forcing themselves upon others.

On the other hand, I do know people who love liberty as an abstraction and who are willing to fight for liberty. I have generally found that these people are more rational and less likely to do harm than those who purport to act out of love for their fellow persons.

When you fight for liberty, you fight for the right of all people to pursue their own lives in their own way; and as a result, you are more likely to have a good effect. But you must make sure that you really are fighting for liberty and not for your right to impose upon the liberty of others with some preconceived notion of your own about how people ought to act.

Reformers and Do-gooders

If we give free time to a political group, write unprofitable books, volunteer to help retarded children, or give money to help the starving, we are likely to end up resenting what we are doing, unless we really love it. We will grow bitter and attempt to exact some covert price from those we allegedly serve out of love if we have not loved the process itself. We can become a menace; failing to have altruism rewarded, we attempt to make our impact through force.

I smell self-deception and fraud when I see a man or woman devoted to a cause when that man or woman neglects self-interest or the mutual interest of those who are nearest and dearest. To reach out to humanity with a hand that trembles from personal failure at home is to defraud ourselves as well as the people nearest and dearest to us.

People who tell themselves "I cannot be happy as long as this or that atrocity exists" do not stop for a moment to examine the implications of their viewpoint. They have consigned themselves and those dependent upon them to misery and frustration throughout their entire lifetimes by making their happiness await the creation of a world free of injustice. They must ask themselves why they have adopted such a self-defeating philosophy.

It is best to devote oneself to the betterment of humankind only if one is already in a position of enormous personal security, and only if one has genuinely reached a spiritual height from which one is able to identify the common humanity and liberty of large numbers of individuals. Most people would do far more good for themselves and for humankind if they spent more time loving and liberating themselves and those nearest to them. My wife, Phyllis, reminds me that, if everyone did this, there would be much less need for reformers.

This brings me to an apparent paradox. I have declared that love for others is the basis for our affirmation of their natural rights and that love of liberty is really an abstract principle that draws upon love for people or recognition of their common humanity. If it is so difficult to love others on a grand scale and if our affirmation of human rights in general depends upon this attitude, how and why do people respect the rights of others?

In reality, there is little love for others in life, and there is little respect for their rights. We live in a world in which most people pay little or no heed to the rights of others. Most of what passes for concern for the rights of others is little more than guilt combined with fear of them, or fear of the law, or fear of some tyrannical religion. This is a wretched situation to say the least, but it is the situation.

Is the solution to this the encouragement of guilt and fear? These oppressive solutions have failed throughout time, and they will continue to fail. They do not serve the general interest nearly so much as they serve the interests of those who elevate themselves to positions of authority as politicians, priests, psychiatrists, and other secularly empowered moralists. We would do better without these alleged benefactors of mankind. But the need for authorities in society is a complex political and economic question — one that we need not solve in order to apply these principles to our personal lives. I am sure that anyone with enough sense and rationality to read this book would do far better in life if he or she gave up being controlled by authorities, or by guilt and fear, and instead relied upon his or her own rationality.

Practice the ethics and discipline required to love yourself and your own liberty. Start with self and gradually expand the circle of your interests to those whom you have learned to love. Give as much as you feel and no more.

The Equality of Selves

Are some people inherently unlovable? Are they as individuals somehow unlike the rest of us, somehow malevolent in their essential nature? If so, it would seem rational to see them as devoid of natural rights. It might even seem rational to use every means at our disposal to stamp them out. This is the attitude that the individual must assume if he or she is to encourage the destruction of other individuals. Instead of loving them as people with inherent goodness, he or she must hate them as people with inherent evil.

I believe that we are born with the capacity to do good or evil, rather than with any specific inclination to do either. We are born with a moral capacity, not a specific morality or lifestyle.

Evil is a choice, and a few people choose a wholly evil life. The most Hitleresque individual usually reserves an area of life for creative self-expression with one or another person, with plants or animals, or even with some element of the physical universe that he or she recognizes, understands, and hence treasures.

Even when people fail to display any vestige of decency, they retain the capacity to choose to do good. They continue to have free will and therefore the potential to change. I believe it is possible for one to stay in touch with everyone's essential humanity and therefore to respect the natural rights of all human beings.

Assume that people are lovable, even if you lack the desire to feel it or to act upon it. Recognize their right to life and liberty. Do not make yourself into an omniscient god who can determine whether another human being deserves love from anyone. Do not take it on yourself to declare any life devoid of all potential value. Do not be the one to decide that a person has no redeeming human value. Never do this to yourself or to anyone else, no matter how badly you or anyone else has conducted his life.

Remember that you are a person too. If you take it on yourself to judge others to be of lesser *inherent* value, you may be tempted, at times of disappointment and frustration with yourself, to make the same ill judgment of yourself. Only if you wish to make yourself a murderer or a suicide victim is it useful to think that any person can be inherently and irredeemably evil; only if you wish a person to kill himself or herself is there any purpose to convincing that person that he or she is essentially evil.

Love Is Created, Not Learned

On occasion when I speak in public about the capacity to love as an inherent human potential, someone will retort that love has to be learned and that you cannot expect a person to love if they have been abused throughout life. Not long ago, a person stood up after one of my talks and declared that I was contemptible for implying that the battered, abandoned, or poverty-stricken child had a chance to become a loving adult. He told me that my emphasis upon personal sovereignty and free will in the face of miserable or wretched childhood conditions was insulting to the poor and the deprived on the earth. But this person's viewpoint is the one that degrades and demeans people who have gone through wretched childhood experiences. It states that they cannot pull themselves through and become loving.

Spiritual leaders have risen from deprived backgrounds. Often it appears that men and women who strive to contribute to the world derive their motivation from a decision to change precisely those abuses that they themselves once endured in excess. What marks the person who values others is not that he or she has been valued by others but rather that the person has decided to love and to improve the quality of his or her life and the lives of others.

Most loving persons will know what I am talking about; life is too tough and too frightening for most of us to become loving without mustering a great deal of courage. We encourage helplessness and failure when we encourage adults to look anywhere other than toward themselves as the source of their ability to love.

Within my hierarchy of values, it is much more important to love than to respect. A person who acknowledges love for himself, for others, and for life is far ahead of the person who feels respect with little love. Love is the first principle of life. Animals feel love, while it is highly doubtful that they feel esteem. Children feel love long before they can feel esteem. Two people often fall in love long before they develop esteem for each other. Love is an affirmation of life; it is the starting point for every rich personal experience.

The Love Wavelength

In my own personal life and my psychotherapy practice, I refer to being on the love wavelength. A person on the love wavelength glows with a feeling of warmth for people and, in particular, for the people nearest to him or her. The loving person radiates a feeling of interest and delight in life that draws others to him or her and that lends him or her a special aura. People tend to feel good around such a person and he or she tends to feel good around other people.

The question, "How do I become more loving?" can now be answered. Begin with yourself. Base your life upon self-love and the pursuit of self-interest. As you become more willing and able to take care of yourself and to fulfill your own aspirations, you will increasingly find others with whom to share your mutual interests and aspirations. Self-recognition will lead you to recognize others and to love them.

Love is our spiritual connection to life: the more we feel it, the more worthwhile we will feel and the more productive we will be in our own interest as well as in the interests we share with others.

Love for life itself may be the highest ethical or spiritual attainment, for it means that we feel joy over existence itself; but it can only be achieved on the foundation of love for self.

Unconditional Love

The more value you or I place upon life or the more we love, the less vulnerable we become to the vicissitudes of life. When we discover that love is fully self-generated, it becomes unconditional, or noncontingent, and our capacity to remain loving becomes relatively independent of circumstances.

The more independent we become as loving persons, the stronger the sense that we are the source of our own feelings, regardless of what is going on around us. We discover we can maintain our love in the face of rejection, disappointment, or loss.

The concept of unconditional love is pivotal in understanding personal failure. All personal failure derives in part from a denial of love toward oneself, another person, or an aspect of existence. These denials begin with decisions to withdraw love or value in response to fear, disappointment, or frustration.

When love becomes conditional or contingent upon others and their reactions, or upon circumstances, one's own mental stability is thrown into constant doubt. To leave one's affirmation of life up to changing conditions is to place one's existence at the mercy of these conditions.

There are so many dangers and uncertainties in choosing to cherish a single other person with all our hearts that no one would ever dare do it if he or she focused solely upon the conditions or circumstances in life that surround loving. Every human being, you and I included, must face the fact that death can rob us at any time and without any warning of the person whom we have chosen to love. We can be robbed of almost anything we hold dear, including our children, our parents, the health of our bodies, or the aspirations we have tried to fulfill.

The only way to love fully is to make love unconditional — independent of both circumstances and the reactions of others. Love for a person must be so unconditional that it does not depend upon that person's willingness to love in return.

I want to be very specific about this, because it is at the root of most failures in longterm love relationships. If a parent truly loves a child, or if a man loves a woman, he must recognize and accept this as his self-generated feeling toward the other person, rather than as a trade or reciprocal of the other person's love. Only in this way can a loving relationship survive.

The self-defeating tendency of conditional or contingent love can be simply illustrated. If a woman's love grows in doubt whenever her husband's love for her seems in doubt, the relationship will spiral downward at the first sign of uncertainty on his part. Similarly, if she develops some doubts about her love for him, and he backs off defensively, then again they enter a collapsing cycle that can come to no good end. In a loving relationship, each person must take sole and absolute responsibility for staying in touch with his or her love for the other person. A love relationship is not an affair of 50-50 sharing, but of two fully independent loving individuals.

Unconditional love does not create a trap for the loving person. This person does not have to remain in a relationship that proves too one-sided, too frustrating, or too oppressive. The loving person may wish to withdraw and seek another person who can return love and help create a new and deeper love. But, even in the act of leaving a relationship in which one's love has not been reciprocated, the person must not make believe that he or she no longer loves the person he or she is leaving. Instead, one must stay in touch with being a loving person while nonetheless determined to look for a better relationship. This may lead to great pain, but it will not lead to psychological collapse.

The trap is not in loving but in making one's love dependent upon others. If I will not love people unless they are available to me, then my sense of loving becomes dependent upon them. I then easily become their victim. I am trapped by my dependency.

Let us say that I love a close friend who unexpectedly changes and does nasty things to me, so that I am forced to keep my distance from him, if only to protect myself. I have at least three options. First, I can decide I never did love him and that my evaluation of him before his nasty conduct was false; I can throw into doubt my own previous perceptions. Second, I can decide I no longer love him, in which case I have lost touch with a person who has the potential to lead a creative life, and who still may do so. Or, as a third alternative, I can decide that my love can remain as real and alive as ever, even though I cannot now get close to him or approve of his present conduct.

To the extent I am able to pursue the third alternative, I will experience myself as a person who is loving, and I will experience a rich sense of my relationship to others, independent of the vicissitudes in their conduct. In doing this, I leave myself fully open to the return of my friend, without embitterment and recriminations, anytime he should choose to change.

By remaining loving, I also keep open the possibility that I, too, have been wrong in my actions or feelings and that my own conduct may have helped create the current distrust or pain. By remaining in touch with my love for the other person, I help maintain an atmosphere in which he may be able to love me as well, despite my real or imagined offenses against him. I leave open the possibility that I too may be the beneficiary of an unconditional love that perceives my true good nature despite my weaknesses or liabilities.

Upon first hearing, the concept of unconditional love can evoke a frightening specter of bondage. This is because love is confused with enslavement and with need. To understand unconditional love as a freely chosen and self-fulfilling attitude, we must understand voluntary exchange (chapter six), the context in which it is most safe to *express* or to *act upon* love.

Chapter Five

The Supremacy of Reason over Emotion

Emotions are feelings; they have a bodily component. Sometimes this component is more obvious than it is at others, but it is usually perceivable. Positive emotions, such as self-esteem and self-love, are associated with good feelings within the body, and negative emotions are associated with unpleasant feelings within the body. Emotions are reactions; they are largely involuntary. They can function as signals about our state of being, but they cannot make decisions for us.

Emotions as Reactions

Many psychological theories postulate that emotions are closely related to involuntary bodily reactions. The identification of emotions with bodily reactions is important, but it is certainly an oversimplification. What we usually call emotions have many highly intellectual and even rational colorations to them. When I *feel* love, I am not merely sensing physical reactions. I am experiencing a whole realm of intellectual, emotional, and bodily responses. Nonetheless, especially in the simpler emotions, specific bodily components can be identified, such as sympathetic nervous system arousal in fear. Thus, when you or I become afraid, certain bodily reactions automatically take place and heavily affect the feeling of fear.

Despite the complexity and little understood nature of emotions, it is important to underscore their more or less automatic nature, and, in the case of the more highly developed emotions, such as love, hate, and happiness, to understand their dependence upon specific volitional thoughts, or the choice-making process.

Emotions and their bodily responses can sometimes be changed merely by *deciding* to change one's thoughts. As a child, for example, I learned that I could control my heart rate by evoking fearful or calming thoughts that would alternately speed up or slow down the rate. Mystics and others who have trained themselves to control their so-called involuntary or autonomic nervous system probably do so by a similar method of controlling their thoughts. This leads to changes in their emotions, or at least in the physical reactions associated with their emotions.

While it is possible to change our emotions by changing our thoughts, it is rarely possible to change an emotion by merely "thinking it away." This is not because emotions dominate thoughts but because our thoughts are so interrelated with our lives and our lifestyles that it is no easy matter to consistently change a pattern of thought. In regard to important thoughts, we may have to change a whole way of life.

Suppose that a person is afraid of snakes. In some cases, this fear might be controlled by the thought "There are no dangerous snakes around here." But as hard as the person may try to think this thought, he or she might fail. Perhaps there is a lingering suspicion that poisonous snakes are indeed in the area. Or perhaps the fear of snakes bears no relationship to reality. It may be rooted in some earlier fearful experiences with snakes that the individual has never mastered, or it may be a symbolic defense against more complex and overwhelming childhood fears. In either case, the individual may not be able to "will away" the thoughts of snakes (and the corresponding fear reactions) without dealing with earlier experiences in which the fear originated. Nonetheless, it is the thoughts that stimulate the fears, and these thoughts can ultimately be changed by rational processes, including discovery and mastery of the original fears.

Because psychologists and psychiatrists have failed to see that so-called involuntary emotional reactions stem from specific kinds of controllable thoughts or mental decisions, they have tended to think of the emotions as dominating the intellect, reasoning, and choice. Few people ever attain sufficient voluntary control over their minds to control their emotions with any regularity or certainty, but this merely confirms the lack of personal sovereignty in the typical individual's life. As personal sovereignty is strengthened, emotional control is strengthened. This does not lead to robotlike unspontaneity but, rather, to the mature ability that we call emotional control.

This view of emotions as subject to control indirectly through the intellect is foreign to many individuals. But without this understanding the individual remains the victim of haphazard and often painful and conflicting emotional reactions to a poorly controlled mental life.

Emotions as Signals

The most refined or complex emotions, such as esteem and love, can be understood as reactions that signal whether or not our decisions and actions are consistent with our values and ideals and also consistent with values and ideals that promote our best interests and our happiness. The problem becomes very subtle and complicated in human beings, because the human being can gain some satisfaction from fulfilling chosen values, even when these values are ultimately misguided, in the sense that they affront important aspects of human life, such as love for oneself and others and respect for one's own rights and the rights of others.

By paying close attention to emotional reactions within oneself, the individual can develop a better idea about how well he or she is doing in "living up" to his or her own values. When these values are "lived up to" and the individual nonetheless remains unhappy, it may then be necessary to make a further evaluation of the values themselves to see if they are inconsistent with personal happiness. If an apparently successful life culminates in unhappiness, this signals the need for a re-evaluation of the values that the individual has thus far successfully pursued.

It is not always so easy to know or to recognize one's emotions. All unconsciousness partially involves an attempt to avoid a painful emotion, just as all consciousness involves recognition of emotions. Furthermore, emotions may be in conflict. It may feel good to eat or drink a great deal or to indulge in promiscuous sex, but it may feel bad to live with the after-effects. Furthermore, our values may be self-destructive, confused, or unethical, so that the good feeling we get in fulfilling them runs smack into negative feelings associated with their very fulfillment.

Some emotions deserve more attention than others because the actions that cause them are more relevant to the person's most important values, including self-interest and survival. Thus, the emotions related to love and esteem are among the most important. But this is itself a judgment requiring reasoning. It is a judgment about life. Emotions themselves are reactions. It requires reason to disentangle, identify, and rank them in order of importance.

Some very potent emotions have no direct relationship to self-esteem and self-love; but like all emotions, they reflect the positive or negative state of the individual's life. Pain, for example, is a very powerful and compelling reaction to physical hurt. Hunger, sex, and other so-called drives, when satiated and unsatiated, have their corresponding positive and negative emotions. These emotions are important signals regarding actions that will harm or serve the person. But even the emotions associated with hunger, sex, or physical injury take a back seat to those associated with self-esteem or self-love. This can be easily demonstrated by the fact that people will endure starvation, sexual abstinence, or great pain in order to maintain their self-esteem and in order to love and, conversely, that failures of self-esteem and perversions of love often motivate persons to seek self-inflicted starvation, sexual abstinence, and pain. The human being is so oriented to himself or herself as a moral agent with free will that he or she embellishes sex and hunger with subtle meanings before fully enjoying them. A person can even enjoy pain in the pursuit of these pleasures if the pain serves to relieve any guilt or inhibition associated with them.

Emotions are signals, but they cannot become guides. Emotions may light up a problem, as pain discloses injury and anxiety discloses a threat to oneself or one's values, but reason must be used to choose a better path — to analyze the confused or self-destructive values that lie at the root of the emotions and to select better, more consistent ideals or goals.

The lack of self-direction and personal satisfaction in some contemporary individuals has been reinforced by popular psychologies that place feelings above rational thoughts and the expression of feelings above rational discourse and ethical self-control. The most important feelings of all, love and esteem for oneself and others, require a high degree of rational self-determination within a carefully developed ethical system.

Emotion versus Free Will

We now have the information to solve a paradox within the psychology of everyday life — that people have free will and yet their emotions are largely involuntary, biological reactions.

When a person feels anxious, his or her body pours out epinephrine, causing a dry mouth, sweaty palms, and a rapid heart beat. Anyone monitoring his or her pulse, respiration, or other physical signs might be able to guess that this person is anxious.* Guilt also has a set of somewhat less specific physical responses. When it reaches the proportions of depression, the person's entire body seems to slow down, particularly the digestive system. Appetite declines, the bowels become sluggish, and the skin loses its luster. In the case of shame, the response can be highly specific: the body blushes.

We can struggle against these involuntary reactions, and with grave concentration and some practice we can modify and control them within narrow limits. We can become especially good at hiding them from others, but we are fighting a losing battle against our own nature. If we succeed in suppressing one set of physical responses, we may end up with another in the

---

*Because the emotions are so complex and highly integrated with volitional and intellectual processes, the guess might be wrong. The person might be experiencing another emotion with similar bodily signs, or the person might have his or her own particular emotions in regard to bodily signs usually associated with other emotions. See Peter Breggin, "The Psychophysiology of Anxiety" (1964) in the bibliography.

form of palpitations, gastritis, or something as mundane as diarrhea.

This may dismay and disappoint people, but it is the truth; we cannot escape the reality that emotions are determined by how we choose to think and to act. We cannot eradicate painful emotions with drugs or spiritual-therapeutic trickery. We cannot even overcome them by willpower. Instead we must exercise free will and reason to change our ethics and conduct in the direction of greater self-determination and self-interest. Ultimately, this generates self-love and self-esteem.

Emotion versus Reason

By *reason* I mean rational thought, including discrimination, inference, logic, and all other systematic intellectual functions required in the attainment and evaluation of truth or knowledge. Reasoning is an orderly, systematic process that can be examined, dissected, or studied for its inner consistency and step-wise progression.

We may not always reason in an obviously orderly or systematic fashion; intuitive leaps or sudden insights can put together an understanding in the twinkling of an eye. But the final product of this short-cut process must meet the test of orderly and systematic reasoning. Our intuitive leaps must meet the standard of rationality, even though we have been able to skip a few intermediate steps in coming to our conclusions. Those in the philosophy of science who have touted the flash of insight in the scientific method have wholly neglected to mention that many millions of people have flashes every day but that few of these flashes are then integrated into a rational system that includes relevant elements of earlier thoughts and that can be communicated to others for rational analysis and criticism. Ultimately, all "flashes of insight" must be subjected to the highest human process, abstract reasoning, or the capacity to make generalizations or to extract principles from perceptions of existence or reality.

Despite much romanticizing by others to the contrary, abstract reasoning is the most necessary human capacity. All the higher animals can feel. My dog, Ted, demonstrates unbounded enthusiasm for life and responds to the slightest affection with an outpouring of affection in return. I love Ted, but I would not rely on him to discriminate too carefully among people or to rationally judge my relationship to him. An unscrupulous master could make sport of Ted's feelings, manipulating him in moments from a happy, jubilant creature to a skulking, fearful, and unhappy beast. Ted is nearly all reactivity. While he does have a very particular style of relating in a very warm fashion, he rarely modifies it to fit changing circumstances. His lifestyle is rigid; there is little choice in it. He neither sets his own standards nor decides how seriously to pursue them. Rare is it for him to rise above his reactions to make choices that change his behavioral direction. It is rarer still to see him sit in contemplation before making a decision about how to govern his conduct. Mostly, he rests or he reacts.

Precisely because animals are dominated by emotional reactions rather than by reason, they can be manipulated by people and in many cases domesticated for human purposes. So, too, people who allow themselves to be dominated by feelings or emotions rather than by reasoning can easily be controlled by others who play upon their emotions. Sometimes these individuals believe that they have achieved a degree of strength and even independence by virtue of their relatively unbridled emotions. The man who is easily provoked to feel rage against others may believe he is "strong" or "independent" in regard to others. In reality, he is dominated by the people who can stimulate him so quickly and easily to rage. He can only become strong and independent by subjecting his emotions to conscious control or self-determination.

In brain damage, the superordinate function of reason and abstract reasoning is confirmed by its loss. The frontal lobes fill up the forehead region, distinguishing the human being from all the flat-foreheaded animals, and are required for the proper functioning of reason. When these highest human centers are damaged, abstract thinking is the first and most obviously impaired function. The individual loses the ability to think about himself or herself, to anticipate the future, to plan ahead, and to make generalizations or draw abstract principles from his or her inner experience or from the outside world. The lobotomized person especially loses those more abstract emotions associated with free will and ethics, such as esteem and love or guilt, shame and anxiety. As the husband of a lobotomized woman told me, "She cannot love anymore." The lobotomized or brain-damaged person often experiences a marked loss of self-determination, rendering him or her more docile and easily controllable. This unfortunate outcome has been repeatedly and systematically used by psychiatrists to gain control over difficult or rebellious patients.*

Reason is linked inextricably to free will. Reasoning, unlike feeling, is a series of choices. The individual chooses between one alternative and another in creating a rational process of thought. The individual who seems dominated by feelings seems to move from one reaction to another without making choices and without reasoning; his choices and his reasoning processes have been relegated to the unconscious. In reality, he is dominated not by emotion but by hidden, obscure, or unconscious reasons and values. He is dominated by his own chosen helplessness, his own unknowingness, which then brings chaos to his feelings. Faulty reasoning and self-defeating standards or ideals are at the root of his emotional turmoil.

---

*See Peter Breggin, *The Crazy from the Sane* (1971), *Electroshock: Its Brain-Disabling Effects* (1979), and *"Brain-Disabling Therapies"* (1980), in the bibliography.

Reason and emotion are not necessarily at odds with each other; but to repeat an all-important point, when reason and emotion contradict each other, reason should take over. Let us say that a man loves a woman, but his reason tells him that this woman fails to meet his most important standards. She is nasty, cold, unreasoning, stupid, and abuses her children; but he feels he loves her. What is he to do? He must use his reason to discover the cause or source of the reaction he is feeling. Perhaps he has misidentified his emotion and he feels guilt instead of love. He feels bad about not loving her the way she loves him. Or she evokes in him a childhood commitment to rescue his mother and save his younger brother and sister. Having realized this, he becomes free to leave her. Or perhaps she has some genuine qualities that remind him of a woman whom he truly loves. Knowing this, he can then decide to seek out this more valued person.

A woman may feel like killing herself and yet rationally conclude that this would only serve the interest of her enemies. A man may feel like giving away his fortune but decide he has been trying to assuage guilt from childhood. Often a new, rational understanding conflicts with emotional reactions to earlier irrational thoughts, actions, and values.

Think about the last person you saw who praised emotion over rationality. The odds are that this person was an oppressor, the victim of an oppressor, or both. Oppressors play on emotions to control the reactivity of their victims, and the oppressed in turn play on the guilt of their oppressors in order to remain helplessly dependent. Suppressive fathers pretend to be rational with their children, but their alleged reasoning is but a flimsy cover for guilt-provoking moralisms. Oppressive mothers may pretend to be rational with their children, but this is a cover for their spiritual rejection of their children.

The fundamental relationship between oppressor and oppressed manifests itself as an emotional one devoid of rationality. Oppressed people — like their oppressors — often suppress themselves by luxuriating in emotion. They drive themselves sexually, take drugs to give themselves feelings, and indulge in mystical games. Feeling helpless, they give up their rationality to authoritarian philosophies or political systems, to oppressive religions, to irrational and self-destructive love affairs.

Intense emotions lend color and much of the beauty to life. Beautiful emotions — such as those associated with a sexual climax or with a musical crescendo — are the product of a highly rational person. At their most exalted, these emotions are earned by an individual who has rational understanding of love or music. Anyone who thinks that he or she has achieved great heights of emotional experience in sex or in music in proportion to personal ignorance, rather than in proportion to understanding, has fooled himself or herself. He or she is missing out on life's peak experiences and doesn't dare to admit it.

People mistakenly equate rationality with emotional coldness because rationalizing or false reasoning is often used to disguise lovelessness and authoritarianism and to enforce oppression. Children are taught that it is irrational to want sex, to be bored by school, or to desire respect from their parents. They are *told* it is irrational, but no rational explanations are given. Rationality is more often on the side of the child who realizes that the authority is not working in his or her self-interest or in the interest of anyone over whom the authority is exercised.

Resentment over Controlling One's Emotions

Many people resent the need to control their emotions. They want to say anything they feel or to act on any feeling under conditions in which greater responsibility is required. In most life situations outside the home, these people realize that they cannot give free play to their spontaneous or momentary feelings. On the job, shopping, in a restaurant, and in numerous other circumstances, other persons would not put up with their displays of emotions. But in the home with their loved ones, especially their children, and in therapy, they express their resentment about self-restraint and try to act upon their most irrational feelings. As one mother said to her daughter, "If I can't show you exactly what I feel, who can I show it to?" Of course, she can only get away with it with her daughter. Similarly, husbands and wives who are models of deportment in public dump their emotions on each other endlessly in private. New clients in therapy, who restrain themselves everywhere else, may anticipate the therapy as the one place where there are no restraints and where they can "unload" on the therapist with impunity.

In the early stages of therapy, it may be necessary to explain the importance of rational conduct and ethics during the therapy session and to remind the individual that therapy is a place to learn self-control rather than to forsake it. Clients may ask me, "Do you want to hear everything I have to say, even if it's going to hurt you?" I don't respond, "Oh, yes, fire away at me." Instead I suggest that these clients impose rationality upon their feelings and present what they have to say in a manner that will communicate their inner state without unnecessarily antagonizing me. Therapy, as well as our intimate personal relationships, requires us to be rational and to be ethical in order to preserve its integrity.

Sometimes a client will protest that I don't want him or her to be "honest" with me or with his or her loved ones. This is true if by honesty is meant unbridled emotional destructiveness. Emotions do not reflect "the truth." A person can choose the manner in which to express or to describe what he or she is feeling. If a person is feeling nasty, he or she can explain that feeling without becoming nasty. If a person has hateful thoughts, these thoughts can be presented objectively without becoming hateful. Their unethical nature can be acknowledged as they are described. Instead of "emotional honesty," I favor emotional control through reason and ethics.

The individual who wishes to ventilate emotion may believe that self-control is a form of self-suppression or loss of liberty. In actuality, the compulsion to express all emotions regardless of their nature or effect usually stems from feelings of helplessness and frustration developed in childhood. The individual may be reacting to parents who refused to tolerate the expression of any emotion. Or perhaps the individual was encouraged to act irrationally in order to justify the parents' desire to treat him or her as a child. The possibilities are infinite, but all attempts to tout emotions at the expense of reason and ethics are rooted in helplessness and frustration.

In therapy, I encourage my clients to feel as fully as they can. If they are talking about childhood losses or painful conflicts, I will gently urge them to express their feelings. It is possible to express these feelings powerfully without succumbing to them. It is possible to express the pain without actually becoming its helpless victim all over again. Clients must keep an adult perspective on the pain they are experiencing or the experience will only reaffirm their helplessness.

Is Life Fair?

You can decide for yourself to develop your capacity to reason in the pursuit of self-interest. You can become a self-determining person, and you can find others to love, in accordance with reason, self-love, self-interest, and your other self-determined values. Or you can take the other road. You can choose not to love yourself. You can choose not to use reason to pursue self-interest. You can become other-determined. Ultimately, you will find others will hate you as much as you hate yourself. Each of us must choose how to live life, and our choices will influence the quality of our lives, as well as the quality of every other life we touch.

While we can use reason to improve the outcome of our lives, I do not wish to imply that life is fair in the sense that life deals us all the same cards. Some people have the deck stacked against them from the start; they are born into conditions that guarantee them short, painful lives. Others are born into conditions that provide many opportunities for long, productive, and healthy lives. Nor are the cards dealt out evenly after birth. Some people are lucky in avoiding accidents, ill health, and war, while others are not. Only the most mystical religions claim that such obvious injustices have some hidden justice within them. Only the most utopian political ideologies claim that most or all injustice can be eliminated through radical political solutions. The unfairness of life will be with us for the foreseeable future.

I do not wish to suggest that all religious attempts to deal with the injustice of life are necessarily stupid or pernicious. Nor do I wish to suggest that we should give up the search for better political solutions. What I do suggest is that there is a definite boundary between the inherent, objective injustice in life and the type of justice that the person may achieve for himself or herself through personal actions. The psychology of self-determination is solely concerned with the *latter* — the justice a person can achieve through his or her own rational thoughts and deeds. This is why it is psychology and not politics or religion.

In order for there to be justice in any situation, the situation must be under the control of the individual. Then and only then is the individual responsible for the outcome. The task of each person is therefore to increase control over the internal and the external world and to impose as much rationality upon it as he or she is able. This cannot be done by complaining about the "unfairness of life," which is already apparent to anyone who bothers to look around. It can only be done by giving full attention to whatever justice the individual can create within his or her own life as well as within the lives of those with whom he or she shares mutual interests and love.

You cannot know your own limits in determining the quality of your existence, but you must set your personal standards as best you can. You cannot know whether tomorrow will be threatening, opportune, or indifferent; you must have courage. But the more you exert rational control in the pursuit of self-interest, the more you increase your chances of enjoying a happy life and the more you will succeed in making the most of whatever life turns out to offer.

Chapter Six

Libertarian Ideals to Live By

Given that we have free will, what sort of relationships should we choose to build with other human beings? What do we owe our husband, our friend, our business partner, or our child? What do they owe us? Is it every person for himself or herself? How do self-love and love for others get translated into ethical conduct?

Voluntary Exchange

When people get together of their own free will, they usually have an exchange in mind. They expect to get something in return for giving something. In happy personal relationships, the exchange usually involves intangibles, such as companionship, sex, relaxation, entertainment, and security. While love is unconditional and not dependent upon an exchange, loving persons surely *hope* for an exchange in which both partners feel love for each other. Because self-esteem and personal happiness are so much at stake in these personal relationships, I'll focus upon them, although the libertarian principles examined apply equally to business and professional exchanges.

Principles of free will and personal responsibility lead inevitably toward the ideal of voluntary exchange or voluntary relationships, whether these relationships are as personal as romantic love or as political as the enforcement of a Bill of Rights or a Declaration of Independence.

A voluntary exchange is one in which both partners are able to exercise free will, personal sovereignty, and personal freedom. Two conditions must be met before any relationship can be called voluntary. First, the relationship must be free of force or coercion or the threat of force or coercion. This rules out intimidation, scare tactics, and extortion, as well as outright physical force. Second, the individual must not be kept from knowing the nature of the relationship that is being entered, otherwise he or she cannot be said to be entering it voluntarily. This means that there must be no lying, misrepresentation, fraud, or other tactic that pulls the wool over the eyes of either participant. In short, for a relationship to be voluntary, it must be free of force and fraud.

In our personal lives, force and fraud are more commonplace than meets the eye. A man wants sex from a woman and bullies her physically in order to obtain it. More subtly, a man who wants sex may lie and say that he loves a woman in order to talk her into it. More shamelessly, he may play on the woman's guilt in order to get her to satisfy his needs. In either instance, he imposes a morally or psychologically involuntary relationship upon the woman. More subtle forms of manipulation, such as playing on guilt feelings, may not fit into a political definition of coercion, but in the context of self-determination, emotional manipulations can be as coercive as outright force or fraud.

People forget that an involuntary exchange is invariably an unjust one from the viewpoint of the individual subjected to it, otherwise the individual would have made the exchange on a voluntary basis. Whenever you pressure someone to do your bidding by playing on guilt feelings, by ridicule or shame, or by misrepresenting the nature of the exchange, you have usurped the other person's personal sovereignty and personal freedom. You commit a moral crime any time you form a relationship in which the other person has anything less than full knowledge of the conditions that you plan to impose. You commit a moral crime against the other person any time and to whatever extent you form a relationship by any means other than by reason and by a fully explained, aboveboard voluntary exchange.

Involuntary impositions upon us harm us regardless of their apparent outcomes, because we have compromised our personal sovereignty and personal freedom. If against our better judgment we are pushed into a business deal that turns out well financially, we have nonetheless given up self-determination and self-esteem in the process. If we spend an evening with a person because we felt too guilty to turn him down, we nonetheless suffer even if we turn out to enjoy the other person's company. We have let ourselves slide in the direction of other-determination and inevitable personal failure, especially if we use the good outcome to justify further forfeiture of personal sovereignty.

Fortuitous benefit from involuntary exchange will at best be very rare in most of our lives. Only voluntary exchange opens the way for individuals to use relationships to get what they want. On the personal level, you can establish expectations and criteria for what you will accept in any given friendship, love affair, or marriage. Since the relationship is voluntary, you cannot impose your expectations upon the other person — but you can refuse to enter into a relationship if you don't like what is being offered, and you can terminate the exchange if it fails to meet your expectations.

Many people think an individual has a right to a fair return in his personal relationships. It seems to them that a father should expect a reasonable amount of attention from his children, and that a wife should be fair in her expectations of love from her husband. This concept of fairness encourages personal failure, for it is bred of guilt and shame over the wholehearted pursuit of one's own self-interest. More maliciously, it is bred out of a desire to force more out of the exchange than the other person is willing to give. Unless you have made a legal contract, "fairness" should rarely enter into negotiations between friends. Friends should give what they want and not what one partner deems is fair. An individual can and should seek a maximum exchange in every relationship, but he or she must fully respect the other person's desires.

If the individual is not free to seek everything he or she wants from a relationship, then the relationship is not fully voluntary. Furthermore, if the individual does not attempt to use this freedom to obtain everything he or she can from a relationship, the individual stifles himself or herself while degrading the other person by setting limits on that person's potential to give.

How a person can go about pursuing self-interest without abusing others will be the subject of much that follows; but basically he or she must not attempt to pursue self-interest through force or the threat of force, or by more subtle forms of coercion, such as fraud, dishonesty, and deception.

People grow afraid that this ideal of voluntary exchange will end up with one individual or group dominating and exploiting another in the pursuit of self-interest. Whether or not this is true in the political world, in your personal life you do not have to become an exploitative or coercive person, nor do you have to put up with it. You can find friends and loved ones with whom to establish voluntary relationships that satisfy your self-interest and your ideals, while reserving your right, and your friend's right, to withdraw anytime the relationship becomes disappointing, coercive, or simply boring.

You will get more — and you will give more — once you make your personal affairs as voluntary as possible, and once you demand the highest possible standards. As you begin conducting your personal life upon choice and upon your right to maximum exchange, you will become a happier and a more productive person. You may have to disappoint someone, such as an unrequited love who has been trying to force an exchange from you; but you will make others still more happy as you offer yourself to them freely in a mutually agreed upon fashion.

Libertarianism

Voluntary exchange is a libertarian principle. According to *The American Heritage Dictionary,* a libertarian is:

> (1) one who believes in freedom of action and thought; (2) one who believes in free will.

This two-part definition is commonly given by dictionaries and exactly represents my usage in the psychology of self-determination. Note the connection made between free will and personal freedom. Natural rights theory, as developed by philosophers, observes that human beings are endowed with the ability to choose and to reason and that this is the unique attribute through which the human being reaches his or her full potential. Given this capacity to choose and to reason, the human being must therefore have the right to express his or her choices and reasoning processes through freedom of action.

You were born with the ability to make decisions based upon your reasoning processes and you have the right to do it — regardless of what anyone else says to the contrary. Self-liberation involves throwing off the influences of those who have suppressed your natural rights and, in particular, throwing off your own tendencies to suppress your natural rights in your efforts to get along with your oppressors in your childhood, in your home, in the office, or within the wider world.

Libertarians believe in a society in which individuals can determine their own lives and pursue their own self-interest or happiness without interference from others. They believe that force is never legitimate, except in self-defense. Libertarianism has been variously described as the philosophy of *voluntary association, noncoercion, and individual freedom.**

The definition of what constitutes aggression, force, or coercion is central to libertarianism and will be developed from a psychological viewpoint throughout this book. But while libertarians dispute various subtleties, they agree that there is entirely too little freedom in the world today. Libertarians want to maximize personal freedom far beyond the usually acceptable limits in modern politics, philosophy, and psychology. From your viewpoint as a person, this means that any legitimate libertarian psychology promotes your ability and your right to become far more independent and free than any other philosophy or psychology.

---

*For an application of libertarian theory to a general critique of psychiatry, see Peter Breggin, "Psychiatry and Psychotherapy as Political Processes" (1975), "Needed: Voluntaristic Psychiatry" (1975), and "Therapy as Applied Utopian Politics" (1974), as well as other relevant titles in the bibliography.

Unconditional Ethics

As moral agents, people conduct their lives on the basis of ethics. Their conduct is determined by their principles of right and wrong. But in most cases, these ethical principles are inconsistent, poorly articulated, contradictory, and often destructive to themselves and to others. The typical person goes from one situation to another in life without a consistent philosophy of life.

When I use the term *ethics,* I will usually have a more specific meaning than ordinary dictionary definitions. I mean *rational* ethics and I mean *libertarian* ethics. By ethical conduct I mean libertarian conduct. In the psychology of self-determination, "ethical" does *not* mean "in conformity with community standards of right and wrong"; it means "consistent with rationally self-determined ideals or values."

In the psychology of self-determination, ethics are unconditional. This means that the individual can and should remain self-determining under any and all conditions, while respecting the equal right of others to remain self-determining. This is another way of saying that libertarian values and ethics can and should be applied without compromise to daily living.

Here are four applications of the principle of unconditional ethics that will clarify its intent.

First, under no circumstances treat others by antilibertarian standards. Regardless of their bad conduct toward you, and regardless of their bad conduct toward themselves, you must not be seduced into treating them unethically. You must not use force against them, except in defense of your own liberty or the liberty of others.

Second, under no circumstances permit others to treat you without respect for your freedom. Even if you have done something dreadfully wrong, do not let others use this as an excuse to abuse you. Never let your mistakes become a justification for succumbing to others.

Third, never assault your own freedom. If you have done something wrong, understand it, undo it if possible, and determine not to do it again. But never make yourself feel miserable over anything you have done. Never abuse yourself.

Fourth, under no circumstances compromise your own ethics, even though many others are compromising theirs. Rampant dishonesty, fraud, or brutality all around you is no excuse.

Conducting yourself according to the principle of unconditional ethics is the backbone of self-esteem — confidence and respect for yourself.

The unethical conduct that we see around us is used by nearly everyone as an excuse or rationalization for continuing or increasing one's own unethical conduct, and this leads to spiritual deterioration and to personal failure. Such conditional conduct in effect puts you at the mercy of any unethical person who comes along. He can make you become like him! A liberated person concentrates, first and foremost, on his or her own feelings, thoughts, and performance, regardless of the conduct of others.

You are probably breaking the principle of unconditional ethics whenever you think, say, or act upon any of these excuses:

> He made me do it.
> Under the circumstances, I had to do it.
> He did it to me first.
> She deserved what I did to her.
> They don't deserve to be treated any better.
> Anybody would have done the same under the circumstances.
> I shouldn't have done it, but everyone else was doing it.
> Nobody can be good all the time.
> I'm only human.
> I wasn't old enough (or didn't know enough) to understand what I was doing.
> How was I to know it would turn out so badly?
> I had to get even.

Remember that the principle of unconditional ethics applies to yourself as well as to others. Therefore, you are aggressing against yourself if you begin muttering anything like the following to yourself or to others:

> I guess I had it coming to me.
> How can I feel good knowing what I did to you?
> I deserve to hate myself.
> I am hateful, worthless, etc.
> I expect too much of myself.
> I need to be punished.

The idea that we should never aggress against ourselves reflects self-love and is more radical than the idea that we should never aggress against others. Yet the most common form of personal failure — guilt and depression — is closely related to a conviction that we *should* suffer.

The principle of unconditional ethics is most difficult to apply where the individual is most personally involved — in family conflicts. During separations and divorces, it is not infrequent to see people go crazy as they up the ante in abusing each other to make up for real and imagined abuse from the past. It is rare indeed when one partner steps outside the arena and determines to no longer give or take abuse, but such an action is the only sane or self-liberating one. Similarly, children who grow up with a realization of how they have been abused sometimes hang onto their parents in order to gain vengeance on them. Typically, an individual cannot get free of his or her parents precisely because he or she can't bear to let them get away with what they have done. The old family in-fighting continues when the now-grown child could step away from it.

The principle of unconditional ethics is at the opposite pole from all ethics that tell us that we are or should be reactions to our environment, to reward and punishment, and to the ailments of our brains and bodies.

The principle of unconditional ethics raises many concerns in individuals who distrust the capacity of the free individual to choose and to reason.

First, it is objected that unconditional ethics will foster a zealot who remains unwilling to listen to others or to modify his or her own views. But a conviction that one must remain ethical at any and all times should instead encourage a person to face the truth at any and all times, as painful as it may be.

Second, it is objected that great misadventures and even atrocities have been committed by people in the name of carrying a given ethic to its logical extreme. While this is true, it does not argue against unconditional ethics. It only demonstrates the power of ethics, and the importance of good ethics. Since time immemorial and to this very day, dictators and ruling classes have slaughtered, crushed, and subjugated their fellow humans beneath antilibertarian, totalitarian philosophies; it is time that women and men espoused liberty with equal zest, consistency, and devotion.

Third, it is objected that unconditional ethics place a great burden upon the individual, who must make sure that his or her actions will not bring unnecessary or unjust harm to others. This is true — but that same burden always remains upon the individual, whether he or she adopts a traditional ethic or one of his or her own devising. More important still, it is the intent of unconditional ethics to place full responsibility in the hands of the individual, with the single imperative that he or she not use force or fraud against others.

In addition to these and other objections, there is the general reluctance to adopt any "ism," including libertarianism. I believe that all isms are dangerous, with one exception, and that is the ism that supports individual freedom. Libertarian philosophy is based upon the conviction that liberty is the highest moral value and the context within which human beings thrive.

Some of the most practical concepts in personal liberation are based upon unconditional ethics, including the unconditional right to self-defense.

The Unconditional Right to Self-defense

The unconditional right to self-defense is one that you can use every day of your life. When you have mastery of it, you will be far more able and secure in any life situation. Its application may do more to improve your life than any other single principle.

The unconditional right to self-defense declares that, whenever you feel attacked, harmed, or threatened in your personal relationships, you have the right to use the minimum necessary force to protect yourself and that you and only you must be the judge of when you have been attacked, harmed, or threatened. The unconditional right to self-defense in personal relationships is:

> an ethic advocating the right of the individual to use the minimum sufficient force in personal relationships to defend himself or herself from harm under any and all circumstances, as well as the right of the individual to decide independently when and if something is harmful or destructive to him or her.

There are several important elaborations of the unconditional right to self-defense:

> The individual has the right to protect himself or herself from any kind of harm, including harm inflicted by (a) those with good intentions, (b) those with legitimate grievances, (c) those whom the individual has harmed in the past, and (d) those who harm the individual unknowingly, unwittingly, or unintentionally.
>
> The individual has the right to determine on a purely subjective or idiosyncratic basis that an action or a relationship is harmful or no longer worthwhile.
>
> The individual has the right to terminate any personal relationships with friends, spouse, or parents, even if the partner in the relationship believes that the termination is unfair, too painful, or devastating. The only exception to this is that parents may not reject their dependent children.

It is most important that the individual use only the minimum necessary or sufficient force in self-defense. In voluntary relationships, terminating the relationship is usually sufficient to end all aggression between the partners and ordinarily constitutes the upper limit on the amount of justifiable force.

While these definitions provide wide latitude in determining when one has been aggressed against, they place stiff restrictions on the degree of force that can typically be used against an aggressor. If a relationship is voluntary, or if escape is possible from an involuntary relationship, the direct infliction of harm upon the aggressor will rarely be justified. Only when one individual is *physically trapped* by another individual are inherently damaging means of defense justified. In personal relationships there will almost never be justification for harming an aggressor beyond the indirect harm caused by backing off or by removing oneself from the situation or the relationship. My intention is to emphasize the individual's *freedom of choice* in choosing lifestyles and companions, including the freedom to personally reject any and all persons from his or her personal life.

Most people doubt their right to make a subjective judgment about what constitutes harm to them. They feel they have no right to pursue their own personal desires to be left alone while watching television, to eat dinner free of harassment, to wear the sort of clothes they wish, or to have their own idiosyncrasies. They are ashamed to admit that it bothers them when their wife makes jokes about their weight or when the boss treats them like a dummy or when their girlfriend is late for every date. They also assume that they deserve punishment even if they know that they never again plan to repeat the actions for which they will be punished. If they are children, they also assume that the authority of their parents is legitimate, even though they had had no choice in selecting their parents.

Self-interest and Self-defense

The unconditional right to self-defense is a requirement not only for the pursuit of self-interest but also for love for others. You cannot begin to love to the fullest until you can protect yourself to the fullest. In all ways you will be more able to enter into life and to participate actively with other human beings in cooperative ventures when you are sure of your right to defend yourself under any and all conditions.

Most people want to be creative and want to love. They want to venture out into the world more courageously, and they want to relate to others in a free manner. None of this can begin until the person has embraced the right to defend himself or herself. But once a person has begun to act upon this principle, the person rids the space around him or her of harassment, ridicule, chronic putdowns, and any other unwanted control or manipulation. As much as possible, the person learns to clear his or her space of everything that seems offensive.

Civil Disobedience in Personal Life

The right of the individual to become his or her own authority and to reject oppression in his or her personal life is equivalent to civil disobedience in political life. Happily, the hazard of applying this principle in one's personal life is far less than that of applying it in the political arena. Recognizing the pun on *civil,* we can become civilly disobedient toward our friends, spouses, or parents with much greater ease and with much less cost than we can become civilly disobedient toward the tax collector. But since most personal misery evolves from our personal lives, we can apply civil disobedience where it will most markedly and quickly benefit us as individuals.

Remember that you have sovereign authority to break any contract that turns out to offend libertarian principles. If you discover that you have knowingly or unknowingly given away your right to self-ownership or to self-defense, unilaterally break the contract.

Even the courts recognize that a person cannot legally sign himself or herself into slavery. Slavery is illegal; the individual cannot make it legal. The individual may act like a slave, if he or she so chooses, but the individual cannot create a legal condition of slavery by signing away his or her life to another person. If the other person tries to implement it, the courts will refuse to honor the contract.

This should be as true in your own personal relationships. If you discover that you have pledged yourself to a personal relationship in which you have been coerced or defrauded — such as a typically oppressive marriage — you have the right to terminate it, regardless of how many promises you have made or how many papers you have signed. If the courts do not recognize your legal right, you retain the moral right. Your problem becomes a practical one — how to evade imperfect legal justice — rather than a moral one. You have the right to be a free person, regardless of what the government says.

Limits on Self-defense

The unconditional right to self-defense as a libertarian ethic is subject to a most important condition — the individual cannot use force *except in self-defense*. Furthermore, you cannot indulge in "overkill," but must restrain yourself and use the minimal necessary force. Any use of excess force makes you an aggressor. The fact that the man attempted to rob you, for example, does not give you the right to rob him after you have subdued him. You only have the right to take your own money back and to bring him to the authorities for trial.

That your daughter has hit you does not give you the right to spank her once you have stopped her aggression against you. That a man has defrauded you does not give you the right to defraud him after you have discovered and stopped him. Vengeance always indicates excessive force or coercion.

The principle of minimal force also applies to those who feel the need to defend themselves against you. If you have insulted or harmed someone, he or she has no right to insult or harm you beyond that which is necessary for self-protection. Your bad conduct does not justify bad conduct toward you — only the minimally necessary force to stop you from continuing what you have been doing.

Here is a vignette to illustrate the principle. Your girlfriend has said that you're a male chauvinist pig, and you feel offended.

"Maybe I ought to show you what a pig I can be," you declare, and you make a menacing gesture at her with your fist.

"Don't ever threaten me with force," she declares.

She is invoking the unconditional right to self-defense. She may have offended you, but she must defend her own dignity and physical integrity regardless of what she has done.

If you catch on, you might now apologize: "I'm sorry, I won't ever try to intimidate you again. But you must stop calling me a pig."

If she disregards your dignity, she might go after you again. "But you are a bully! You proved it when you shook your fist at me."

If you have your ethics in order, you will disregard her argument and will insist, "You must stop calling me a pig, regardless of what I've done in the past."

If you and your girlfriend can agree that both of you have the right to preserve your freedom and dignity, you will be on the way to building a decent relationship. But you can only do so when each of you is willing to break the cycle by stopping all attacks, regardless of what has been done by either of you in the past. The only justification for an attack is the need to defend oneself.

The Captive's Rights

You cannot apply the unconditional right to self-defense while you hold someone captive. Even if you seized the person's liberty for a justifiable reason, you cannot then permit yourself a freewheeling right to determine, upon a subjective basis, when he or she has aggressed against you. Only if the person is free to leave you can you feel free to use force to protect yourself against any and all kinds of subjectively defined harm.

Let us say that you are holding prisoner a man who has repeatedly brought physical harm to other human beings. Under a libertarian system of justice, it might be justified to keep this man in jail. But once in jail, the prisoner becomes subject to your whims; he has no capacity to protect himself against your arbitrariness, because he cannot leave you if the relationship is not to his liking. Therefore, as his jailer, you cannot decide that you don't like the way he smiles or that you dislike the hook of his nose and that therefore you have the right to use force if necessary to get him out of your sight. In a free society, you could decide to get him out of your sight: you could walk away from him in public places or keep him off your private property. But when he is in jail, you must respect his right to be himself, regardless of how offensive he may seem. You must limit your self-defense to very specific and narrowly defined objective criteria, such as your right to be free of physical assault from him.

This limit on the unconditional right to self-defense in jailer-prisoner relationships or in any involuntary exchange is very important in our society. Hundreds of thousands of inmates are confined in mental hospitals, institutions for the retarded, old age homes, and prisons. More important, the world's children are captives in almost every aspect of their lives. They cannot choose their biological parents, they cannot legally flee from their parents until they have reached adulthood, and they are virtual prisoners all day long throughout their schooling.

Adults must be very cautious in utilizing the unconditional right to self-defense against children. If you decide that your child is offensive to you, for example, and you refuse to feed him, you have threatened your child's life. If you banish your son to his room, you have inflicted the punishment of solitary confinement. If you spank your daughter, you have committed assault and battery. Since she cannot leave you, she has little or no ability to defend herself against this drastic measure, and so it is unjust to rationalize the spanking as the minimum necessary force required to carry out your wishes.

Nor can you invoke the rule that you can defend yourself regardless of the pain it inflicts, if the alleged aggressor is a prisoner or a child. If you leave your husband, you may inflict great pain upon him. He may even kill himself in outrage and anguish over your abandonment. You nonetheless have that right to leave any voluntary adult relationship. But if the prisoner will starve to death or the child will be abandoned to an institution upon your departure, then you cannot invoke the unconditional right to walk away. I will examine the ethics of parent-child relationships in separate chapters. Here I want to reiterate that the unconditional right to self-defense only applies when you do not have the other person trapped in an involuntary relationship.

No Assaults on Personal Sovereignty

The concept of minimal necessary force implies that the effects of any force used in self-defense should be as reversible as possible. Killing a person is a last resort indeed. But within the psychology of self-determination, there is more to a person than the vegetative existence of his or her body. There are the individual's human capacities, in particular his or her ability to make choices, to reason, and to feel. The existence of these capacities is fundamental to the existence of the human being. Therefore any attempt to cripple these capacities must be viewed as seriously as murder.

The distinction between personal sovereignty and personal freedom helps define acceptable types of coercion in self-defense. Force in self-defense should aim at limiting personal freedom rather than personal sovereignty. It may be acceptable to imprison a murderer, but it is wholly unacceptable to intrude forcefully upon the sanctity of his or her mind with drugs, electroshock, or psychosurgery.

When to Stand and Fight

The use of minimal necessary force also means that, if you can walk away from a conflict, you are rarely justified in fighting. If you attack and harm a person whom you could walk away from, you have become an aggressor. Pride and other ego gratifications are false excuses for attacking a person, even in self-defense. Since it is not an aggression to leave a free adult, leaving someone will almost always be available as an alternative before the use of more directly aggressive actions. It provides an upper limit short of directly harming the person.

This is a radical principle; its application would put almost all hostile, self-defeating relationships out of business. People resent this concept because they do not want to give up the endless variety of hostile, punishing techniques that they use against each other. They do not want to face the challenge of relating through love and through reason. Nor do they wish to face the anxiety and the guilt involved in leaving unhappy, frustrating relationships. Modern psychology balks at unconditional self-defense, because it negates nearly all the games the people play and makes clear that we have no right to take any of our frustrations out upon others.

I can imagine some circumstances in which you are free to walk away from someone but might choose to stay and fight, if it were in your own self-interest or in support of your ideals of liberty and love. Let us suppose that you frequent a favorite restaurant, hotel, or museum, and another frequent visitor insults you every time you meet. You could choose not to return, but that would gravely compromise your self-interest. You might, therefore, use force to prevent the individual from carrying out his offenses against you, either by confronting him verbally or by calling upon the authorities within the establishment to protect your rights.

There is another circumstance in which an individual cannot and should not walk away from a fight: when it takes place upon his or her own property. Most libertarians believe that private ownership of property is the next most important right after private ownership of body and self. Only if a person has the right to own property can that person protect personal privacy. The public world places multitudinous constrictions upon us, if only upon our desire to avoid people who conduct themselves in ways that we do not find attractive or dignified.

I believe in the right of a person to smoke cigarettes or to drink, but I do not have to grant this right when he or she is visiting my home. I also believe in the right of individuals to dress as they please, to eat what they please, to say what they please, and to play any games that they please. But I am not required to cater to their idiosyncrasies when they are on my turf.

Frequently, my clients let all manner of abuse take place in their own homes. Practical jokers make mayhem at their parties; their parents visit ad libitum and ad nauseam; their own children ruin their favorite pieces of furniture. Obnoxious strangers keep them standing at the door listening to selling spiels; gossipy neighbors waste their hours in discussing trivia. Their telephones are hotlines for anyone with a problem. They cannot say "I'm busy now"; "I want to get off now"; "I don't want to listen to any more of this; get off my phone." They have never hung up a telephone on anyone in their entire lives.

Some readers may wonder if I envision an ideal relationship as one in which two otherwise loving people are forever baring their teeth or shaking their fists at each other and at their friends and relatives, constantly invoking their right to self-defense. In reality, two individuals who maintain their personal right to self-defense will rarely find themselves invoking this right. Fighting will be minimal, for well-exercised self-defense does away with the need to exercise it often. Two people who frequently attack each other are two people who do not respect their own or each other's rights to be free of bullying. If you find yourself in frequent combat within the sanctity of your home, either you are inviting the wrong people onto your property or you are a very hostile person.

The Oppressor's Fear of Self-defense

Many people who fail to defend themselves are hiding the fact that they themselves are oppressors. These people are afraid that any insistence upon being treated better by others will only make more apparent their own tendencies to abuse these same others. "If I tell my wife never to yell at me, then I'll have to stop yelling at her; if I insist that my children always speak to me respectfully, I'll have to treat my children with respect all the time, too."

A husband takes abuse from a wife because he knows he has been unfaithful, unloving, or disrespectful toward her and doesn't want to change. A wife takes abuse from a husband because she knows she treats him no better. A parent accepts maltreatment from a child because he knows he has failed in his responsibilities toward the child. A boss lets an employee get away with goofing off, because he takes advantage of the employee whenever he can. To insist upon being treated well is to establish a standard for one's own treatment of others.

Accepting abuse because one is abusive never does any good. It is an unethical way of assuaging guilt. It is an attempt to handle one's own guilt by accepting arbitrary punishment rather than by reforming one's own conduct.

In therapy this often comes out openly. When I encourage a client to exercise the unconditional right to self-defense, my client may quickly disclose that he or she can't because he or she has been abusing the other person and deserves what is being dished out in return. My client is unwilling to change the conduct that has brought this abuse from the other person; instead, my client accepts punishment, all the while continuing to conduct himself or herself badly.

Sometimes a person is reluctant to implement the right of self-defense because "I'll be fighting all the time with everyone" or because "the arguing will only get worse." This is a dead giveaway that this person is already leading a very unethical, conflict-filled life. Anyone who is afraid that self-defense will bring about constant struggle or escalate the struggle to new heights is already under heavy attack and is attacking others as well, not in an ethical fashion aimed at self-preservation but in a hateful fashion aimed at supporting a style of personal failure. Such a person is invariably locked into an unfree, unsatisfying relationship, a trade-off of abuse for abuse. Such a person needs to look out for his or her true self-interest through voluntary relationships based on sound libertarian ethics. Then he or she won't be fighting all the time.

The failure to defend oneself is closely linked to the overall attitude of self-oppression and especially to guilt, which will be explored in the following chapters. In the meanwhile, it can be stated as a general principle that the more you exercise your right to self-defense, the more you will increase your sense of safety and your self-esteem. Others will also show you more respect. You will be more willing and more able to make decent relationships and to reach out in a loving fashion to other people when you know with certainty that you will defend yourself from every threat.

Chapter Seven

Self-oppression — How People Choose to Fail

That most people make the greatest contribution to their own misery is both dismaying and heartening — dismaying that human beings do such terrible things to themselves, and heartening that much human unhappiness can be overcome by the individual's personal efforts.

The notion that individuals choose their personal problems not only defies much of modern psychology; it may also seem outrageous to any specific individual with problems. If we confront individuals about their self-defeating lifestyles before they voluntarily choose to examine them for themselves, they will often argue with all their might to justify or to prove why they must remain miserable, self-hating, and helpless. They will *choose* the depressed, paranoid, or anxious lifestyle — marshaling every argument they can to show that they have good reasons to feel that way.

Personal Failure

In its most literal meaning, personal failure is:

any failure attributable to the person himself or herself rather than to forces beyond his or her control or responsibility.

Personal failure is self-determined. Out of fear or cowardice the individual betrays himself or herself, refusing to exercise rational, conscious decision making in his or her own best interest and instead lapsing into helplessness. He or she becomes irresponsible and self-defeating.

Personal failure is typically brought about by a psychological process that will be defined and described as *self-oppression*. This understanding of personal failure is intended to encompass most of what are typically called psychological or personal problems, including the entire range from minor inner tensions and conflicts to so-called neurotic and psychotic disorders.

Personal Failure versus "Mental Illness"

The concept of personal failure vastly differs from the concept of mental illness in two ways. First, it does not mix metaphors but adheres closely to the language and categories of persons, personal relationship, and ethics. Second, it does not suggest that any personal failures are caused by real brain diseases. Brain diseases may cause stresses that the moral agent, or self, must respond to, but brain diseases cannot bring about specific human actions. (See "Awareness of Self as Separate from One's Body," in chapter two.)

What then is the common ground of the concepts of personal failure and mental illness? At times, traditional psychiatrists use the term mental illness to describe thoughts, feelings, and conduct that I would also consider reflective of personal failures. I also share use of the terms depression, paranoia, and anxiety. I also believe that the term "schizophrenia" does reflect to some degree upon a human phenomenon, an extreme of utter irresponsibility that I prefer to label "craziness." In part, I use terms similar to those used by traditional psychiatrists to make clear that I am talking both about minor human failures and about major ones, such as psychiatrists routinely see in mental hospitals.

Similarly, I speak of "therapy" when I do not mean a medically oriented or traditionally psychiatric relationship, but a conversation between equals concerning the personal successes and failures of the client. I continue the use of the misleading term because I do not have a better one.

Mental illness and personal failure are very different concepts with a very narrow common ground. Mental illness as a concept is a self-contradictory, mixed metaphor: a nonphysical concept (the mind) is given a physical description (illness). As Thomas Szasz first analyzed in *The Myth of Mental Illness,* to speak of a mental illness is like speaking of a "sick economy" or a "sick joke." Economies and jokes are products of human action. They can be "bad," or they can be "poorly organized," or they can be failures; but they cannot literally be sick. To speak of someone who is mentally or morally depressed as being ill is no more sensible than to speak of a financially depressed economy as being literally ill.

Sometimes, the term mental illness is used not as a mixed metaphor but as a substitute for "biologically ill." It is presumed that the mentally ill person actually has a brain disease. For example, it is assumed that the psychotic who claims to be Jesus is caused to make the claim by an as yet undetected molecular defect in his brain. But a person is not *caused* to imagine or to claim that he is Jesus; he *chooses* to do so. Not only is evidence lacking for the molecular defect theory, but it also defies rationality. As Szasz has observed, biological explanations for delusions will only be possible when we also have biological explanations for other forms of human thought and action, such as rooting for the Yankees or believing in Christianity. The difference between believing in the divinity of Christ and believing in oneself as Christ is merely a difference in "religious viewpoint." There is no more reason to explain away the latter as a molecular defect than there is to explain away the former.

Personal Responsibility

Personal failure can be understood as a failure to take responsibility for maximizing personal sovereignty, personal freedom, or self-determination.

Personal responsibility has three separate but related meanings that will be used in the psychology of self-determination:

> (1) the capacity for self-aware rational thought and action; (2) the capacity for making conscious ethical decisions; and (3) the capacity to be a self-aware active force or to be a conscious cause of something that happens.

Unhappily, in dictionary and common usage, responsibility is also equated with duties, obligations, burdens, and sacrifice. Responsibility is also equated with blame or guilt. This is so ingrained that the question "Who is responsible for this?" is likely to conjure up the implicit question "Who's to blame?" or "Who's guilty?" If I ask a client if he or she wants to become more responsible, I am likely to be greeted with a sour face as the person conjures up burdensome duties and guilt. When the implications are thus confused, it would be better to ask, "Do you want to be self-determining?"

The Unconscious

The unconscious is that area of a person's life for which he or she has refused to accept responsibility as a self-determining person. It is made up of personal experiences and decisions that the person does not want to call his or her own.

Unconsciousness is self-deception or lying to oneself. While lying to others may at times be a necessary action for the survival of oneself or one's friends, lying to oneself is never a good thing. It can be said, "Behind every personal failure, there is a lie."

The murderer or the rapist may claim that he or she was "driven to do it." He or she may even pretend not to remember what went on leading up to the offense. If this person is as dishonest with himself or herself as with other people, the person may actually become *convinced* that he or she is unable to recall anything surrounding the crime.

Similar self-deceptions are not at all uncommon in daily life and in therapy. A woman who cruelly spanked her child a few moments earlier in the waiting room will deny any knowledge of how or why she did it, but a couple of well-put questions will lead her to disclose exactly why she struck her child. She was angry and was unwilling to act with love and with restraint.

Similarly, a man may strike his wife during an argument and then deny any capacity to recall why or even when he did it. He only knows about it because she has shown him her black-and-blue marks. But again it may take but minimal therapeutic skill to encourage the individual to see that it is in his own best interest to become more aware of himself. Once convinced, he will manage to recall the beating he gave his wife in all its gruesome detail.

It is true that many of our self-deceptions are more difficult than this to reverse, but we miss the point if we envision the unconscious as a foreign or alien element within us that pushes us in one direction or another against our will. Instead, the unconscious is a creation of our will, a private hell into which we have relegated our most painful memories and our most agonized choices. It is a darkroom, a closet, a basement, or an attic built upon the premise, "out of sight, out of mind." But "out of sight" must also mean out of rational control. We cannot rationally control that which we have decided to ignore or to relegate to oblivion.

In most lives, the unconscious has been heaped so high with self-deceptions that it must be approached gradually, as if turning over one page at a time in an encyclopedia. Attempts to open the entire book through drug experiences or other artificial means can result in horrendous psychotic experiences. Psychosis itself can be understood as the expression of a great deal of unconsciousness in everyday living.

In ordinary usage within psychology, the *unconscious* is:

> (1) that part of the mind that is out of awareness or not immediately accessible to the individual; (2) that part of the mind that has been repressed or pushed into unawareness as a result of associated emotional pain or conflict.

In the psychology of self-determination, the individual is held responsible for the unconscious, which is explained as:

> that part of personal experience for which the individual rejects responsibility; that part which the individual wishes to disown or to declare beyond his or her control; that part in which the individual wishes to deny his or her own participation as a person with free will; that part about which he or she wishes to remain unknowing, stupid, or dishonest with himself or herself.

The unconscious can be understood as an involuntary relationship with oneself. It is chosen servitude to one's own cowardice.

In my own practice, I never use hypnotic techniques, for I see little purpose and many pitfalls in encouraging an individual to give up personal sovereignty to me or to shift from self-determination to other-determination. There is little or no good in passively recalling that which one has previously chosen not to recall. It can become terrifying, encouraging further helplessness and dependency upon the therapist's authority.

The process of overcoming the unconscious should be one in which the individual freely chooses to become more and more aware of his or her past and present functioning in the interest of becoming more self-determining. This can only be done in a libertarian or nonauthoritarian context. It can only be done through hard work and self-determination.

A man who has built himself a large unconscious has a big task ahead when he decides to become self-determining. His unawareness has piled up on itself much as an accumulation of bad debts and bad deeds. Like the thief or embezzler who is in constant danger of discovery, he has created new deception upon new deception to fool himself and others about his failure to control his life. He becomes increasingly afraid to look within to confront the sum total of everything he has sought to avoid throughout his entire life, until he finds himself riding upon a monster. He feels it getting out of control beneath him. Because of his history of cowardice, he must now deal with a creature whose size and virulence far exceed that which he originally conceived.

Sudden psychotic breaks and bad trips on drugs can be understood as unexpected encounters with the accumulated denials and personal frauds of a lifetime. More typically, the transition into psychosis is gradual as the person increasingly refuses to put order into his everyday thoughts and actions.

Like psychotic thoughts and actions, garbled and confused dreams often are expressions of personal life for which the individual will not take responsibility. Early in therapy, a woman may tend to take no responsibility whatsoever for her dreams; she cannot and will not remember them. Later she begins to recall them, but they are crammed with unintelligible thoughts and actions, often smacking of chaos and destruction. Then as this woman dares become more aware of herself, her dreams become valuable to her as indicators of what she thinks and feels. These new dreams do not seem crazy, incomprehensible, or morally chaotic. They make sense because sense has become the individual's way of life.

Unconsciousness is probably the most important example of what I call self-oppression.

Dreams

I believe that dreams remain an area about which we know very little. Why do we put so much energy into them? What overall function do they serve? What is their relationship to craziness or personal failure? How and why are they so intimately involved in processes and contents that often seem to reflect very irrational and even infantile areas of life?

In some of his earliest work, Freud concluded that dreams reflect wishes, that these wishes are repressed, and that the dream therefore disguises these wishes from us as a kind of compromise with ourselves. This is not an exact rendering of Freud's views, and it may be generous in its straightforwardness. But there is a kernel of truth in that summary statement. Dreams often contain wishes, suggestions, or hints that the individual seems unwilling to recall or to otherwise deal with in waking life. Dreams in this sense are stories that we tell ourselves when we are not sure that we wish to hear what we have to say. They are inner conversations with a person who is both afraid to speak and afraid to listen. This does not provide a full explanation of dreams, but it is the most useful one I have found.

When a person is especially unwilling to face himself or herself, he or she may fail to recall any dreams at all. I have already mentioned how the client in therapy often starts out with no awareness of recent dreams. But as therapy progresses, dreams will be recalled; and as self-understanding increases, the dreams tend to become easier to understand. It is as if the individual's "personal conversations with himself or herself" no longer must be kept a secret from himself or herself. At this point, dreams may display valuable hints, suggestions, or pointers about what is really on the person's mind.

My own experience with dreams may vary from that of other persons who have studied the subject. Freud, for example, saw "Freudian symbols" everywhere in dreams. In a more sophisticated manner, Jung saw Jungian symbols everywhere. Perhaps patients produce dreams compatible with the needs of their therapists. I am not the first to suggest this. Dreams often express those childhood experiences in which we were heavily under the influence of others, and, even more surely, they often reflect our current tendencies to suppress ourselves. It is therefore not surprising if they also express our self-oppressive desires to submit to and to please current authorities, such as our therapists.

The Unconscious and Creativity

I have not been impressed with the relationship between relatively unconscious processes, such as dreams and daydreams, and the individual's higher creative processes. The higher processes have much more to do with crystal clear consciousness and rational thought. While dreams and daydreams often smack of helplessness and self-oppression, consciousness and rational thought move toward mastery.

Dreams and daydreams must be distinguished from creative play and imaginative fantasy. Play and fantasy are very active. A conscious act of will initiates the process, and conscious intelligence guides it. While the individual may be surprised and pleased by the direction that play or fantasy takes, the individual will not feel overwhelmed by it. Nor will the individual feel that the product is alien or bizarre. Ultimately, play and fantasy are joyful and satisfying, while dreams and daydreams are almost always in part painful and frustrating. A self-determining person chooses to play or to pursue a fantasy; a helpless person lapses into daydreams.

Sometimes a dream or daydream may become an inspiration for a creative work, but the ground will typically have been prepared by many previous hours of hard conscious work devoted to the area in which the dream or daydream now provides a stimulus. The stimulus itself, such as a fragment from a daydream, may be one among dozens or hundreds that the individual has previously recalled and rejected as uninteresting or fruitless. Again, the rational mind determines which hint becomes an inspiration. The creative individual must then develop the stimulus in a whole new context and present it in a manner satisfying to himself or herself, and to others. Dreams and daydreams, then, are grist for the mill of the creative mind; but the individual's finest creative moments will come when he or she is best prepared, most disciplined, most awake and alert, most rational, and most eager to face difficult challenges.

Creativity involves the full play of personal sovereignty and personal freedom; it is that area of life in which the individual as a self is most fully explored and expressed. If these seem like rather empty statements, I believe this emptiness lies not so much in my concepts as in the nature of creativity. Creativity is precisely that process whereby the individual produces or generates in a manner in which others have failed to produce or to generate. Creativity is unique and it expresses uniqueness. It cannot be explained; it can only be recognized. In this it resembles both free will and courage, to which it is so closely linked.

Craziness — the failure to create anything of value in life — is much easier to understand. That is what this book is about. The understanding of self-oppression and personal failure can be used to help liberate oneself and others to become more creative, but even this is not a very enlightening statement. Creativity often seems to rise up in response to the most oppressive conditions; it then makes its appearance entwined with anticreative, self-oppressive tendencies. Nonetheless, I believe that creativity exists in opposition to self-oppression and that it thrives in proportion to the extent that the individual has overcome guilt, shame, anxiety, and other manifestations of self-oppression.

Creativity cannot be pursued for its own sake. Like happiness, it is achieved as a by-product of ethical, brave living. Find what interests you in life and pursue it with all your love for life. To concern yourself with whether or not you are being "creative" in the process is distracting and demoralizing. Such a preoccupation can lead to trivial or contrived attempts at newness and cleverness. It can turn your head more toward your critics and your fans than toward yourself and reality. Beware if you yourself or anyone else gets caught up in your "creativity." To bring forth anything original that will stand the test of your own rational mind and maturing judgment requires a mighty effort, wholly absorbing in itself.

Attitudes toward Time

Attitudes toward present, future, and past time tell a great deal about a person's attitudes toward personal responsibility. Typically, a person who is not self-determining will see the future as bleak and hopeless and will neglect serious planning. This attitude of helplessness can easily be distinguished from realistic appraisals of the future. For example, a woman may correctly identify that inflation is eating up her income. She displays helplessness or lack of responsibility if she continues to think and act as if "money matters" are beyond her understanding.

Attitudes toward past time also express a person's attitudes toward personal responsibility. If a man does not want to think about the past because "I made some bad mistakes" or because "It wasn't worth thinking about," he is avoiding learning the lessons of his own past life and is probably doomed to repeat his mistakes.

Ultimately, present time is the most important, and a person who will not focus upon his immediate surroundings and his immediate actions has dug himself or herself into an extremely helpless position. This person is extremely frightened and will benefit most immediately from experiencing a "safe space." When you find yourself, a friend, or a client in this state of mind — wholly unwilling to take control of the most immediate life events — focus upon immediate actions aimed at making life less threatening. This may mean stepping away from a very oppressive individual who is making the person's life feel so unsafe. It may mean pointing out that extreme depression, paranoia, or anxiety is not rooted in the present but is driven by as yet unidentified horrors from the past. Sometimes a very careful analysis of the day's events will help. A person must feel able to determine the outcome of the most immediate events before any safety can be experienced and before personal responsibility can become any kind of a reality.

The concepts of personal sovereignty and personal freedom can also be useful at times of extreme fear, helplessness, and irresponsibility. The individual must distinguish between his or her own inner experience and events in the outside world. This distinction, when blurred, indicates a terrible state of fear and confusion and leads to further helplessness. Thus you can tell yourself or another person, "You can separate your own thoughts and feelings from what is happening outside you. You can see that you are feeling one thing even though your husband is feeling another. You can see that you desire to take such-and-such an action, even though it may be hard to carry out such an action in your current situation. You can be firm in having your own inner life, and you can begin to straighten it out, even before you can begin making changes in your situation." While very simple in appearance, these distinctions can be lifesaving for the person in a state of panic.

Oppression

Self-oppression is at the heart of every personal failure and every negative personal emotion, such as self-hate, guilt, shame, and anxiety. To understand self-oppression, we must first begin with oppression itself. Since the beginning of recorded history human beings have oppressed each other. Most obviously they have beaten, assaulted, raped, and murdered each other. They have stolen from each other, and they have cheated each other. They have taught each other evil, self-destructive philosophies with which to distort rational thinking and to turn individuals against their own best interests. They have threatened physical violence and imposed emotional violence at every turn.

Humanity's crimes have become especially atrocious as people, typically males, have gained imbalances of power in relation to each other. Large bands of men have abused smaller bands of men; masters have abused slaves; the rich have taken advantage of the poor; the many have bullied the few; males have suppressed females; and in every class and in every age, adults of both sexes have taken out their frustrations upon their children, mistreating them far more miserably and far more consistently than any other underprivileged or minority group. No slave, no victim of poverty, no abused woman has been so powerless that he or she could not, in turn, abuse children.

One only has to look at the major authority systems in any society to locate the sources of greatest abuse. Governments have abused their own citizens as well as the citizens of competing governments. Religions have abused their members, armies their soldiers, schools their pupils, and families their children. From cradle to grave, in every age, the average person has been forced to deal with chronic oppression.

In some eras, oppression has seemed more rife than in others. Whole societies have turned themselves morally inside out, destroying or castrating entire classes, such as their religious minorities, their slaves, their lower classes, their women, or their children. Entire societies have turned upon each other in wars of annihilation and enslavement. But even in times of relative peace, oppression has ground down the average, ordinary citizen with relentless regularity and monotonous repetition. Even in the most free of nations, such as the United States of America, the average citizen is burdened from childhood on by a host of suppressive agencies, starting with his family, his schools, and his religion, and culminating in his too-powerful government.

It has never been possible — and it may never be possible — to grow up within any society on earth without being forced to endure chronic assaults on oneself. From the perspective of self-determination, the most destructive of all influences is that of the family. The self-liberating individual can benefit most from confronting, understanding, and overcoming oppression where it has hit the hardest — within the confines of his or her own family. Until the effects of oppression during the early formative years can be undone, the individual will find it difficult to become fully effective in any other area of his or her existence. If a man grows up believing that his father's word is law, he will never become fully rational in understanding the oppressive effects of authoritarian religious, educational, or political institutions, and he may be tempted to indoctrinate his own children in submission to authority. If a woman never clearly perceives her own mother's role in submitting to her father's sexist views, she may never find the strength within herself to stand up to her father or to her husband. The variations on these themes are endless, and so the principles must be grasped and then applied to each person's life.

In the psychology of self-determination, oppression is the implementation of antilibertarian values; it is an assault on any of the principles of self-determination through force or through propaganda. *Oppression* is:

> any use of force or deception, or any enforcement of an involuntary relationship, except in self-defense; any infringement on an individual's unconditional right to self-defense; any imposition upon an individual's personal sovereignty, even in self-defense; any other-determined, antilibertarian, or unethical action or relationship; any undermining, disparagement, or discouragement of the principles of self-determination.

This is a broad definition that far exceeds the libertarian political injunction against force or fraud. By this definition, even voluntary relationships become oppressive if they promote, encourage, or propagandize against the various principles of self-determination. This is a psychological definition of oppression, not a political one. Ethics and the law do not coincide; ethics defines what is right, while the law defines what is allowed. Many things must be allowed in the interest of freedom, even unethical conduct.

The third part of the definition, "any imposition upon an individual's personal sovereignty, even in self-defense," reiterates the principle that impositions upon personal sovereignty are never justified, even as a police measure or even if the imposition falls short of outright coercion or the threat of coercion.

Loss of Liberty Hurts

Loss of liberty hurts. Because humans require freedom for the exercise of their faculties, imprisonment is even more demoralizing to most persons than to most animals; and human zoos, such as prisons, mental hospitals, and public schools, are more desperate places than animal zoos.

The human desire for freedom is proved by the extreme measures that must be taken in mental hospitals, prisons, and schools to make sure that the inmates do not attempt to escape. Massive indoctrination programs, as well as great threats and grave punishments, are required to force an individual to continue submitting. Authorities must rely on inculcating self-oppression, or else police controls by themselves will fail. Prisons, mental hospitals, and schools attempt to make their inmates stupid, guilt-ridden, ashamed, and anxious, all to counteract their aspirations for freedom.

An angry response to oppression is not only natural, it is good — for it reminds the individual that he or she has free will and longs for personal freedom. If this anger is suppressed, it will show up as personal failure, for its suppression involves a self-crippling decision by the individual to give up personal sovereignty. No philosophy, psychology, or religion should try to suppress the expression of anger over loss of liberty. It cannot be successfully accomplished without in part destroying the person and driving him or her into robotism. If a woman lives in slavish obedience to her husband and a daughter remains in slavish servitude to her ailing parents, it is far better for these women to feel outrage, for their humanity remains alive, signaling their distress to them and keeping alive their potential for seeking freedom.

Self-oppression

In the psychology of self-determination, self-oppression is the concept which explains personal failure, including so-called personal problems — problems in living, inner conflicts, and craziness. It is the self-imposed crippling of the individual by himself or herself in an attempt to live with and to accommodate real or imagined oppression.

Self-oppression makes an external conflict into an internal one. In her efforts to survive within close proximity to her oppressive mother, a woman puts herself into conflict with herself by hating herself rather than putting herself into conflict with her mother. She thereby becomes her own enemy in her effort to avoid confronting her real enemy. She grows toward unconsciousness instead of consciousness, toward helplessness instead of control, toward irresponsibility instead of responsibility, and toward other-determination instead of self-determination.

Self-oppression is ultimately caused by the individual, not by threats made against him or her. Afraid of the price of self-determination, the person compromises by subduing himself or herself.

To become a self-oppressor, the individual must not only change his or her conduct or actions but also change basic attitudes toward himself or herself. There are many occasions in which an individual must sacrifice personal freedom in the interest of survival, and he or she can do this without becoming a self-oppressor. A man victimized by a gunman may hand over his money rather than risk getting shot. A young woman bullied by an oppressive parent may do what she is told rather than endure a brutal beating. The victim of political totalitarianism may keep his or her rebellious thoughts hidden rather than go to the firing squad. These compromises become self-oppressive only to the degree that the victim enlarges his or her unconsciousness by sacrificing self-knowledge or self-awareness or by denying that he or she longs for justice and freedom.

The principles of voluntary exchange clarify the nature of self-oppression. Confronted with coercion, the self-oppressive person coerces himself or herself in order to avoid conflict with the feared authority and, in effect, creates a self-imposed involuntary exchange by using fraud against himself or herself. If he is a man who was "overprotected" or overcontrolled as a young boy, in adulthood he may continue to place self-imposed restrictions on his own personal freedom. He may do this by refusing to stand up for himself or by refusing to grant himself the right to seek better opportunities in life, even after his parents have died or have otherwise lost their ability to influence him directly. He becomes his own jailer. At the same time, he defrauds himself by keeping from himself knowledge of his true aspirations, as well as knowledge of how destructive to him his parents have been. The result can be an individual who goes through life as bent and broken as if someone were standing over him with a whip or club.

The self-oppressor actively creates involuntary relationships for himself or herself and acts as if he or she cannot leave mother or father, spouse, or job. It may be a woman who refuses to identify how bad her parents' marriage was, and now she continues to act as if life must remain one unending and unendurable burden. Confronted by a therapist or friend about how she actively maintains her own enslaving marriage, she denies that free will and freedom exist. She says she has no choice in the conduct of her life. Often this person ends up seeking out truly involuntary relationships, such as a husband who threatens her life or a psychiatrist who locks her in a mental hospital. These oppressive settings make it easier for her to hide from her failure to love herself enough to pursue her own self-interest in the face of fear.

The tragic disaster for the self-oppressor takes place as he or she grows from childhood to adulthood. In every area in which he or she became a self-oppressor in childhood, the grown adult continues to remain ignorant about his or her self-defeating lifestyle. He or she will persevere or sustain the same chronic pattern of self-denial and personal failure even in the absence of powerful oppressors.

The most catastrophic form of self-oppression or self-betrayal is the denial of the existence of free will and choice. The person negates himself or herself as a choice-making entity in order to facilitate subjugation to the feared oppressor. Closely related to this in importance is the self-denial of rationality or reason, the human's most important technique in the pursuit of self-interest. A woman, for example, long treated as an "air head," takes on the role to avoid conflict and acts stupidly and irrationally, rather than daring to confront this sexist attack on her.

Few people go all the way in self-denial to the point of exterminating their awareness of themselves as living beings with some degree of free will and rationality; but in the anguish of growing up, all people deny many of their most painful childhood experiences, along with the reasons they developed in childhood for betraying themselves and the principles of self-determination, liberty, and love.

Obsessions, Compulsions, and Phobias

The obsession, compulsion, or phobia reflects an earlier self-oppressive decision to cripple oneself rather than to face a severe conflict, usually with one's parents. It is a self-imposed unfreedom that distracts the mind, focuses attention on the absurd and the safe, and reduces the individual's freedom in the interest of avoiding conflict.

One of my clients was crippled by multiple obsessions, compulsions, and phobias. From her earliest memories, she had been tormented by her mother about most of her life functions — eating, sleeping, walking, going to the bathroom, dressing, talking. The mother nagged, bullied, screamed, and threatened physical violence any time her daughter took an independent action that suggested self-ownership. Through it all, her father acted like a kept man whose only defense was to fall asleep upon his return home from work.

During her early adulthood, my client had denied the existence of her life-and-death conflict with her mother and, instead, enslaved herself to a variety of obsessions, compulsions, and phobias, plus a general lifestyle of failure. She would feel obsessed with keeping herself clean; she would feel phobic about germs or sweat; she would feel compelled to wash herself and change her clothes in lengthy rituals. Sex was made almost impossible. In childhood, these preoccupations had kept her menacing mother from utterly destroying her with her own obsessions, compulsions, and phobias. The young girl enslaved herself rather than defy her mother's attempts to impose insane standards upon her. In adulthood, her preoccupations continued to save her from facing her mother or anyone else in an all-out conflict, but the price was high. One function after another was self-oppressed, until she had little idea of herself as a thinking, feeling human being with free will and personal responsibility.

In therapy, we faced months and months of what might be called "mopping-up operations" as we sought the origin of one self-oppressive activity after another, and as she struggled to enlarge her freedom of choice and action. But this was secondary to her larger struggle to accept responsibility in general and, in particular, to embrace her power to make choices and to liberate herself. To accept this responsibility, she had to overcome a lifetime of accumulated copouts, as well as the terrifying childhood experiences that had motivated her cowardice. Especially, she had to face her unwillingness to use her newly recognized power and freedom as an adult to make her own decisions about her familial, sexual, and professional life.

Phobias can also appear in apparent isolation within a seemingly well-functioning person. Whenever medical or behavioral models for human unhappiness are promoted, allegedly isolated and inexplicable phobias are cited as "symptoms" that cannot be explained or ameliorated in terms of ethics. I recall a psychiatrist in an audience telling me, "A middle-aged lady is afraid to go out of the house for fear she's left the gas on. What's that got to do with freedom?" But even the casually interested observer should be able to imagine how a person, overcome with guilt about serving others, with resentment over housekeeping, and with fears about confronting her guilt and resentment, might begin to preoccupy herself with leaving the gas on instead of with rebellion against housework.

One of my clients told me about a humiliating phobia over being "closed in" in elevators, the back seats of cars, restaurants, or movie theaters, with people on both sides of him. He would go through various embarrassing maneuvers to get an aisle seat in a movie, an open table in a restaurant, or the front seat in a car. This man had not come to therapy for the "cure" of his phobia, which he felt beyond his control and beyond treatment, and he did not return to it as an issue for several months, when it was exacerbated by an impending visit from his mother.

Systematic inquiry into the past disclosed some of the origins of the phobia. During his childhood my client, like all children, had a variety of bodily needs that should have been under his own control but that his mother sought to bring under her control. If they were sitting in a crowded theater, in a restaurant, or driving on a long trip, mother didn't want her son "having to go to the potty all the time." The result was frequent times of actual physical torture from a painful, bursting bladder or a stomach nauseated with car sickness. Not only did his mother ignore his needs, she would make fun of his complaints, often in front of friends or strangers. As in the later phobia, not only the closed-in place but the presence of other people became crucial to the pain and humiliation.

My client dreaded talking about the phobia, in part because of the humiliating feelings associated with it, but also because confronting the phobia meant confronting maltreatment at the hands of his mother. Because of religious as well as parental influences, this man was terribly afraid of saying anything negative about his parents; and because of his stored up resentment, he was afraid that examining his childhood would lead him to "hate" them. Only as this person's confidence grew in his right to criticize and confront his parents was he able to examine the origins of the phobia more fully, in terms of the constant, harping criticism to which he was exposed as a child. Now he was able to understand his phobia as a defense against the great fear and humiliation he experienced in proximity to other people, in front of whom his mother had often shamed him. With his awareness of his mother and his fears of people in his consciousness, he could now enter a previously phobic situation without resorting to crippling defenses. Eventually he was able to look around in such situations with a full realization that he was no longer a child, that his mother could no longer oppress him, and that the people surrounding him were in no way waiting to embarrass and humiliate him. He could achieve this position because he no longer oppressed himself into unconsciousness about his mother's role in his life and his own abject submissiveness to her.

Phobias are self-imposed unfreedoms. They help the individual avoid facing oppression and self-oppression. They are a self-crippling compromise. They are easily passed off as inexplicable symptoms, because both the patient and the therapist too often are unwilling to go through the difficult, time-consuming, and painful task of exploring childhood amnesia in the interest of uncovering submission to parental oppression.

Chapter Eight

Three Basic Lifestyles of Self-oppression — Paranoia, Depression, and Anxiety

There is a great deal of resistance to the idea that extremes of craziness are no different in quality than any other personal problem. We want to relegate extremes of human misconduct and personal misery into another universe. Instead of labeling this universe mystical, mysterious, or religious, as in days of old, we now label it medical and scientific. We turn personal failure into mental illness.

Mental illness, like earlier devil concepts of human misconduct and misery, is an empty notion used to bolster the authority of psychiatrists, much as the devil concept was used to bolster the authority of priests. It also serves to distract us from the humanity of each person and from the realization that each of us lives along a continuum of responsibility, with spiritual integrity on one end and craziness or nervous breakdown on the other. We want to believe that the worst spiritual or psychological states are separate from us and that they can only be understood with reference beyond our everyday experience of ourselves. We want to trust authorities to manage our lives if we fail to.

I want to reiterate that I have hesitated to use terms such as *paranoia* and *depression,* which smack of the myth of mental illness. Yet these terms also describe, however poorly, aspects of human ethical failure. I use such words as paranoia and depression not to justify psychiatric authority or to rob individuals of their personal freedom or moral responsibility, but only to make clear that I am indeed concerned with the most serious expressions of human self-destructiveness when I talk about lifestyles of personal failure.

Blaming Others as a Lifestyle (Paranoia)

The three most characteristic lifestyles of self-oppression or personal failure are *blaming others* (paranoia), *blaming self* (depression), and *blaming no one* (anxiety).* Blaming others is perhaps the easiest of the three to understand as a moral failure. We are accustomed to recognizing that "paranoid" tendencies are a means of avoiding personal responsibility for one's failures.

In blaming others as a lifestyle, the individual refuses an awareness of self-determination by blaming others or the outside environment for his or her helplessness. The individual says, "*They* are after me," or "Someone is poisoning my food," or "I am controlled by radio waves from outer space," or more simply, "You have made me miserable."

These statements are paranoid only if the person misidentifies the true source of the problem or misuses a proper identification in order to justify helplessness. What characterizes the paranoid style is the placement of cause or blame outside oneself, plus a helpless refusal to identify the true source of difficulty or to correct it.

The key to blaming others, as to all self-defeating lifestyles, is the misuse or abuse of reason and reasons in the interest of maintaining a helpless, dishonest, or cowardly stance. Blaming others is nothing more than a particular style of excuse-making in which the excuse is found outside oneself.

In a therapy session, it is commonplace to witness the clear connection between a "paranoid symptom" and a refusal to take responsibility for oneself. A man with an elaborate paranoid system may come in stating that his drink was poisoned at a party. How did he know? "I found myself attracted to several girls at once." Why does this require a far-out explanation about something put in his drink? "Because I don't have sexual feelings like that. Women almost never turn me on." With some work in the session, this individual may acknowledge that his last therapy session had encouraged him to think more freely about women but that he had been unwilling to handle his feelings at the party, so he shifted blame to an unnamed persecutor who had allegedly poisoned his drink.

Even people who are very paranoid are likely to realize the absurdity of their delusional system at times. They often smile characteristically as they tell their tales of persecution because they know they will not be believed, and because they don't fully believe them either.

When looking at paranoia within yourself, it is extremely important to distinguish between the truth of your general observations and the use you then make of them. You may have endured the worst parents on record. Your mother may have been an overwhelming, castrating person, and your father may have been a spineless sponge. Accept the facts of your situation, but reject your use of the facts to justify continued helplessness.

---

*The term *lifestyle* was originally coined by Alfred Adler. The analysis that follows is my own.

Many personal failures have a strong element of this paranoid tendency to shift blame outside ourselves as we beat a cowardly retreat from difficult confrontations. Artists and writers, for example, frequently evolve elaborate theories to explain why the public or the publishing industry will not heap praise upon their work. Such preoccupations become paranoid when used as excuses for giving up the challenge of communication — precisely that challenge for which artists and writers are supposed to take responsibility. The artist's role is the creation or recognition of values that have eluded others — including art critics and publishers — hardly a task for which he or she can expect instant and general acclaim.

Paranoia as excuse-making comes up in a person's job. A man is afraid to leave a job because he lacks courage; he is unwilling to take the risks or to do the work involved in finding new employment. So he elaborates a systematic explanation for his failures in terms of his boss, his colleagues, the stupidity of businessmen, or whatever. The issue — as in the artist's or writer's case — is not the relative truth or falsity of the perceptions. The issue is the abuse of reason to justify or excuse continued helplessness or lack of courage.

We find the same phenomenon in marriage. Very frequently, a woman will use otherwise valid perceptions of women's liberation to justify her failures of self-determination. Instead of demanding equality, instead of choosing to face the fearful stress of changing her role in life, she labels all men "MCPs" and uses this to explain her own continued escapism.

Probably the most vicious and yet most frequent expression of paranoia is the tendency of parents to blame their children for problems that originate with the parents. In extreme cases, parents who have been crazy before their children were born nonetheless convince their children that they are the sole cause of parental unhappiness. It is commonplace to find minor examples of this in the typical family.

The parent's abuse of his or her child brings up one last element common to most irresponsible lifestyles. They can and are used as techniques for bullying or controlling other people. The paranoid father, for example, coerces his children by making them feel to blame for his problems. In marriage, this individual spends more time attacking his wife than examining himself; on the job, he spends more time pointing out the inadequacies of others than in doing his own work. In the most extreme examples, the paranoid man kills an innocent victim as a sacrifice to his need for deluding himself about the cause of his own failures.

Because the paranoid person is so obviously hostile to others, it is easy to forget that paranoia, as much as any other self-defeating lifestyle, is a form of self-oppression. The individual makes himself or herself helpless through irrationality and unconsciousness. That this person injures others as well should not distract us from the fundamental principle that he or she is self-defeating. This is especially important if you are trying to help yourself or anyone else overcome tendencies to blame others. You must first be able to convince yourself or the other person that blaming others is not a form of triumph but a form of defeat.

Blaming Oneself as a Lifestyle (Depression)

While paranoia is a form of excuse-making in which the individual thrusts the excuse outside himself or herself, depression is a form of excuse-making in which the individual locates the excuse within himself or herself.

Often the depressed person appears to be acting responsibly when blaming himself or herself for everything. But the individual does this to avoid becoming self-determining, as his or her self-accusations and self-hate become a rationalization for not improving: "I can't do it because I'm no good." The statement may be morally correct, but it is used as an excuse.

Blaming oneself for everything is typically a partial or entire misidentification. Lacking the courage to identify and confront the actual issues, the depressed person blames himself or herself in a vague and helpless fashion, as a relatively easy way out — a way out that leads nowhere, for it is born of cowardice. Like the paranoid person, the depressed person misidentifies, acts helpless, and abuses his or her reasoning abilities to justify inaction.

Most human beings have gone through periods of depression. The man or woman who loses a lover or a job and lapses into helplessness and apathy exemplifies depression. The helpless apathy hides a cop-out or a series of cop-outs. The depressed woman does not want to see that she could have anticipated losing the person or the job if she had only been honest with herself at the start. Perhaps her lover told her at the beginning that he could never love her; perhaps her boss made it clear that she could only have the job for a limited time. Perhaps her lover had a long history of leaving people as soon as they became interested in him, or perhaps he was already in love with someone else or had a bachelor career already planned for himself. Perhaps her boss had a reputation as an S.O.B. who fired people willy-nilly.

Often the depression is a repeat of earlier depressions over previous losses, indicating a pattern or lifestyle that the person does not wish to face. A man who becomes depressed after the failure of another love relationship may have again made it impossible for a reasonable woman to stay with him because he becomes insanely jealous or helplessly dependent whenever he gets involved. Perhaps he begins ridiculing his loved ones or physically abusing them. The possibilities are endless. The important point is that his self-blame and depression reflect a self-oppressive failure rather than an honest assessment of how he has caused himself to lose another relationship.

Like the person who has chosen paranoia as a lifestyle, the depressed person can be very good at marshaling evidence in support of his or her helplessness.

A middle-aged man who wallows in depression may find many reasons for it in the outside world — he has lost several friends or family members through death, his business has failed, his body is in poor health. Like the paranoid, he may point to the social and economic condition of the world to justify depression. But while the paranoid puts the blame on others for his condition, the depressed person ultimately comes down to blaming himself. He feels magically at fault for killing the people he has lost; he feels guilty about the poor and the starving masses of humanity and cannot enjoy his own life. Does he do anything about all this? Not much, other than to recount his own guilt.

The depressed person, like the paranoid, is often a great bully. Depressed lovers try to control their partners by acting as if they will die without them. Depressed parents will self-righteously moan to their children, "I'm a bad mother; I admit it; I don't deserve to be a mother." This will be repeated piteously until the poor child, in desperation over the parent's pain, becomes willing to do anything he or she can to make mother feel better. Everyone who has ever lived with or tried to help depressed persons knows how powerfully they use their pain to draw out the last bit of guilt from whomever they are dealing with. This may be one reason why depressed people are so often the victims of cruel treatment with electroshock or psychosurgery; they drive their therapists into spasms of guilt until the therapists turn, in equally unethical outrage, on their patients. Depression can become an irresponsible style, then, not only because it fails to identify the correct source of the problem, and because it smacks of self-defeating helplessness, but also because it is used to make the innocent feel miserable. This is as true of the psychotically depressed person as it is of the person who is merely irritable or disagreeable with friends, family, or coworkers.

Most people have vacillated at one time or another between depression and paranoia — between a futile and helpless blaming of others to an equally futile and helpless blaming of oneself. Before your eyes, you can watch as a client or friend swings from blaming self to blaming others, each time failing to face life with a willingness to become self-determining.

Blaming No One as a Lifestyle (Anxiety)

Along with paranoia and depression, chronic anxiety is the third major lifestyle of personal failure. It completes the trilogy of blaming others, blaming self, and blaming no one as styles of avoiding self-determination.

What makes anxiety different from paranoia and depression is the person's refusal to identify *any* source for his or her problems, either from within himself or herself or from without. Anxiety shows up in vague feelings of uneasiness and nervousness and in physical symptoms such as trembling, sweating, dryness of the mouth, and palpitations.

In the extremes of anxiety, one sees either panic or so-called catatonia. The woman who collapses in a panic gives up her ability to perceive and to identify herself and her surroundings and may shut off almost all her mental functioning. Anyone can recognize this as a total failure to be self-determining. In catatonia, the individual freezes and refuses to do anything at all on his or her own. In the textbook case, the catatonic person permits others to manipulate his or her arms or legs at will and to place them in any position. This person literally gives up determination of his or her own body out of an unwillingness to confront the sources of his or her problems and to take an action.

Severe anxiety is one of the most painful and intolerable of all experiences, and a person will try to find a way out by blaming others in a paranoid fashion or by blaming himself or herself in a depressed fashion. If, instead, this person decides to identify the source and to take an action, he or she will move quickly toward self-liberation.

That most people walk around with a rather high level of anxiety — characterized by tenseness, uneasiness, tiredness, sweating, and a variety of digestive and cardiovascular ailments — suggests how much most people exist in the dark about themselves. This darkness is born of compounded years of unwillingness to identify the conflicts in their lives and to take action to resolve them in a manner consistent with their own self-interest. Anxiety is transformed into fear when the individual takes this responsibility.

Fear can be distinguished from anxiety. The fearful person is still willing to identify the object or source of the threat, and unless the fear deteriorates into anxiety, he or she will take remedial actions. This is not a matter of semantics and definition but a matter of reality. Fear takes on the quality of anxiety at precisely the moment that the individual refuses to confront that which is causing the fear.

In therapy, one can watch the development of anxiety in direct relation to threats that the individual refuses to identify and to confront. A chronically anxious man may be near to realizing that he hates to work for his father, but he won't let the idea remain in his consciousness out of a cowardly unwillingness to stand up to his father and out of fear over stepping out on his own. In therapy, if I touch on the issue by asking, "Does the idea of quitting work for your dad sound like something you don't really want?" the anxious person may refuse to hear what I have asked. He may change the subject. Upon my repeating the question, he may say something like, "I hear your words, but they don't register." On being pressed, he may say, "You're making me anxious. I don't know what's going on, but I have other things to talk about." This evasiveness can become comically apparent. If the client is a person who is becoming more responsible, he may break into laughter as he sees himself characterized by his refusal to hear what is being said. This can be a turning point if he decides to confront that which he so greatly fears.

Evasiveness like this is characteristic of every lifestyle of personal failure. A person who chooses the paranoid lifestyle will begin to blame outside forces or circumstances, such as, "I can't quit working for my father as long as the economy's so bad . . . or as long as the future's so uncertain . . ." or, in more extreme instances, "so long as 'they' are after me." The depressed person instead will turn to statements of self-hate and self-loathing when confronted with the question of no longer working for his or her father. Remember, however, that the issue is not whether the economy is really bad; nor is it the issue of whether the depressed person really needs self-criticism. The sign of irresponsibility is the use of reason in the interest of excusing helplessness in the face of challenges or threats that must be met if the individual is to survive and to grow.

You can test the function of anxiety in your own life. The next time you feel anxious, search yourself for the cause of it; in particular, look at the few moments preceding the anxiety to check out what you were thinking, hearing, doing, or watching.

You are very likely to find something you do not want to face. Sometimes you will be able to laugh at your own cowardice and to take an action. At other times, the source of your fear may be deeply hidden beneath years of unconsciousness, and you will have a lot of digging ahead of you.

Signs of anxiety within oneself, like signs of depression or paranoia, can be used as signals for the need to face up to threatening challenges. Self-liberating individuals can make progress with themselves when they accept that behind each "symptom" or excuse there is something worth looking at. Anxiety can become a welcome sign that it is time to look into oneself to overcome a long-denied fear.

Just as paranoid and depressed people use their styles as techniques to bully others, so too does the anxious person. Anxious persons will cook up a storm of panic in a therapy session in the desperate hope that it will force the therapist to take over responsibility for their lives. A therapist bullied in such a fashion may find himself or herself pushed to saying, "All right, I'll give you the drugs you want, or lock you up in the hospital, or tell your mother to leave you alone, or make your wife give up her lover," and so on, endlessly. Many people fall victim to anxious friends who call them on the phone in states of panic demanding that they do something to take care of them. Frequently, a person is inhibited in a decision to leave someone because the bereft person promises to collapse in anxiety.

I don't believe there is anything inherent in paranoia, depression, or anxiety that makes it inevitable that people utilizing these lifestyles become bullies. Some people do suffer and make excuses quietly to themselves. They are self-oppressors in the privacy of their own minds. But people irresponsible enough to live a life of paranoia, depression, or anxiety are also frequently irresponsible enough to bully other people. Look at your own reactions under stress to see if you have a tendency to take out your frustrations on others. It goes hand-in-hand with being anxious, paranoid, or depressed.

Helplessness: The Common Denominator

Helplessness is the key to every lifestyle of failure. Every lifestyle of failure is a lifestyle of helplessness. Helplessness is the opposite of self-determination, but it shares with self-determination the element of choice. Helplessness, despite the individual's protests, is a *chosen* way of life. Indeed, when first confronted with his or her helplessness, the individual sometimes clings to it adamantly, resenting any and all attempts to reform. When confronted rationally, the individual with a longterm style of helplessness will argue cogently and persistently in justification of it. He or she may be able to draw upon modern psychology itself, which often reinforces the lifestyle of helplessness by means of its emphasis upon the human being as a reactive mechanism trapped by its instincts, its genetics, its unconscious, or its environment.

Why do people cling to helplessness? Beneath helplessness, there lies fear — fear of self-determination and the pursuit of self-interest (see p. 104).

Whether the individual is trying to liberate himself or herself, or whether the person has sought help from others in the form of guidance or psychotherapy, little or nothing can be gained until the core of the helplessness has been confronted. Approaches that pamper helplessness or ignore it, as well as approaches that delay confronting it in order to build "rapport," are doomed to failure. As long as the person maintains a helpless viewpoint, everything that the person perceives will be distorted and fed into that viewpoint.

I have occasionally made this mistake in therapy: I make an interpretation about childhood oppression before the person has dealt with his or her helplessness, and the interpretation will be used to bolster the person's helplessness, typically by turning the childhood experience into one more excuse for helplessness or by making it another excuse to avoid self-analysis for fear of "hating" or "upsetting" Mom and Dad. Before getting anywhere, the individual must have an idea about the central feature of his or her problem — the tendency to think and act helplessly.

The major lifestyles — blaming self in a depressed fashion, blaming others in a paranoid fashion, and blaming no one in an anxious fashion — are obvious manifestations of helplessness. The individual shifts responsibility in order to avoid facing the true sources of his or her distress. But there are many more subtle expressions of helplessness that are easier to overlook.

Feeling sorry for oneself is a major expression of helplessness. It is one thing to recognize or to understand the sad or tragic elements in one's life; it is another to feel and to act in a pitiable fashion. Nothing is gained from feeling sorry for oneself, and the therapist or friend who feels sorry for somebody else is doing that person a great disservice. By feeling sorry for ourselves or others, we imply that the objects of our pity have no recourse with which to redeem their life or situation. If I should ever develop a dread disease or lose a loved one, I hope my friends will do anything but feel sorry for me; I hope they will encourage me to make the most of whatever life I have left. Similarly, if one of my clients is confronted with a tragic situation, such as the loss of a loved one, I understand the sorrow which he or she experiences, and I acknowledge it; but I do not feel sorry for the person. Instead, I continue to analyze any manifestations of this self-destructive tendency.

Whimpering and complaining are other manifestations of helplessness, and they grow precisely out of the child's desire to communicate pitiable helplessness to the adults around him. There are two kinds of complaints — the first is forthrightly expressed with an intent to find a remedy, and the second is deviously expressed in order to gain pity or to aggravate the listener. The two have entirely different tones to them. Similarly, there are two kinds of crying — the first expresses a deeply felt sorrow or pain and has no manipulative element, and the second is a whimper aimed at communicating "Poor me, I am hurt; you should feel guilty; you should do something for me."

The "So what?" syndrome is another frequent manifestation of helplessness when a person is seeking guidance or therapy. If I make what seems to me to be a series of useful comments, and if the person I am talking with "admits" that the comments sound valid and enlightening but continues to say, in effect, "So what?" or "What good is that to me?" or "What can I do with that?" I then begin to suspect an underlying attitude of helplessness. The individual *resents* any knowledge about the origins or nature of his or her lifestyle of failure because the individual has taken a helpless viewpoint toward the possibility of overcoming the lifestyle. The moment this is picked up, the focus must shift to the person's sense of helplessness, hopelessness, or futility. Sometimes this new focus will enlighten or inspire the individual, and he or she will become willing to look at the childhood roots of this helpless attitude. Recognition that the helplessness originates in the past is a potential antidote to the idea that it cannot be overcome; an attitude with its origins in childhood is more obviously irrational and not the product of those current real-life events that seem to cause the individual's despair. Of course, this is helpful only if the individual has decided to make some inroads into his or her own helplessness.

It is equally true that the helplessness behind paranoid, guilty, or anxious communications must immediately be dealt with if it is presented as a "reality" rather than as communications about a recognized problem that the individual is intent upon handling. A person may say, "I'm scared, and I can feel myself blaming others," and in effect acknowledge his or her tendency toward helplessness. The fears themselves can be investigated. Similarly, the person may say that he or she feels unrealistically immobilized by anxiety or guilt, and the psychological work can proceed. But if the person presents the paranoia, depression, or anxiety as a reality that cannot be escaped — e.g., "I'm too anxious to think about that," or "What's the use, I'm no good anyway," or "What difference does it make — they always get you in the end" — then the element of helplessness must be recognized before any further work can go on.

In effect, the helpless person is *not trying* and is *not willing to try* to overcome his or her lifestyle of helplessness. In therapy, it may take months for the person to realize this, but it is crucial. The realization that one has been helpless, and that one can become self-determining, is often the most important insight in life. It has a "conversion" element to it, for it transforms the individual's entire view of life for the better. But it is not a typical "religious conversion"; the individual who gives up helplessness gives up reliance upon any and all authority — including the authority of a therapist — and, instead, determines to use his or her ability to reason and to choose in the creation of a better life. A therapist or a friend may be useful in the process, but only to the extent that the therapist or friend encourages an end to helplessness and a greater reliance upon reason and the pursuit of self-interest.

Ed, the Maniac

Because psychiatric propaganda is so pervasive in our society, it is hard for many sophisticated individuals to believe that psychological and ethical explanations for irrational, destructive conduct apply to the most extreme examples of human aberration. This is why I want to tell the story of "Ed, the Maniac." Were Ed a client of mine, I would never tell his story in such detail, regardless of whether or not he gave permission. I believe in confidentiality. Instead, Ed approached me after one of my speeches to tell me his own story, and since then we have become good friends. With his permission, and with suitable disguises of his identity, I want to tell you about a man who in no way looked "insane" to the casual observer, but who almost became one of those sensational newspaper accounts of the "model citizen" who murders his wife and ends up in a hospital for the criminally insane.

When I first met Ed, he was forty-eight years old and had already come through his crisis. He could therefore provide his own independent viewpoint of what had happened, and the account that follows has his approval as an accurate interpretation of his conduct. Ed had spent most of his life perfecting himself and preparing for the future. He had always been an outstanding student and had graduated from college with high honors. He had then taken a master's degree and finally settled on the law as a profession. He graduated from law school at the top of his class and then took still another year of "preparation," becoming the national expert in a specialized legal field. Upon graduation, he knew he could command a very high salary in a prestigious law firm. The years and years of study, the financial suffering and deprivation, the postponement of rest and relaxation, the delayed entrance into adulthood — all would at last be compensated for with guaranteed success.

But as graduation approached, Ed began to feel that the years of sacrifice had been a catastrophic mistake. The idea of joining a law firm to make a lot of money and to find security loomed up as one more step in the never-ending subjugation of his spirit. He was excruciatingly dissatisfied but did not know what he wanted to do with his life. He felt like starting over again. His fantasies included the usual flight to a tropical island or into a mountain retreat; but even less radical possibilities, such as teaching in a small university or starting his own practice, seemed utopian fantasies. He could not bring himself to throw away the years of sacrifice. How could he say, "I don't want fame and fortune; I want to be free to do the work I enjoy and to find love"?

Ed had been married throughout his entire training period but felt no more love for his wife than for his many years of higher education. He had chosen her largely out of need for someone to keep him company during his lengthy, agonized suppression of himself. Now he daydreamed of finding a happy, romantic relationship, while it seemed to him that his wife dreamed of reaping the rewards of sacrifice.

Worse still, he had a son whom he loved dearly. How could he break up a marriage? How could he do it to his wife and son, let alone to himself? How could he become "one of those men" who leaves his wife after she had "suffered for him"? Ed couldn't face it as graduation approached. He determined to stay with his wife and to join one of the several law firms that were courting him. He would pay off his debts, put some money aside, and at some later unspecified date, he would think about what he wanted to do with his life. He would continue endlessly preparing for the future.

Then one night when Ed was nearly overcome with physical exhaustion, sleeplessness, and tension, he became involved in a violent argument with his wife. He was about to tell her, "I quit. I'm leaving," but instead he suppressed his rage and stalked from the room. As he sat alone, he panicked, no longer able to remember his name, or what he did each day, or what year or place he was in. He forgot that he had just been enraged at his wife and that he was physically and mentally exhausted. He believed he had been poisoned or that he'd become insane. He was afraid he would never return to reality.

When his wife came into the room, he saw not a person but a terrifying, menacing monster. It was not as if he thought he saw the monster face — he actually saw it. The new reality was more vivid than his ordinary experience of sight under ordinary circumstances. He managed to make the hallucination disappear and then clung to his wife, sobbing and begging her to tell him who he was and what was happening to him and when it would be over. He thought of turning himself in at a mental hospital.

His confusion and terror lasted for many hours, until he fell asleep late at night. Even in the morning, he felt as if someone had taken control of him the night before. He felt he would never be the same.

One month later, he was sitting alone with his wife in their home. He felt an urge to make love to her and, at the same moment, felt revolted by everything their relationship represented to him. Then he abruptly felt the same crazy sensations coming on, only this time, instead of seeing his wife's face turn into a monster, he saw her. As if for the first time in his entire life, he saw her desperate need for him, her panic over any hint of separation, her fearful need for him to pursue his career, her terror about having to face herself. He saw it all and knew he did not love or respect her. But he was as frightened and panic-stricken as his wife and did not have the courage to leave. Now he wanted to kill her. He began to hallucinate cutting her head off. He saw her in vivid detail, bleeding on the floor.

The struggle within him was so touch-and-go that he dared not go near the kitchen and the knives for many hours. For several hours he kept repeating to himself again, "I love my wife the way she is; I must be a good man." It was a chant, a magical incantation to suppress the terror within himself. He remembers making weird associations between life and wife as the words clanged like cymbals in his head.

That night, when he had calmed down, he made his decision. He would do what he had to do, regardless of his guilt and terror. He would uproot his entire life — leave his wife and quit the new job. He did not know what he would do thereafter; he only knew he must be free to pursue his own goals.

When I met him several years later, Ed felt grateful for his two "nervous breakdowns." They reflected utter failures to be brave in the pursuit of his own life, but he had listened to himself and decided which way to go. He was now divorced, very much in love with another woman, and happily making his way in his own small, but self-determined practice of law. He saw his son frequently and felt proud to set him an example of liberty and love.

Ed knew that he had come very close to becoming a very evil person — a man who would murder his wife out of helplessness rather than choose his own freedom. His confrontation with himself as a potential maniac had made him take more seriously his own potential to do good or evil. The vivid, surrealistic, lurid, and murderous quality to his personal crisis made clear to him that he had reached the limits at which he could suppress himself without dire consequences. More than that, these breaks with reality gave him a sense of how profoundly suppressed he had made himself; he realized that he had been out of touch with his outrage and pain.

It would require an entire novel to describe how Ed had worked himself into such a state of self-oppression, but a few highlights can be mentioned. Ed had lost a beloved aunt who had raised him in his wealthy mother's home until the age of three, when she unexpectedly died. He then found himself thrown into intimacy with his divorced mother, a virtual stranger, who discovered, to her outrage, that her little son loved not her but her dead sister. She ranted and raved about his deep grief for his aunt, compared him to his "no-good father," and, in one horrible scene in the kitchen, she brandished a knife and threatened to "carve you up, you little bastard" for not loving her.

Ed was already a tough little guy, and his first impulses were to fight back. He could recall the scene, standing before the demented mother while she brandished the carving knife. He had responded with catatoniclike petrification and then later stole his mother's letter opener and slept with it beneath his pillow in case she came in the night to carve him up. All this at age four. But he saw the obvious futility of fighting back and, instead, suppressed his love for his aunt, which now became unconscious. It would be decades before he ever recalled her again. Instead, he created the facade of a superdutiful son who would do anything to please his mother. His life depended on it.

As Ed grew up, life became one endless effort to please one woman after another. He would do anything to avoid being like his "no-good father." His unconscious decision drove him to placate his mother and then his wife in utter suppression of himself, while he became a superachiever and superprovider for his family.

This facade broke down in his early thirties, when he could no longer stand to deny his desire for personal fulfillment and for love. He thought, as the child had thought, that he must kill his mother and now his wife, from whom he could imagine no escape. Nor could he muster the courage to face the world without these women in his state of crippled self-oppression. But he was even out of touch with this basic terror and largely experienced his conflict as guilt over being a "bad husband."

Too afraid and guilty to step alone into the world, he had almost opted instead for the mutual destruction of his wife and self, leaving the true oppressor — his mother — to go free. His ethical sense had won out, however, even before he understood the deepest roots of his conflict. He had separated from his wife and broken away from his still vengeful mother to enter the world alone, though it brought him face to face with a storm of fear suppressed from earliest childhood.

Ed's story is little different from the horror that remains locked within the childhood amnesia of many, many people. Similar and sometimes more bloodcurdling stories have been discovered within the childhoods of most of my clients who have reached adulthood in states of severe self-oppression.

Life is a morality play — a drama in which the individual, faced with enormous conflicts and stresses, must choose his or her solutions. Ed had mustered the courage to stare at his own evil solutions, and he turned his back on craziness and destructiveness.

Ed's life may have been saved by a decision to stay away from traditional psychiatric therapy until he had gained control over his craziness. Had he been in treatment with an ordinary psychiatrist during either one of his crazy episodes, the odds are overwhelming that he would have been put into a mental hospital against his will and subjected to high doses of mind-blunting tranquilizers. Had he resisted this treatment, he might have undergone a downhill course, with psychiatry completely breaking him down with humiliation and drugs, and even with electroshock, much as I describe happening to patients in my novel, *The Crazy from the Sane*. He might have even killed someone in his frustration. After his mind had been blunted by months or more of psychiatric assault, he certainly would have begun to look as if he suffered from an inexplicable psychotic disorder, unapproachable by psychotherapy or self-liberation. Yet he had liberated himself without professional help.

Craziness as a Failure of Nerve

Those of us who are unhappy most of the time are usually being cowardly most of the time. If you end up feeling like a personal failure, it will come as the endpoint of a series of cowardly decisions that you have made. Craziness is a failure of nerve. It is a betrayal of oneself as a moral agent, as well as of personal sovereignty, personal freedom, and self-determination.

When we are cowardly, we resort to confusion, misidentification, and helplessness as methods of handling conflict. To overcome fearful helplessness, a person must determine to face his fears, his unethical deeds, and anything else that he has been trying to avoid.

Insanity is cowardice; utter insanity is utter cowardice. The person who is constantly anxious or who races from one delusion to another or from a paranoid blaming of others to a depressed blaming of oneself refuses to be brave about handling anything, including his own mind. People who are grossly deluded and hallucinating are grossly cowardly and have forfeited responsibility for the control of their own inner life.

But doesn't everyone have a breaking point? Don't some people deserve to be crazy, considering how they grew up and considering what has happened to them?

Even if each person has a limit, that limit will be set by the individual person. Under similar circumstances, one person will become unethical and cowardly, ultimately going crazy or killing himself or herself or others, while another will rise to new heights of ethical conduct. Even in the most extreme circumstances, such as facing death, some collapse morally and die helplessly, while others maintain their dignity and responsibility. The outcome in death may be the same, but the quality of life to the last minute will vastly differ.

A Dismaying Fact of Life

This is a fact of life: some men and women are more willing than others to think and to act bravely. They provide us with our ethical models.

Nowadays, craziness too often becomes our ethical standard. Faced with a morally reprehensible act, such as a vicious murder, we try to understand and to sympathize over the poor fellow's childhood or current deprivations. We give ourselves and our children a sense that any conduct, however bad, can be justified, if only the excuse is good enough. We have become a society of excuse-makers.

Any psychological or therapeutic model that undermines the ideal of bravery and ethical transcendence robs the individual and the society of its verve or spiritual strength. Recently, a client began therapy with me by protesting that he did not wish to look into his childhood to find the causes of his current problems. At first, I thought he was advocating helplessness in an effort to avoid confronting himself and his life history, but it became apparent that he had been in close contact with a number of psychiatrists at social gatherings and had frequently heard them talking about public figures or criminals in terms of how their backgrounds had caused them to act irresponsibly or criminally. He was afraid I might turn out to be one of these excuse-making therapists, and he told me, "I had a deprived background, too. I was poor, my mother drank, and my father was like a robot. But I didn't go out and rape or kill anyone." My new client wanted recognition of his identity as a person with free will, responsibility, and courage. Once he made this clear to me, he was more than willing to examine the influences his childhood had upon him, as long as his own chosen responses to these influences were not ignored.

Courage

The *American Heritage Dictionary of the English Language* defines courage in a manner largely compatible with my own usage:

> the state or quality of mind or spirit that enables one to face danger with self-possession, confidence, and resolution; bravery; valor. Courage suggests a reserve of moral strength on which one may draw in time of emergency.

In the psychology of self-determination, courage is:

> the willingness to face danger and to take risks, or the determination to remain ethical, sovereign, and free under any and all circumstances.

People who believe that they lack courage often ask, "How do others get it?" or "Where does it come from?" The answer that "people must get it from within themselves" usually proves most unsatisfactory and even provocative, although it is the only answer that can be made. It is ironic that people are so jealous of others for possessing and displaying that which lies within themselves for the taking.

"Where does courage come from?" is not very different from the question, "Where does free will come from?" There are many puzzles like this in life. Why are some people determined to be loving at all costs? Why do some people hold onto their ethics to the bitter end? Why do some people try harder than others at everything?

Modern, sophisticated individuals want answers to these questions, but I do not have them. I begin with the reality that you and I make choices that govern the outcome of our personal lives. Whether you will love yourself sufficiently to take the necessary risks must remain entirely up to you. I do not discount the importance of encouragement or moral support from our friends and associates; but when all is said and done, each person must search within himself or herself to decide if life has spiritual value and if it is worth living to the fullest. Each person must decide whether it is in the realm of moral and mortal possibility to face everything, from death to authoritarian parents to totalitarian governments, by loving oneself and others.

I am reminded of a friend of mine who almost became one more statistic verifying the high rate of suicide among psychiatrists. He sat one late evening in his study with a .38 caliber revolver in his hand wondering if he should end his troubles. He imagined the sound of the shot echoing through the house and felt a vengeful satisfaction at what the event would do to his wife and parents. But then he envisioned his young son and daughter awakened by the same shot. Now bereft of their father, they would be more at the mercy of the very people who seemed so oppressive to him: his wife and his parents.

No matter how much he was suffering, and no matter how much revenge appealed to him, he would not do this to his children. He not only felt responsible for them as beings he had brought to life upon earth, he also loved them. Instead of shooting himself, he determined to change his life — to break with the people who he felt oppressed him and give himself more to those whom he loved. Actions that once seemed too terrifying to contemplate now became possible because he had accepted responsibility for his children. Ultimately he would discover that he must apply the same principles to himself — moral responsibility for his own welfare and love for himself. He was on the way to transforming his life.

Chapter Nine

The Emotions of Self-oppression and Personal Failure — Guilt, Shame, and Anxiety

We are now able to bring many of the concepts of the psychology of self-determination together into a comprehensive understanding of self-oppression, the specific styles of personal failure, and the emotions that are generated by these failures. We are in a position to improve our understanding of guilt, shame, and anxiety.

Self-esteem has already been examined as the good feeling generated by the conscious exercise of free will, reason, and self-determination. Low or negative self-esteem is generated by the failure to think and to act in this manner. Each of the lifestyles of failure or self-oppression generates a particular kind of low self-esteem: guilt, shame, or anxiety.

Guilt is the feeling of low self-esteem generated by blaming self (depression) as a lifestyle; shame is the low self-esteem generated by blaming others (paranoia) as a lifestyle; and anxiety is the low self-esteem generated by blaming no one (anxiety) as a lifestyle. While these emotions, like the styles themselves, will often be mixed together and will often become indistinguishable, these distinctions nonetheless stand up remarkably well.

Blaming Others and Shame

Shame is most closely associated with blaming others as a lifestyle because the paranoid is preoccupied with others and with their view of him or her. Shame is the fear of being ridiculed, humiliated, or disgraced by others and in comparison with others. It is the sense of being small and impotent in relation to others. Much more than guilt, shame involves publicity or discovery, an awareness that others are aware. It is closely related to that more mild state called embarrassment, wherein the person feels displayed in a foolish or stupid manner. As in guilt, the person may believe that he or she deserves to feel shame or to be derided, censured, and ridiculed. The difference is not in whether or not the person accepts the negative feelings but in the specific quality of being thoroughly discredited, utterly disgraced by others and in comparison to others and their standards.

A woman chooses not to face her lack of self-determination. She shifts blame to the outside world and thereby vests it with enormous power, making herself impotent by comparison. She does not dare to appear soft, tender, or easily hurt. She is certain she will be victimized and be made to feel ridiculous if she admits she wants help or love.

This woman may try to compensate by building a glorious pseudoimage of herself. Her impotence is transformed magically into potency, and she becomes the center of vast but ill-defined plots to do her harm or to elevate her to a special status among people. This is small compensation for her self-oppressive failure to be self-determining.

Blaming others and shame are closely related to loneliness. The man who makes a life of blaming others feels that all of his most private experiences would be ridiculed or belittled if anyone else became aware of them. He hides deeply within himself, never daring expose his private life even within the intimacy of his family or his friends. Privacy becomes his most prized possession, to the exclusion of intimacy. He is petrified of publicity. But worse still, he compromises himself, suppressing anything about himself that might spring to light unexpectedly; he loses touch with his own feelings, suppressing every aspect of himself that does not meet standards imposed on him in childhood. Originally afraid that no one will take him seriously, he no longer takes himself seriously and begins to feel shallow and hollow inside. If he is ever to overcome this awful sense of loneliness and emptiness, he must dare to take himself seriously, and he must be prepared to weather any shameful rejections that may come his way. He must be determined to deal with his real oppressors.

Shame is so painful we seldom wish to admit to it. Most people believe that we suffer much less from shame than from guilt. Yet shame plays a most important, if silent or inapparent, role in inhibiting our personal aspirations. We are ashamed to admit that we dream of being great artists, movie producers, architects, builders, athletes, or executives. We are ashamed to admit that we believe deep down inside that we are very special beings endowed with enormous creativity, if only we could get it out. We are ashamed to admit that we do not love our current lifestyles, our jobs, marriages, and friends, and how much we long for a much better life. We are ashamed to admit that we wish to be loved, cared for, or helped. We do not consciously feel shame over ourselves because we do not take our secret wishes seriously enough to envision the need to feel or to overcome our shame over these aspirations. In therapy, for example, a person's most honest desires for himself are often prefaced with, "You might think this is ridiculous," or "I know this sounds absurd, but . . . " Then he declares that he would like to quit his job and change his life or that he really thinks he is capable of great achievements.

Whenever any degree of publicity is involved in an activity, as in public speaking, writing, painting, singing, athletics, or dancing — shame becomes especially easy to detect. The inhibited performer is afraid to subject himself or herself to ridicule. Whenever our aspirations are for greatness among other men and women, shame again rears its head quite obviously. Shame is the greatest inhibitor of romantic love and creativity. We become so afraid of how we will look to others, we dare not aspire toward our most prized and precious goals. If we feel no shame, it is because we never tempt ourselves to overcome our inhibitions.

Self-esteem versus Paranoid Pride

Self-esteem must be sharply distinguished from pride. Self-esteem results from ethical self-determination. The autonomous, self-governing person feels self-esteem. Pride results entirely from other-determination and is closely related to shame and the paranoid lifestyle. The prideful person is ultimately afraid of being overwhelmed with humiliation or ridicule. Pride is reactiveness to what others think. It is subjugation to the standards set by others.

The prideful person works against his or her true self-interest and is a self-oppressor. Instead of backing away from a fight he did not start, a young man tries to prove that he can stand up to a bully. Instead of leaving the scene with his body intact and with the knowledge that he has refused to participate in someone else's destructiveness, he gets into a brawl. Win or lose, he has lost; he has permitted an irresponsible person to draw him into his destructiveness.

A woman becomes enraged when she discovers that her lover has been having sexual relations with another woman. Instead of searching herself for her own contribution to the failure of her love affair, and instead of confronting her lover's deceitfulness, she concentrates on getting even with the other woman. She feels put down or shamed by the other woman and becomes involved in acrimonious backbiting and hatefulness. She corrupts her own character and fails to deal with her personal failure to understand herself or to create a worthwhile romance.

Pride can drive a person into conquests or feats of daring that give the individual ephemeral ego-gratifications. But the man who feels "I showed *him*" has really become his victim's victim. He has let himself become preoccupied with triumph over an individual for whom he has little or no respect. This is a terrible irony: our prideful conflicts almost invariably bind us to people for whom we hold no respect. Given that a person voluntarily wastes himself or herself through entanglements with those whom he or she disrespects, it must be suspected that this person holds still less respect for himself or herself.

Differences between Shame and Guilt

Guilt is the emotion generated by the lifestyle of blaming self. It too is a form of low self-esteem. The guilt-ridden person believes that he has fully adopted an appropriate moral code. A man in his thirties, for example, may be anguished by his desire to leave his wife. He "knows" how bad he is and believes that others will agree with him that he is bad in desiring his freedom and another woman. Convinced that his standard is universal, he may be eager to tell anyone who will listen how bad he feels about himself and may experience some redemption through his confessions. He will do this until he reaches such a depth of depression that he loses all hope and becomes stuporous and uncommunicative.

The shameful person, perhaps a shy, fearful young woman, feels more like an outsider who is damned by her inability to meet or to understand universal standards. Unlike the guilty person, she feels that confessions of her inferiority will humiliate her. Certain she falls short of the mark, she is afraid to tell anyone about her smallest blemish or peccadillo. She shrinks within herself and is reluctant to talk about herself at all. She only begins to communicate when she has reached such a depth of paranoia that she must tell the world about the plots against her.

These differences are apparent in the language used to enforce guilt and shame. Guilt is imposed through remarks that appeal to the child's own inner sense of right and wrong. "That was bad," "You did a wrong thing," "You know that's not right," "You are naughty," "You are selfish," "You really want to hurt your mother," "You don't care how you hurt us," "You are bad," and so on. The expectation is for the child to feel like a moral being who knows he or she is bad. This child is at least being taken seriously.

Shame is imposed through remarks or actions that make light of the child's sense of right and wrong and that compare him or her in a belittling fashion with the superior authority of adults or with the standards of other persons and other children. Whereas the guilty child feels he or she is bad, the shameful child feels out of place, insignificant, and unable to use his or her own judgment. The shamed child is made childish rather than bad, small and inferior rather than evil. Shame is stirred up by remarks such as, "I can't believe you would do anything like that"; "Nice girls don't do that"; "Mommy feels so embarrassed about the way you behave"; "Nobody will want to play with you"; "You should never say anything like that in public"; "See how you look to everyone"; "You're making a fool of yourself"; "Hide

The Emotions of Self-oppression and Personal Failure   103

your face."

Of all the belittling experiences in life, being ignored may be the most devastating. Whereas being ridiculed at least suggests that the victim merits some attention, being ignored states clearly that the victim is worthy of nothing, not even notice. The child who experiences this is likely to be hard pressed to rationalize or understand it. One of my clients declared it a "mystery" at an early age and projected this mystery into life as an adult. If slighted by someone, she would experience emotional devastation. Her defensive attempts to fathom the "mystery" bordered on paranoia, until she was able to recall the childhood origins and to discover some of the family interactions surrounding this dreadful humiliation.

The guilty man sees people scowling; they know he is an evil force. He has a sense of potency, if only to do evil. He can take himself seriously. The shameful woman sees people laughing at her; they know she is of no account. She feels impotent, even unable to do evil.

In guilt, the masquerade of personal sovereignty and personal freedom is most thoroughly maintained. The guilt-ridden person feels inner-directed. His morality seems like his own. He may declare that he feels free to do anything he wishes with life, even while he rules out all happiness for himself and sacrifices his freedom to his parents, his spouse, and his children. He may declare himself sovereign over all his life, even as he kills himself.

Guilt typically begins in childhood when a parent rants and raves against a child in an attempt to limit the child's sense of responsibility. Remember, I am defining responsibility as an awareness that you can and should be in charge of your own thoughts, feelings, and conduct. If the child accepts self-blame and its associated guilt, he will give up responsibility for the actions he originally chose to take. Most likely, they were actions that promoted his own self-interest, but soon he will not even recall that he once was motivated by such "selfish" ideas.

Psychotherapists usually interpret guilt and depression in adulthood as a "reaction to loss," without concerning themselves with the individual's betrayal of self-determination and self-interest. They encourage the depressed person to express or "abreact" his or her feelings about the loss. This can only be of temporary help. The depressed person must face his or her own helplessness and, especially, must recognize his or her "reaction to loss" as a repetition of a lifestyle of self-oppression and guilt that reaches back into childhood.

The woman who cannot recover from the loss of her husband turns out to have oppressed herself in the marriage, much as she was oppressed by her father. Her exchanges with him were often painful, oppressive, and humiliating. With his death, her rage and resentment are reactivated, not only toward her husband but toward her father; but she is a cowardly self-oppressor. Instead of feeling "I'm glad to be rid of them," she becomes still more irrational and helpless in their absence. She "recovers" only by finding another oppressive man to couple with her self-oppression. Or perhaps she never even makes such a sham recovery and instead sinks into chronic depression.

Blaming No One and Anxiety

Anxiety is the emotion associated with blaming no one and nothing as a lifestyle. Anxiety is generated by acting and thinking in a generally stupid, bewildered, unknowing, or confused fashion.

The anxious young man may tell you that quite the reverse is the true case: his anxiety *makes* him feel stupid, confused, bewildered, and so on. In reality, this person makes himself blind and ignorant and turns his fear into anxiety.

Very often individuals can be seen to actively encourage anxiety in each other by sending confusing and baffling messages. Parents will often maintain a child's state of helplessness and dependency by making constant communications about how the world is frightening, dangerous, and chaotic in a way that cannot be understood or managed. The parent who encourages anxiety wants above all else to make sure that the child never gets his or her mind sufficiently organized to become independent of the parent.

Fear as the Root of Guilt, Shame, and Anxiety

As helplessness is the common denominator of all lifestyles of failure, fear is the common emotion beneath all guilt, shame, and anxiety. Helplessness is the attitude and fear is the motive that lies at the root of all personal failure. Nothing is more important than a clear understanding of these relationships.

Guilt, shame, and anxiety are derivatives of fear. Anyone who feels guilt, shame, or anxiety and who seeks to understand it must find the fear that lies beneath it.

Here is a simplified example. A man in his forties acts as if he can never get angry at his wife. He feels terribly guilty whenever he gets near to being angry. That is, he talks to himself in a manner that is very hostile. He calls himself names and finds himself immobilized by a feeling of gloom and despondency at the mere thought of getting angry at his wife. A first level of analysis disclosed that he is afraid of the consequences of any encounter with her. Specifically, she threatens to leave him. So instead of facing that threat, he attacks himself. Once having faced that fear, however, he discovers that it would be no disaster if she left. It might even be a relief. Still he remains afraid to take action. He remains helpless.

It turns out he feels guilty over getting angry at any woman — a generalization he learned in relation to his mother at an early age. When he got angry at his mother, he instead turned on himself and felt very guilty. He cannot even recall showing any anger toward his mother. At last, however, he traces back his life history to a period of grave conflict with his mother when he was three, four, and five years old. Whenever he got angry at her, she threatened to leave him. Twice she literally abandoned him in strange places — a store and a restaurant — when he got "nasty" with her because he was tired and irritable. Beneath his guilt is a fear of abandonment by his mother, as well as a complex of other fears learned in childhood.

Ultimately, guilt, shame, and anxiety as forms of self-oppression are attempts to deal with specific fears. Sometimes the threats that arouse the fears are very obvious — physical punishment, abandonment, harsh words, and the like. At other times, the threats are more difficult to define — a barely discernible expression of disapproval on a parent's face or a withdrawal of love so subtle that only the child senses it.

To repeat, a good or thorough examination of any guilt, shame, or anxiety will take a person back to the original fear. The guilt, shame, and anxiety are self-induced attempts to deal with the fear or with the threat that induced the fear.

Too often, therapists go back to the sources of guilt, shame, or anxiety and think they have solved the problem. A man's sense of guilt is traced back to a time when his mother repeatedly told him he was no good. A woman's sense of shame is traced back to her father's communication that women are inferior. Another person's anxiety is traced back to a persistently anxious relationship with his mother and then his wife. None of this is sufficient. The hardest work remains to be done. What *fear* induced the son to accept his mother's statements that he was no good? What fear caused the daughter to accept her father's insinuation that women are inferior? What fear caused the man to accept anxiety-generating relationships with his mother and his wife? At the point of looking at the fear, there will often be a great deal of resistance or cowardice. But it is important to get at the root fear. It dispels the idea that guilt, shame, or anxiety are somehow so natural to persons that they will adopt them without great cause. There is always great cause — great fear — behind the adoption of such a self-destructive attitude toward oneself. Therefore, the child's great vulnerability to fear or to *real threats* is key in understanding the commonplace development of such great overloads of guilt, shame, and anxiety in the life of the typical child.

The Fear of Death

The most debilitating fear is the fear of death. While I am hardly the first person to make this observation, the fear of death is usually overlooked in seeking the childhood origins of guilt, shame, and anxiety. When most people try to recall the fear of death in their own lives, they remember specific incidents, such as the death of a friend from illness or the threat of a serious personal illness. Others may think of adolescent ruminations about life and death, or about middle-aged fears of growing old. But the fear of death begins early in life,, and much of the conduct of small children as young as four or five years old is influenced by this fear.

Very often when I help clients reach back into the forgotten past to a time when an all-out confrontation took place with their parents, they recall that a parent "threatened to beat me to death" or "to leave me to starve in the street." Even in the absence of outright threats, the child may have become aware of violence lurking within the parents — a dread that the fights between mother and father could have been turned against the children, or that the hysterical spanking could have turned into a severe pummeling, or that Mom or Dad might have lost control and bashed in a head with that uplifted frying pan or whiskey bottle.

Often the issue of death comes up in therapy when I suggest to adults that they did have choices in childhood and that they could have stood up to their parents. The response will come spontaneously from the heart, "Yeah, I could have told Dad to shove off, and he would have killed me," or "Yes, I could have stood up to Mom when she got hysterical, but she would have wrung my neck." Sometimes, thorough questioning will elicit lurid details of violence perpetrated by the parents against other members of the family, friends, pets, or inanimate objects, such as furniture or walls. Sometimes the threat will be more vague but pervasive: an attitude of brutality rather than perpetrated brutality.

When I deal directly with youngsters or their parents, often I will witness these threats firsthand. As the adolescent attempts to become independent of the parent, the parent begins to threaten physical violence. More frequently, the parent directs a withering hatred at the child — an obvious, if unstated, death wish toward the child.

Parents connect death to "being bad" by encouraging children to believe that misconduct (meaning disobedience) can cause them to be sick and to die. Sometimes the connections are made directly, such as attributing colds and stomach aches to failures to follow prescribed rules of dressing or eating. Instead of treating any real connection as a factual matter that the child should learn about, such as eating too much junky candy can make you sick to your stomach, the parent treats the matter as a lesson in submission, such as disobeying Mommy leads to stomach aches. Many Western religions also encourage this connection between being bad and dying, or being bad and going to hell.

Existential Anguish

Existential psychologists emphasize dread and despair in relationship to human mortality and the human condition. These psychologists make explicit that thoughtful persons will necessarily suffer from these agonies as they become aware of death and the alleged "meaninglessness" of life.

If there is an existential anguish associated with life, it has not played a large part in the painful emotions suffered by the people I have come to know closely. Human suffering is not proportionate to human intelligence or wisdom but to the misuse or abuse of human rationality. Alleged existential anguish has usually turned out to be a rationalization for not facing real life problems, such as miserable marriages, unsatisfying jobs, and lifestyles of failure pursued since childhood. The failure to love, or to place a high value on oneself and selected others, is a personal failure that lends itself most easily to rationalizations about the inherent "meaninglessness" and "alienation" of life.

If existentialists remain mired in guilt, shame, and anxiety, it is because they pursue philosophies and lifestyles that are hostile to their own self-interest and oppressive towards others as well. A brief review of well-known existentialists will show that their viewpoints are often closely linked to religious and political philosophies that are anti-individualistic and that call for personal self-sacrifice and submission. In psychiatry, existentialists have found no difficulty associating themselves with involuntary treatment, authoritarian psychoanalysis, and the use of drugs and electroshock for subduing unhappy, difficult human beings. In politics, they are often sympathetic to collectivistic solutions that inevitably lead to the undermining of individualism and even to totalitarianism. In religion, they confuse love with obedience to Judeo-Christian authoritarianism.

The main similarity between my own libertarian viewpoint and existentialism lies in the common emphasis upon "responsibility" and upon the individual as a moral agent. But responsibility, for the existentialist, is often laden with "accepting human helplessness" and even with "accepting guilt." Too often the existential guru replaces traditional authority with his own authority. He encourages followers or disciples similar to those in any authoritarian system.

When an individual seems to be facing an "existential crisis," including preoccupations with death and with "meaninglessness," it is time for the individual to take a more honest look at his or her current life to see wherein he or she is failing to pursue self-interest in an ethical manner. If the person feels paralyzed by anguish, he or she is probably becoming helpless in the face of a lifestyle that leads straight back to an oppressed childhood. Before labeling anyone's pain as "existential," make especially sure it hasn't been experienced many times before, even as a child.

There is a more abstract "existential" anguish that individuals sometimes endure, but again, it is not inherent in life or in humankind's nature. It is the anguish of pursuing false, contradictory, or self-destructive values. When a person feels disillusioned with life, he or she is often disillusioned with a specific set of values that he or she has mistakenly identified with "life." This individual needs a new set of values with which to understand and to approach life.

Typically, a person disillusioned with life has been pursuing some variation of the ethics of altruism, with a heavy dose of self-righteous self-sacrifice. The individual learned self-sacrifice at the hands of parents who taught the child that "selfishness" is wrong and that the needs of others come first. This was then reinforced by church, school, and government propaganda, all aimed at getting the individual to pursue the self-interest of others at the sacrifice of his or her own interests. When others then fail to repay in kind with sacrifices for the altruistic individual, and when altruism per se fails to bring joy, the individual can become embittered, disillusioned, and very vengeful.

Recently, a psychologically sophisticated client came in for a session after a conversation with another sophisticated friend. My client and his friend decided that my client had two "opposing" tendencies: an altruistic desire to sacrifice for others and a selfish desire to take advantage of others. They concluded that each attitude probably reflected the conflicting viewpoints of my client's two parents. Instead, I suggested that the two viewpoints — altruism and a desire to take advantage of others — were cut from the same ethical cloth. Everyone I have known who has devoted himself or herself to altruism has expressed an underlying resentment that the world does not magically repay the altruism with enormous praise and with mutual self-sacrifices made in return by other altruists. Altruists become frustrated and bitter because they cannot survive psychologically when their psychology calls for self-sacrifice. They then blame this personal failure on the failure of others to return their altruism with altruism. It is no exaggeration to say that some of the most frustrated, cruel, and vengeful people I have ever known have preached a philosophy of self-sacrifice for themselves. On the other hand, a person happily devoted to the pursuit of his or her own self-interest is not likely to resent others who pursue their own interests as well. He or she will only resent those persons who use force or fraud to achieve their ends, thereby interfering with the rights of others to pursue their own self-interest free of force and fraud. He or she will note that those people who do use force to achieve their ends are typically people who preach altruism. They use force against others allegedly for the good of others, even claiming that their use of force is a self-sacrifice in itself.

Guilt, shame, and anxiety are self-induced or self-generated attempts to deny real threats against ourselves, our self-interest, and our freedom. The threats evoked fear in us, and when we suppressed ourselves, our fears were replaced by the emotions of guilt, shame, and anxiety, or related feelings of self-hate, resentment, bitterness, and the like. Fear is the foundation of these emotions, especially fear of real and imagined authorities, and, in particular, childhood fears of one's parents. The greatest fears include rejection, abandonment, loss of love, and ultimately death at the hands of these authorities.

Confront your fears, determine *never* to become helpless in the face of fear, and you will make a most important step toward a life of liberty, love, and creativity.

Chapter Ten

Guilt Is an Unethical Emotion

There is only one value to guilt, shame, and anxiety — their usefulness as signals that the person must become more self-determining and more ethical in his or her thoughts and actions. The person who does anything other than use these emotions as signals for the need to change himself or herself has misread their meaning and continues to live a life of self-oppression.

Feelings of guilt, shame, and anxiety are rarely, if ever, rooted in rationality, reality, or sound ethics. Instead, they reflect the individual's need to come more honestly to grips with reason, reality, and the libertarian pursuit of self-interest.

Guilt Fails as a Deterrent

Guilt may help prevent a person from committing one crime or another because the person wishes to stop feeling bad about himself or herself. But it will not help anyone become a more self-determining, self-loving person free of the desire to bring harm upon others. If anything, the guilt-ridden aggressor often tends to feel outraged over the control that his or her victim has gained by "making" him or her feel guilty. Thus, the guilt-ridden person can become more eager to torment his or her victim. Guilt can drive people to express their hostility with increased abandon in an attempt to surmount their guilt or to prove it impotent.

Guilt not only fails to prevent crimes; it can break down completely and result in the most heinous atrocities, as the individual seeks to obliterate his pain by excesses of viciousness. This is one reason why deeply disturbed people commit such apparently senseless crimes.

Guilt is also a poor method of control because oppressors are usually self-oppressors as well, who may welcome the sense of guilt and may seek to increase it. They may *encourage* others to place blame on them.

Guilt is also a poor means of control because it fosters irrationality. Along with shame and anxiety, it blocks out reason, depressing the capacity to think about oneself or about other people. A person burdened with guilt is not in touch either with himself or herself or with other people. The most important barrier to destructiveness — recognition of the community of people, the kinship of humans — is partially or wholly obliterated by guilt.

In myself, my friends, and my clients, some of the most violent reactions and feelings are spurred on by guilt. Typically, a husband takes a patronizing, guilt-provoking attitude toward his wife, and the wife goes on an emotional rampage against him that lasts for hours or days. Or a wife nags at a husband, and he ends up threatening her with physical violence. In each case, the person reacting to the criticism with violence can be found to suffer from an enduring guilt, especially a suspicion that the other person is right. Usually this guilt can be traced back to similar interactions earlier in life, in which a parent also evoked guilt and suppressed rage. Now the guilt is re-stimulated and the violence never directed at the parent is directed at the new guilt provoker. Once this guilt is handled, the patronizing husband or the nagging wife can be dealt with without the use of violence. Even if the individual being criticized decides to break up the relationship, he or she will not feel the need for violence.

The violence of the guilty-feeling person almost always has a strongly self-righteous air to it. The guilt-provoking husband or the nagging wife is thought to "deserve" whatever is done to him or her. Often the violence in action or in covert feeling has the quality of retribution. It is also a statement — "I'm so right that I will use violence." The violence rendered becomes a kind of godlike wrath against the wicked. This attitude can usually be found to one degree or another in anyone who feels or acts violently. To overcome such guilt, the individual must recognize its childhood sources and find the courage to deal more directly with the current oppressor, by confronting or leaving the oppressor (see p. 120).

Authoritarians and totalitarians propagandize on behalf of guilt. They argue that guilt prevents people from harming others. They really mean that guilt manifests the subjugation of the individual — the crushing of his or her spirit of rebellion. These authoritarians want their subjects to suppress themselves on behalf of the authoritarian's oppressive morality. Authoritarians create confusion between guilt and responsibility to bind their victims into a submissive, guilty style of life.

Responsibility is very different. A responsible person feels strong and self-determining, not weak and helpless. A person who feels responsible for an action, good or bad, knows that he or she did it and that he or she had other options.

Sharing Pain as a Form of Guilt

Nobody wants to feel anybody else's pain. Yet almost everyone thinks he or she is supposed to feel someone's pain. This is an especially pernicious and common manifestation of self-oppression and guilt.

Self-oppressed people feel pain when they see someone else hurt. In extreme instances, a person hears about someone else getting beaten up and feels the pain in his or her own stomach. Or this person watches someone else bleeding from a cut and nearly faints. Or he or she sees a dog injured on the highway and is overcome with a sick feeling.

Self-oppressed people also feel emotional pain when they see someone else suffering. A man finds his insides churning up when his wife starts to cry. A woman gets tense when her husband walks into the house in a bad mood. A man who has separated from his wife mopes around feeling sorry for her. A daughter suffers at the thought that her father is old and sick, even though she dislikes him.

"I feel sorry for her or him" is among the most frequent statements made by individuals who suppress themselves in response to the pain of others. "But she's hurting," my clients tell me when I ask why they don't break off with their spouse or friend. "I feel sorry for him or her," they repeat in a dozen different ways.

Many people seem to live on guilt. They build their relationships to others on the basis of sharing pain. They feel very self-righteous about this, without realizing that their viewpoint degrades humanity. It implies that people have no rational desire to help others and that love of people or love of liberty is insufficient as a motive for helping others.

Such people seek out suffering individuals. Millions of couples make psychiatric patients of each other — seeking out each other's pain and sharing it as a full-time occupation. Often my clients talk about how meaningful, important, and close their relationships have been, and every one turns out to be a mutually depressing enterprise in which both people spent most of their time talking about, dissecting, and compounding their individual miseries.

By picking out another self-oppressed person, the individual maintains a myth that all moral and insightful people suffer dreadfully and that pain is the true source of closeness. Such people never get close to each other as people; they only get close to each other as "cases."

Am I saying that people should not care about each other? I am saying that people can care about each other in two different ways — they can seek the free spirit in each other, or they can seek the helpless cripple in each other. The first is a true form of love. It is a joyful reaching out from one person to another. The second is closer to hate. It is a depressing pact to affirm each other's helplessness.

Oppressive people, especially relatives and lovers, use their pain to force others to do their bidding. If a daughter stands up to her mother, mother is likely to begin complaining about how hard her life has been or how tough it is at home with ailing Dad, or how the daughter was so difficult to raise (the pregnancy and delivery were torture!). If the daughter refuses to back down, mother may make anguished phone calls or send guilt-provoking letters about how ungrateful her child is and how all the friends and neighbors think it's terrible that Mom can't visit her daughter anymore.

The oppressor who feels abandoned may even have a nervous breakdown or attempt suicide to force the return of the wayward loved one. In therapy it often comes down to a most excruciating decision — my client must choose her own life over someone else's, when the other person threatens to commit suicide in a last ditch effort to control my client's life.

Think of it this way — the person who holds the dagger to his or her own chest in an effort to coerce you really wants to hold the dagger to your chest, but he or she is too cowardly to do it directly. Unwilling to assault you openly, or knowing that you will refuse to accept direct bullying, he or she assaults and bullies you through martyrdom, hoping to accomplish the same purpose through cowardly indirection. If you submit to this, you not only harm yourself, you encourage the other person to pursue an unethical lifestyle.

Even if it were in the other person's best interest to bully you — you should never respond to it. You should not make yourself a slave to the wretchedness of another human being. Every time you do, you destroy the beauty within your own life in the service of the ugliness within someone else's life. You deprive yourself, and you reduce the overall beauty within the world. You become less able to love not only yourself but others.

Like most forms of self-oppression, feeling someone else's pain begins in childhood. When a child stands up against an oppressive parent, the parent attempts to create pain in the child. The parent may hit the child, threaten to abandon it, or tell it how bad it is and how much it hurts mother. The child at first wants nothing to do with this, and will not hang his or her head over Mom's pain. He or she will not at first cry or cower because Dad is upset, and the oppressive parent may go to any length to make the child apologize, act ashamed, or otherwise become pained. The child who accepts this — and all children accept it to some degree — becomes a self-oppressor. This child inflicts pain upon himself or herself in order to get along with his or her oppressive parents.

Often an analysis of the parent-child relationship in therapy will demonstrate that nearly all communications from parent to child had to do with parental pain, which the parent wished the child to accept as his or her own. The child gained some sense of power and importance in this role of confidant but sold out his or her happiness in exchange. In adulthood, he or she continues to seek out others with whom to share suffering rather than joy.

When a person grasps his or her unconditional right to self-defense, he or she rejects any and all attempts to make himself or herself feel pain. This can create dramatic confrontations. A husband tells his wife that he is going to get a separation regardless of how she feels about it. She in turn tries her same old tactic. Her face grows long, her brow furrows, her mouth trembles, she cries. She is a frail person, a mild-mannered person, a person never prone to violence, but she is a powerhouse at showing pain and she pours it on. But he has changed, and he announces to her: "Your pain is your own. I won't let you make me feel it." He stands up, prepared to walk out of the room, and she breaks all precedent by smashing him in the face with her fist. She has again made him feel her pain; but he at last sees the extreme to which she will go, and he leaves the house.

A young lady returns from college to visit her mother and father at spring vacation. Father is very adamant that she must study on her vacation and that she must not visit with a particular boy, whom he sees as a potential threat to his domination over her. This oppression has been going on for years, but at last she decides to stand up to him. It gives her a strange and painful smarting in her cheeks — a real pain — but she nonetheless defies her father. She tells him she will do what she wishes with her vacation time. He in turn begins the same old harangues about how ungrateful she is. He gets more and more upset, and mother chimes in about how the daughter will give her poor father a heart attack. The young lady starts to feel a pain in her chest as well as in her cheeks, but in a burst of courage she tells her father she will do what she wishes with her life, even if it gives him a heart attack. He lunges at her and slaps her hard across the face. She backs off, turns, and leaves the house. She too is going to leave her oppressor behind. As she drives off, feeling the smarting sensation in her cheek, she recalls for the first time how he often slapped her when she was three and four years old. No wonder she felt pain in her body over every confrontation with him or with any man.

But what about loved ones? Shouldn't we feel their pain? No, we shouldn't. When we feel someone else's pain, we become partially unable to use our powers of reason. If your daughter has got a fishhook caught in her hand and you must be the one to remove it proficiently, you will do far better if you experience not one whit of her pain as you do the job. Parents who become hysterical over their children's pain are focused on their own helplessness, rather than on their children's needs, and cannot perform in emergencies.

If your friend has lost his wife and feels that his world has come to an end, you will be far more help to him if you feel none of his pain. You can, instead, assure him that your own world remains intact and that you will be fully available to him. If your wife feels hurt by her father, you will be more helpful if it does not evoke pain in you over your own parents. You will be more able to see her problem and to help her.

When I was a young therapist, I frequently felt the pain of my clients. I would occasionally cry with them, and I prided myself in how this proved I was very sensitive and human. Often my clients seemed to feel good about my emotionality. But as I became more ethical and more honest with myself, I discovered that there were patterns discernible in when and why I shed tears. It had nothing whatsoever to do with the degree of pain being felt by my clients. It had nothing to do with how much I loved them. It related to one thing and one thing only — how closely their pain touched upon an unresolved pain of my own. I was crying for myself, not for them, and my crying indicated an area in which I myself felt helpless. Needless to say, I no longer felt so proud of myself as a "feeling therapist."

Next I had to face how my feeling pain interfered with my performance as a therapist. At the very moments when I felt I was showing so much understanding through my tears, I was most in danger of distracting attention from my client's pain. Not only would his attention shift to me, but since we were in an area touchy to both of us I might become negligent in pursuing my client's problem to its painful roots. The lesson is this: if you feel pain over someone else's pain, you are likely to want to stop him or her from delving into that pain in your presence. You will therefore shut the person off.

Whenever you feel another person's pain, you will tend to do something to him or her with the aim of removing your own pain. You may end up doing great harm to the person. Psychiatrists drug their patients into stupors rather than listen to their pain. Parents beat their children senseless rather than listen to their crying. I have seen people moved near to murder in order to destroy someone whose pain they have been sharing. This is probably a major cause of mass murders within families. One member of the family can no longer bear sharing the pain that screams out from everyone within the house; the guilt is too great. So he or she kills, in a last ditch effort to remove the pain.

But why didn't the murderer choose instead to abandon the household? Herein lies the key to why people share pain with others: they do so because they are unwilling to face the alternative — leaving the person who is the source of the pain. As children, they suppressed themselves into believing that they had to stay forever with the pain-producing parent; now they carry this helplessness into adulthood.

If you wish to be a feelingful person with your family, friends, or clients, do not add your tears to theirs; love them, and let them have their pain as their own. Let them cry over their own pain while you keep them loving company.

The Fear of Hurting Others

Much as people argue that it is good to feel the pain of others, they also oppress themselves by refusing to do anything that will cause pain in others.

Obviously, there are many circumstances in which it is wrong to hurt others; I have analyzed them in setting limits on the right to self-defense. But the alleged unwillingness to hurt others is among the most common rationalizations for the failure to defend oneself or to pursue self-interest. Although cloaked in the rhetoric of altruism, this rationalization does not stem from a true love for other people. It reflects fear and often hatred of the very people whom the individual says he or she is afraid to hurt. He or she is afraid to hurt them because of childhood guilt or current threats of retaliation.

People manifest this cowardice in every aspect of their lives, in large and small encounters alike. One man cannot enjoy going to the coffee shop in his corporation building because he cannot bear encounters with people who want him to have a cup of coffee with them. He wants to use his coffee breaks to rest and to think through the coming events of the day; but he is unwilling to say to a friend or acquaintance, "Thanks, Harry, but I'd rather sit by myself; I have some things to think over," or "I'd love to visit with you another time, Jane, but I need some time alone," or "Thanks, but I always use this time to be by myself." Another man is willing to make these vague and neutral refusals but is wholly unwilling to choose one group over another at coffee time, for fear of making someone feel jealous or left out.

This same cowardice plays a major role in longterm relationships. Many friendships are based on little more than a mutual inability to tell each other off. Mary and Joe think they owe Joan and Bill a dinner, and so they invite them over. Then Joan and Bill owe Mary and Joe. Thus, ludicrous sacrifices of self-interest can keep unfulfilling relationships going indefinitely because people have rationalized that they do not want to hurt others.

I have observed in dismaying detail how men and women become enmeshed in unsatisfying, self-defeating relationships, only to pursue them to the bitter end through engagement, marriage, and unending misery. A man drinks himself nearly to death rather than face his own cowardice in breaking up a relationship with a woman he disdains. A woman collapses with physical disease and debilitation rather than stand up to her husband and to her own shame about divorce. A bizarre antispiritual adhesive, cowardice attaches people who inherently repel each other and makes strong bonds where reason and a devotion to liberty and to love would cause people to separate.

It is commonplace in therapy to see a client rationalize taking severe abuse from a parent for fear of taking a single defensive stand. Mother visits her daughter's house where she systematically dominates the family's life, insulting her daughter's ability to cook, sew, clean house, and raise the children; downgrading her son-in-law's business acumen or family background; ridiculing her grandchildren and ordering them about — all the while talking a mile a minute, exhausting everyone in the family. Having brought vast harm to everyone, the mother not only goes unpunished; she goes unopposed, because the devastated daughter allegedly "doesn't want to hurt Mom." The daughter, meanwhile, has become so embittered over the years of submission to her mother that she, in turn, commits wretched offenses against her own husband and children, nagging them, belittling them, flying off the handle at them, and even beating the smaller children. She hurts her family as much as she is hurt by her own mother — but continues to submit to the original oppressor. An end to this ugly situation will come when the daughter carefully and scrupulously protects her own self-interest and defends herself against her mother at every opportunity.

Jealousy and Resentment as Personal Failure

Jealousy, envy, bitterness, and resentment deserve special attention as variations on guilt, shame, and anxiety. Just as people tend to justify guilt as a "natural" and even beneficial emotion, so too they try to justify feeling jealous or resentful.

These people commonly focus upon the misconduct of a past or present friend, spouse, coworker, or parent. One woman I know has problems loving her sons because she is jealous of the alleged advantages all men have over women. Another feels jealous of her husband's new success in life. A man wants to kill a friend who had an affair with his wife. A young man hates his father, even though he no longer has contact with him. He still resents letting his father get away with rejecting and abusing him.

Behind every such resentment and jealousy there lies a helpless, fearful refusal to be self-determining. Often the other person is targeted as an escape from oneself and especially one's own guilt. The woman who can't enjoy her sons finds that they remind her of the things she has done to men throughout her life. The man who hates his friend doesn't want to recall that he encouraged his wife to have an affair with him as a justification for his own affairs. The woman who can't stand her husband's new success won't admit she held him back during the marriage, and that she herself is afraid to risk success or failure in the business world. The young man who hates his father doesn't want to face how he rejected his father as a child by siding with his mother against him.

These emotions are multitudinous and subtle in their expression. Sometimes the bitterness is toward life in general, as people go through their brief span of years in resentment over the bad deal they have been given. These emotions are always nonproductive. The individual is jealous because he wants to cover up the fact that he himself has failed to do the best he can with his own life.

When an ethical person works hard but fails to fulfill a dream because of chance, such as an accident or ill health, he or she does not become bitter, resentful, or jealous. While feeling disappointed, he or she knows that ethical conduct carries with it an inherent satisfaction called self-esteem. When the individual betrays self-determination, he or she covers it up with hate, resentment, bitterness, and other expressions of low self-esteem.

Locate someone around you whom you hate or resent because of harm he or she is currently doing to you. You will find beneath your hate a decision and an action that you have been too cowardly to face. Perhaps you are afraid to confront this person; perhaps you are too cowardly to take the same independent actions that you resent in the other person; perhaps you are unwilling to do something about the ill will he or she has spread; perhaps your enemy's bad actions toward you remind you of similar bad things that you yourself are doing to others; perhaps you treat others no better than your adversary treats you. Identify the source of your helplessness, take the necessary action, and you will find that even your worst enemy cannot keep you awake at night with resentment. You will do everything in your power to disarm your opponent, but you'll waste no time getting upset about him or her.

Give yourself no excuses for your failures to take care of yourself. Every time you find yourself rationalizing a failure to defend yourself or to pursue your own happiness, search beneath the helpless excuses — however good they sound — to discover your true fear. You will find yourself afraid to stand up to an oppressor, and ultimately, you will discover that you are afraid to confront your own self-defeating decisions.

Martyrdom and Resentment toward Others

The martyr complex is typically manifested when a person is doing something that he or she really does not wish to do. Often it arises in the context of sacrificing oneself for others or for a cause. A divorced woman may be hard pressed to support her daughter on her own but usually manages not to feel much resentment about it. Then her daughter decides she must have a car, and the well-meaning mother begins to shop for one. Her daughter changes her mind about one car after another until her fickleness drives her mother into a rage. Realizing the inappropriateness of this reaction, the mother settles herself down and has a serious talk with her daughter. Her daughter confesses, "I can't pick out a car because every time I do, you act like you don't want me to buy it." Mother now realizes that she resents "having to buy a car" for her daughter. She can't afford it, and her daughter can do without it. Having determined not to sacrifice herself, she no longer resents her daughter. Nor will she buy her a car.

A man has built an organization whose aim is the reform of some segment of our society. It is an admirable project even by libertarian standards, and the man feels fully justified in flying off the handle at anyone who fails to fulfill responsibilities in the project. He feels awful after these outbursts but justifies them on the grounds that he is working full-time and with full concentration and can expect the same from others. Then he meets a woman who loves him very much, and he is startled when she tells him, "You seem to hate what you're doing." It turns out that, despite his good intentions and despite the merit of the project, he would much rather be doing something else. Having put his own shoulders beneath a self-sacrificing yoke, he profoundly resents it when anyone else refuses. Moreover, since he actually dislikes his day-to-day work on the project, his satisfaction has become invested in succeeding in his efforts. Lacking regular enjoyment in his work, he profoundly resents anyone or anything that keeps him from his hoped-for success.

Whenever you find yourself reacting with violent upset about someone else's goof in regard to your "pet project," make sure your pet has not become a cruel taskmaster. Make sure you don't resent what you are doing even more than you resent the other person's failure.

Love, Hate, and Anger: The Differences Are Real

There was a time when I used to encourage my clients to let themselves feel hate. Expressing any emotion seemed better than suppressing it; and the expression of hate in particular seemed a step toward liberation from the hated person. But I soon discovered that my clients' inherent goodness usually turned them away from such destructive feelings, and I learned a lesson. I also discovered that hate binds individuals to the hated person in a never-ending cycle of vengeance and retaliation. This is hardly freedom or independence.

The binding nature of hate is frequently illustrated in the lives of badly abused children who cannot separate from their parents, in part because they don't want to let their parents off so easily. They want to use their own helpless misery as a means of retaliating. Often, thwarted lovers conduct themselves in the same vengeful way. This kind of hate manifests itself in many lives by a more muted resentment or bitterness toward others. As I have already observed in regard to resentment, any preoccupation with the faults or actions of another should make us suspect that we are trapping ourselves into self-destructiveness out of a deeper fear of facing ourselves.

While love reaches a sense of understanding with other people, hate twists a person away from sharing with others. While love searches for the common humanity within oneself and others, hate gives a person a bad feeling about himself or herself, as well as about others. While love encourages a sense of strength and power, hate breeds personal helplessness and frustration.

Even when combat is required for survival, hate tends to reduce efficiency and effectiveness in fighting. The hateful person is inflexibly obsessed with doing harm, rather than with winning, and wastes his or her energies in over-kill, instead of saving them for future battles. The hateful person is like the athlete who loses his or her head and, hence, the game.

Scratch beneath the psychological armor of hateful persons and you will find helplessness. They blame the hated person for their own failures and give up hope of achieving psychological independence from him or her. They are spiritually dependent upon fantasies of defeating, humiliating, or annihilating the other person. Yet they may also fear the fulfillment of their fantasies, for the destruction of the hated person would rob them of their excuse for failure. Should they somehow lose the object of their hate, they must find new ones in a perpetual pursuit of excuses for their own personal failure to find happiness. Thus, hateful people cannot easily be reasoned out of their positions; they need their much maligned enemies. The more they let themselves hate, the more they become victims; the more they become victims, the more they hate. If hateful persons do translate their fantasies into action, they can become more nasty than their alleged enemy. Such is the downhill course of the hateful lifestyle.

This combination of helplessness and viciousness in hateful persons makes them fit subjects for manipulation by anyone with destructive purposes, including dictators and gang leaders. By stirring up hate in these persons, the dictator or leader can encourage them to ignore their true self-interest and to throw themselves away in the struggle against the alleged enemy.

Because anger and aggression can cause harm to others, they are often confused with hate. But the quality and purpose of hate is unique and separable from that of anger or aggression in its intention to cause harm rather than to facilitate self-defense. Hate is personal — it aims at diminishing or destroying the personhood or actual existence of the other individual. Hate is driven by reasons that the person refuses to acknowledge and expresses an irresponsible refusal to control oneself, no matter what the cost to oneself or others. While anger and aggression may be effective instruments in asserting or defending oneself and one's ideals, hate causes ruinous self-sacrifice. Anger and aggression can be used in the interest of self-liberation, but hate is always a last ditch attempt to deny one's own personal failures.

Having condemned hate — including resentment and any other preoccupation with defects in others — I want to examine its single redeeming feature. Because these preoccupations are a perversion of connectedness to others, they suggest the presence of a strong attachment to oneself and to others. Hate is often a conscious attempt by the individual to keep himself or herself from succumbing as a person. It is a form of defiance. "I hate you" is often a child's last ditch attempt to assert his or her own right to life. It can be a declaration that the individual plans to stay alive and full of feeling no matter what the price.

Violence and Hate

Violence and aggressiveness are often confused. When I speak of violence, I mean aggression born of hate rather than aggression in rational self-defense or the defense of liberty. I do not consider it an "act of violence" to defend oneself, but I do consider it an act of violence to take revenge or to let out one's frustration on a helpless victim.

Many people live within a violent world of fantasy. A mild-mannered professor tells me why he lives in the middle of the inner city: the violence of the city verifies the reality of his fantasy life, which is rife with daydreams about his need to shoot or knife bullies and muggers. Since early childhood he has dealt with his sense of being oppressed by whipping up vicious responses within himself. Now he lives in a violent urban community, which justifies his inner life.

Time and again in therapy I discover that a male client has created within himself a monster to contend with the monsters he fears from his childhood. On a daily basis, he imagines a whole range of violence, from shooting strangers lurking in dark alleys to smashing his wife or boss in one final showdown. Usually we can track such fantasies back to the impotent child's daydreams of killing or hurting Mom, Dad, or an older sibling in revenge for their abuse. In response to parental neglect and even parental hate, the child grows up convinced that violence must be met with violence. Sometimes the family experience is reinforced by further experiences with violent neighborhood kids, classmates, and teachers. Because there is indeed a plethora of violence "out there," the individual easily confirms his fears, if only by watching TV or reading the newspaper.

While violence and violent feelings in women usually take a more subtle form, they play an important role in the life of women. Most often the issue comes up in regard to children, when the harried mother feels barely able or unable to restrain violent outbursts against her small son or daughter. Sometimes the mother will be so appalled by her own desire to express violence that she will inhibit all aggressivity and allow her children to run rampant.

It is easy to be lulled into ignoring the issue of violence when dealing with a gentle or even meek young lady. A woman in her early thirties, whose manner was wholly gentle and sometimes diffident, expressed a fear of physical violence from her mother, even though her mother had not taken any overt physical actions against her since her teenage years. This young woman felt pent-up rage about her treatment as a child and recalled that when her mother would abuse her she would often imagine retaliating by bashing in her mother's head with a heavy object. When she thought about having a verbal confrontation with her mother, she became afraid that her mother would threaten her physically again and that she would then kill her mother. Indeed, the fantasy of killing her mother had some gratification for her, and she was inhibited in dealing with her mother precisely because she was afraid that any encounter might get out of control and lead to her committing murder. This person became able to deal effectively and courageously with her mother only after she promised herself that she would never use violence against her mother, except as a dire necessity in self-defense and then only with as much restraint as possible. Needless to say, such an eventuality never took place, for the mother could sense more than a match for herself in her daughter's new strength. Eventually this young woman decided to have nothing more to do with anyone who had treated her so badly and who still posed a certain amount of threat to her.

Often when we are afraid of violence, we are in reality *planning violence,* if only on a very abstract fantasy level that will never materialize. Even our fear of truly violent people will vastly diminish when we make up our minds that it is rarely, if ever, in our own best interest to meet physical violence with physical violence. Once violence is largely foresworn, the individual is liberated to consider the better alternatives in any given situation. Nonetheless, the need for aggression is sometimes inescapable, especially in the lives of young school-age boys, and I believe that a sense of physical confidence in self-defense is worthwhile for both sexes.

Feeling violent is a terrible burden, but a hard one to give up. It is terrible because an otherwise gentle and loving soul finds himself or herself falling into horrible fantasies of violence and counterviolence. It is a difficult burden to give up because it often becomes inextricably involved with the individual's view of the dangerousness of life.

In helping rid yourself or others of violence, consider its implications. First, to be violent suggests that you feel very frightened and helpless. Examine your fears and helplessness. Second, to be violent means that violence has been perpetrated or threatened against you in your childhood. Look at it, face it, stop hiding from it. Third, if you feel violent, your feelings have adversely affected others. Even if you have never physically harmed anyone, you have undoubtedly done something to embarrass, humiliate, or otherwise hurt others. If you have been actively involved in violence, you have harmed other people because of cowardice in facing your true oppressors, usually your parents. Fourth, to be violent means to deny the reality of other human beings against whom you imagine or perpetrate the violence. You must envision them as unlike yourself or "half-human" or undeserving of any shred of forgiveness or kindness. To be violent, you must cut yourself off from humankind. Decide that it's more important to be in touch with other human beings and face your fears about doing it. Fifth and last, to be violent means that you place little value on yourself. Your violence is rooted in guilt and self-hate.

That idea that feeling and acting violently indicate little self-worth at first strikes the violent person as absurd. The person who harbors fantasies and desires to harm others, or the person who carries out these fantasies, always believes that he or she is "asserting my value" or "my strength." The actual language involves such rationalizations as "standing up for myself," "taking care of myself," "not letting anyone push me around," "proving I'm no pushover," and "showing them I'm not afraid." Everything I have said about hate, envy, jealousy, and other such emotions pertains here. The man (or woman) becomes his victim's victim. He thinks so little of himself that he is willing to risk or to imagine risking his well-being in a confrontation with other individuals whom he invariably dislikes, disrespects, and even loathes. To help another person overcome violent feelings or to help yourself overcome your own violence, you must reinterpret it as a sign of a lack of strength and self-worth. You must find enough love and respect for yourself, and enough concern for others in general, to give up trying to bolster your value through hatefulness and destructiveness, even within the confines of your own imagination.

When Should You Feel Guilty, Ashamed, or Anxious?

When most people feel badly about themselves, they tend to think that they deserve or merit these ill feelings toward themselves. In therapy as well as in everyday life, people are plagued by an inablility to decide if they *should* feel bad about themselves. They believe they have been bad or have handled themselves badly. This is particularly true of the emotion of guilt. Rarely does a person say "I feel guilty, but I know it's irrational or that it has no basis in reality." People also feel this way about shame. It seems to them that they *ought* to feel ridiculous or humiliated, given their true character or their actual mistakes. Anxiety, on the other hand, is vague and unattached to any specific "crimes" or causes, and so it is more rare for individuals to believe it is merited. They are, however, likely to think that it is realistic, i.e., that anyone would feel anxious under the given circumstances. Thus the problem with the guilty, ashamed, or anxious person is how to determine if the emotion is based in rationality or in reality.

I have vacillated on the question of how much negative emotion is "deserved." Early in my career I thought it was often deserved. Later it became apparent to me that, in the vast majority of cases, guilt, shame, and anxiety had no basis in reason, reality, or sound ethics. More recently, with the formulation of my concept of self-oppression, I have come to believe that most or *all* guilt, shame, and anxiety is explainable as self-oppression and therefore wholly lacking in rationality.

My concept that self-esteem is a barometer of the individual's ethical conduct leaves open the interpretation that the individual "deserves" to feel bad if he or she fails to meet certain standards. In this sense the cowardly person who acts helpless and other-determined "deserves" to feel terrible about himself or herself. Individuals do at times tend to feel bad about the way they conduct themselves if they fall short of their own standards or ethics. But in my experience this is usually putting the cart before the horse. The bad feelings are not typically generated by the personal failure itself, but they lie at the cause of the failure. The person who feels guilty about forgetting someone else's birthday *always* feels guilty about such things and, in fact, would just as soon not remember these birthdays if he or she were operating rationally in the pursuit of self-interest. The child who feels guilty about confronting Mother or Father in fact *ought* to confront Mother or Father but is kept from doing so by guilt, shame, and anxiety. The man who has failed in business and feels terrible about it actually was motivated by guilt in entering the business and perhaps motivated by guilt in failing at the business. The actual failure itself is not the cause of guilt. The woman who doesn't want to sleep with her husband and feels guilty about it was actually feeling guilty about refusing sex to men before she got married and really needs to learn not to feel guilty about it. Generally, what *seems* to make the person feel so guilty is actually a defense against looking at the true source of the guilt.

The most common and powerful examples of guilt, shame, and anxiety grow out of relationships to parents. Typically, a person feels very guilty about some transgression against the parents — not inviting them for Thanksgiving, not calling them on the phone, not thinking about them all the time, not professing love for them, not pursuing the life program established by the parents, and so on. This guilty person thinks that the guilt might be relieved if the parents were given more attention, or if their life program were pursued. In reality, the guilt would not be relieved to any appreciable degree by these actions. The guilt instead is generated by the original conflicts earlier in the relationship between child and parents and reflects the child's attempt to control or punish himself or herself in the interest of conforming to the parents. The guilt, if relieved by any given submissive act, would again rear itself the moment the individual conceived again of pursuing self-interest instead of parental interest. Since this desire is likely to lurk beneath the surface most of the time, the individual will go on feeling guilty all the time until the original self-oppressive tendency is disclosed and the individual decides that he or she does not have to go on submitting to the parental will.

The same is true for shame and anxiety. If the individual is ashamed of a recent failure, new achievements will have but an ephemeral effect. The self-oppressed, ashamed person must confront the original source of the shame — humiliation at the hands of the parents, followed by self-humiliation — and determine not to pursue the parental standards of achievement anymore. Similarly, if the person feels anxious about confronting the parents, the individual must see that this anxiety is not rooted in rationality or current reality. The parents no longer have life and death control over the individual. They can be confronted without the grown child's feeling threatened to the core. Again the antecedent childhood events are at the root of the problem, and an understanding of them can relieve the anxiety if the individual determines to act more bravely and with more self-determination in regard to the parents on the basis of this understanding.

I want to repeat and underscore that, in the vast majority, if not all, of the cases in my experience, guilt, shame, and anxiety are not "merited" or "deserved" and have little or no basis in reality, reason, or sound ethics. Most of what most people call "self-criticism" or "legitimate pangs of conscience" is self-oppressive guilt, shame, and anxiety.

But it is not enough to call a feeling "irrational" or unwarranted. We must ask, "By what standards?" Even the term "unrealistic" requires a standard of reality against which to measure actions. My standards are self-determination and the ethical or libertarian pursuit of self-interest. By *these* standards, most people are self-oppressive, and nearly all negative emotions toward oneself are irrational. Self-liberation by these standards means learning to live and to enjoy life in a self-determined, libertarian manner, with wholehearted devotion to one's own self-interest.

The philosophic justification for believing in these principles goes beyond this book and delves into the heart of ethics. Many volumes have been written supporting and criticizing ethical systems that bear similarity to the one I am proposing. The purpose of this book is more practical: to show the feasibility of living by these ethics and to demonstrate that they can maximize self-fulfillment in the life of the individual. I personally believe that these ethics are soundly based in human nature and will serve the society as well as the individual, but I cannot possibily justify such a position without writing still another book. My more limited aim is to show you, as an individual, that you can live fully and happily by a set of ethics based first and foremost on individual rights and individual freedom.

Criteria for Determining the Irrationality of Guilt, Shame, and Anxiety

There is, of course, such a thing as legitimate self-criticism, which may become confused with guilt or shame, just as there is such a thing as realistic fear, which may become confused with anxiety. Genuine remorse or regret is to guilt and shame as fear is to anxiety. Remorse or regret reflects realistic or rational self-criticism. With the caveat that remorse and fear play a small role in most of our lives compared with guilt, shame, and anxiety, I want to outline some of the criteria for determining if a negative emotion toward or about oneself has any basis in reason, ethics, or reality. This list provides a good stepping-off point for any analysis of personal feelings.

First and foremost, if the negative feeling is tinged with self-hate, it has no useful or rational basis. I have already written extensively about this in earlier chapters and here wish to reaffirm that the emotion is self-destructive if it leaves no room for redeeming self-love or if it condemns without any shred of hope for a happier future. Self-criticism that reeks of self-loathing must be treated as alien and irrational. So, too, a sense of doom or dread is rarely useful to the individual and instead must be handled by seeking out and dealing with any real, underlying fear. Usually, the doom or dread is not contained within the current situation but originates in childhood helplessness.

Second, if the negative feeling has a long past history, it is probably not a form of legitimate self-criticism or realistic fear. The person who says, "I've always been a jerk; that's why I hate myself" is very likely wrong in his or her perception of reality. More likely, the person was badly oppressed in childhood and then learned a lifestyle of helplessness. Similarly, if you have "always been afraid" of something, you probably have a lifelong anxiety rather than a legitimate fear.

Third, if the negative feeling has a quality that has been associated with many other circumstances or events, it too is probably irrational. If you feel upset about insulting someone but then notice you have often felt upset about all kinds of interactions with people, you are probably dealing with a lifestyle of self-oppression rather than with a legitimate self-criticism of your conduct toward others.

Fourth, and perhaps most obvious, if your sense of proportion tells you that the pain you feel is inappropriate to the size of your "crime," the pain you feel may have nothing at all to do with the crime. A common mistake is to assume that the alleged crime is, in reality, the cause of the pain and that the pain is merely exaggerated. In reality, the crime itself is probably not the cause of the emotional upset. A woman handles the finances of the household, for example, and discovers an error that has caused a check to bounce. She feels an overwhelming sense of shame and guilt, realizes it is out of proportion, but cannot identify the source of her upset. If she is able to overcome her focus upon the oversight itself, she may realize that she was resentful before she made the error because she does not like doing the family finances. Now she also anticipates ridicule at the hands of her husband, who believes that "women can't take responsibility." The entire episode further restimulates her childhood upsets, watching her father treat her mother like a "dim wit." This woman will not overcome her exaggerated sense of guilt and shame about the bookkeeping error until she realizes that her resentment over doing the books is compounded by her fear of her husband's response and her long-standing resentment and shame about her father's treatment of her mother.

Fifth, deserved or productive self-criticism always contains within it a genuine wish to correct the mistake and, if that is impossible, to make amends and perhaps to apologize. In the same vein, a person who is genuinely contrite about a mistake quickly promises himself or herself not to do it again. If you have angrily insulted your boss and feel terrible about it, be cautious about calling your feeling a product of self-criticism unless your immediate response on self-reflection is a desire to correct your outburst. You may have many complaints against your boss and would rather quit than apologize, and your guilt is actually a fear of the consequences. If you are genuinely sorry about what you did and believe that your attack was unjustified but still feel paralyzed and upset, then you are probably responding to a desire to confront earlier authorities, such as your parents, and instead are taking it out on your boss. Though you have been unfair to your boss, your pain is probably related to fear and resentment toward your parents. If you master that, you will easily apologize to your boss in your own self-interest.

Sixth, when self-criticism or remorse is genuine, looking at the unethical act typically brings relief. If you feel *more* upset after realizing that you have hurt your friend's feelings or falsely accused your roommate of being insensitive to you, then you are feeling guilty, ashamed, or anxious about something other than the immediate object of your concern. In therapy, for example, I will point out to a young man that he is trying to bully a young lady into making love to him. If he falls into a state of self-hate upon being confronted with his unethical actions, he is probably hiding from his true source of guilt. He may even harbor a hidden desire to go on pushing himself on women. It may turn out that his own mother was very controlling and rejecting in physical terms, and he is "getting even" with the women he dates as well as seeking physical gratification without developing intimate, threatening relationships with women. When he deals with his guilt-laden feelings about his mother, he will feel little or no guilt about his unethical actions toward other women; he will feel glad to face his unethical actions and to stop them.

Because confronting one's own unethical actions can bring relief and even joy, self-insight and therapy do not have to be painfully anguished experiences. When one of my clients leaves a therapy session feeling self-hating and unhappy, it does not mean that my client has faced a truly devastating self-insight. Instead, it means that my client continues to remain self-defeating and helpless, and that the true source of guilt, shame, or anxiety has again been overlooked or denied. It is very important to establish with oneself or with a client the general principle that self-liberation is a *happy* experience that *serves one's self-interest* in an immediate and gratifying manner. If the process remains painful, then the causes of this pain must be dealt with until they are understood and mastered. Typically, self-criticism seems so painful because the individual has been horribly criticized by parents and becomes restimulated by any hint of criticism from other people. Ultimately the person has become a self-oppressive self-criticizer who must give up this punitive role toward herself or himself in order to go on effectively with the business of self-understanding.

In summary, there are a number of practical tests for the irrationality of guilt and shame, as well as anxiety. First, feelings tinged with self-hate, dread, and a sense of doom should always be treated as irrational. They are born of helplessness and are a block to self-determination. Second, negative feelings toward oneself, which have a long past history, can probably be traced all the way into childhood and are rooted in conflicts and disappointments with parents and other authorities, rather than in the immediate present. Third, negative feelings that are associated with many different aspects of daily life probably reflect a lifelong pattern of self-defeat and self-oppression. Fourth, guilt, shame, and anxiety that seem out of proportion to the apparent cause are probably caused by something entirely different. Fifth, genuine self-criticism is usually associated with a wish that the act had never been committed, plus a strong desire to make amends, to apologize and to correct the misconduct. Sixth, relief and even pleasure, rather than anguish and self-hate, predominate when unethical acts are confronted.

My major thrust cannot be repeated too often — it is very rare that any persistent feeling of self-criticism or any strong negative feeling associated with oneself is rational, realistic, or ethical in its origin. When a person feels like a personal failure — indeed, when a person is a personal failure — the main emotional charge of guilt, shame, and anxiety is more the *cause* of the failure than the *product* of the failure. Most human emotional pain is irrational in origin and signals a self-defeating thought process.

Ultimately, whether or not an individual *should* feel guilt, shame, or anxiety depends upon one's philosophic framework. When a person describes negative personal feelings to me, I listen to them from the viewpoint of a commitment to self-determination and to the ethical or libertarian pursuit of self-interest. My friends, family, and clients know that this is my belief system. I frankly describe it to them and I make available my writings on the subject. I make no covert manipulations to influence people in my direction. Instead, I present them a standard for living and provide them opportunity to reflect upon their own lives in the light of this standard.

If I find my friends or clients abusing others by these same standards, I will draw it to their attention if they wish to receive this kind of help from me. Similarly, I may ask for help from them in correcting my own conduct if I feel confused about what I am doing. But, in criticizing someone by these standards or in asking for criticism, guilt, shame, and anxiety have no place whatsoever. The guilty, ashamed, or anxious person is rendered less able to pursue rational self-criticism and is greatly impeded in finding a self-determined method of pursuing self-interest. Guilt, shame, and anxiety have no place in a rational, self-determined life.

Guilt, shame, and anxiety are the product of a failure to live by the principles of self-determination and the libertarian pursuit of self-interest. Ultimately, this is a philosophical rather than a psychological statement. It states that people *ought not* feel bad about ethically pursuing their own self-interest. This is why self-insight can and ought to be a happy, productive experience — because it can be based upon the self-determined pursuit of self-interest and personal happiness.

Chapter Eleven

The Oppression of Children

The process of becoming a self-oppressor is a long and painful one. It would probably not be chosen except under drastic conditions. Childhood, for most children, is a drastic condition.

The Totalitarian Situation of the Child

The misery of childhood flows inevitably from this fact of life: parents have unlimited power over their small children. Power does corrupt, and since parental power is exerted in such an intimate setting, where people are bound to conflict in myriad ways, parental power can become more corrupting than political power. Parenthood requires an enormous amount of self-restraint.

Infants are born into their families as helpless and dependent persons devoid of the capacity to protect or to promote themselves. The society and the typical family provide them little or no recourse in those conflicts that inevitably breed within intimate settings, and their parents have little inducement to resort to anything more than outright force.

For the first several years, nearly everything that happens to the typical child is wholly determined by one or two adults, and to a lesser extent, by older brothers and sisters, relatives, and hired help. These people, typically the parents, know that they will not be held accountable for their abuse of power except under the most extreme circumstances, such as outright abandonment, starvation, or near murder of the child, and then only if these atrocities happen to be discovered by interested adults or officials.

The average parent possesses more authority and influence over the details of the life of the typical growing child than does the most potent dictator in a totalitarian nation, and the child is a helpless subject who must adapt itself to this situation or perish. Most personal problems derive from early compromises of self-interest and self-determination made by the child in the interest of surviving the totalitarian situation of childhood.

For most children throughout the world, growing up is one unending subjugation to oppression. The personal sovereignty and personal freedom of typical children are chronically assaulted by the whims of self-oppressed and oppressive parents, and the children are seldom respected, rarely encouraged, and often openly assaulted. Often children hardly seem to qualify as persons or individuals.

The oppression of children throughout the world is so thoroughly accepted that it is used as the model for justifying all other forms of oppression. Men who wish to oppress women attribute to them traits that they also ascribe to children, including helplessness and dependency. Psychiatrists themselves tend to belittle women with a double standard of normality, identifying a normal male with a normal grownup, while a normal female is assigned childlike traits. Mental patients in general are similarly oppressed by attributing to them the traits of children, much as it was once fashionable to justify slavery in terms of the black's alleged childishness.

These so-called childlike qualities have little or nothing to do with anything inherent in children but reflect instead the child's response to chronic belittlement and oppression. This is why chronically oppressed groups develop similar traits. These traits are adopted by the victims to ensure survival at the hands of the oppressors, who demand helplessness, dependency, and even ridiculousness upon the part of their victims, whether these victims are slaves, mental patients, prisoners, women, or children. When the full force of moral authority and social institutions reinforces this victimization, allegedly childish traits become commonplace.

The special quality of parental power over children is confirmed by the impossibility of an oppressor's controlling an adult without first reducing the adult to childlike status. This happens in all mental hospitals and jails, as well as in some of our more totalitarian schools. Its most extreme form in the Western world is found in the wards of mental hospitals.

Under such circumstances, the authorities in charge of the adults must have total power to incarcerate their victims, usually for as long as necessary, and they must have complete control over every aspect of these individuals' lives: everything from their food and clothes to their bedtime and their entertainment. Along with this, the authorities must introduce powerful rituals, calculated to humiliate the inmates and to rob them of their identity as adults. They will be talked down to in the tone used for children; they will be called by first names while required to address their rulers more formally; they will be subjected to humiliating punishments and to equally humiliating rewards, similar to those given to children. In short, the role of the child is the model for humiliation and subservience.

Because of their physical and mental immaturity, children are still more vulnerable than slaves, prisoners, or patients. There is very little that they can do — almost nothing — in regard to changing their environment. They have only two choices — risk disastrous encounters or accommodate. Even with the wisdom, experience, and strength that we adults sometimes acquire, few of us would be able to stand up to the indignities and outright atrocities heaped upon typical small children.

No other minority on earth suffers so consistently and so chronically. Having no power base whatsoever, no minority has so few champions.

Particularly in recent years, successful members of oppressed groups have tended to show some sympathy and even support for those whom they have left behind. We find women and blacks joining in the fight for the liberation of their "brothers and sisters." Ex-prisoners and former mental patients maintain their identities as prisoner and patient after release in order to defy the stigma and to help liberate other incarcerated prisoners and patients. But how many among us want to maintain our identification with children and childhood? The humiliation associated with being a child is far greater than that associated with being a patient, a prisoner, or an oppressed woman. Few adults are willing to admit their identification with children by joining with them in their defense. Childhood is forgotten, the agonies of children are rationalized, and the self-oppressed adult goes on to lord it over another generation of helpless children.

The Severity of Childhood Oppression

To demonstrate the degree of brutality and abuse heaped upon the sort of person who routinely seeks psychotherapy, I will review a series of clients seen during one typical week several years ago in my practice. I will mention each of the six people seen that week.

As a very young child one of these clients had been sexually used by his father and probably by his mother, although the contacts fell short of incest. Both parents had inflicted severe physical punishments during conflicts, the mother beating him with sticks, the father twisting his ear, dragging him about by his ear, and slapping his face during crucial showdowns over authority. A second client had been incestuously used by her father throughout childhood and again late in adolescence. She had been forced to gratify him sexually and to do this in a submissive and personally frustrating manner. She had been deprived of any privacy in her home life and was often forced to function in place of the chronically depressed mother. A third client was brutally assaulted, often daily, by her blindly enraged mother. These attacks went on through childhood and early adolescence, resulting in bruises and cuts and constant terror. Following these attacks, her mother would fill the house with wailing over her own plight at being damned with a child whom she had to beat with her fists. Her father always ignored these beatings or accused her of upsetting her mother. He himself would drag her physically out of bed in the morning when she delayed getting up to face her mother. A fourth client was only occasionally spanked but remembers such chronic humiliation and ridicule from her father, as well as a lurking sense of pent-up rage, that to this day in her professional work she is inhibited from showing anger toward men for fear of her life. A fifth client remembers such constant, withering hate and hostility from his father that to this day he must struggle with a morbid fear of retaliating against any men in authority who antagonize him. A sixth client lived with a psychotic mother who attempted to control every detail of her life, again while father sat back impotently. She daily endured a constant harping, threatening, guilt-provoking outpouring from her mother.

Perhaps most startling to the inexperienced observer of human misery, each of these clients came from a family that looked highly respectable to the outside observer, and several of these clients originally thought they had good parents who exposed them to no abuse or brutality. Such is the strength of denial and amnesia in regard to childhood.

Nor are these unhappy circumstances limited to those who become patients of psychiatrists/and other therapists. Many of my own clients are more competent and more happy than the average person; they have set higher standards for themselves and hence seek help.

Considering the dimensions of childhood oppression, it is remarkable that civilization had to await Freud and modern times for a systematic analysis of the importance of this misery in the formation of the individual's character. It is equally dismaying that many of my psychiatric colleagues still harbor the notion that we need genetic causes to explain a considerable portion of the personal misery seen in a typical psychiatric practice.

One reason psychiatrists and others continue to deny the importance of childhood is a general tendency to underestimate the strength of childhood amnesia. Most people, including typical clients, have little initial recall for what has happened to them prior to age ten, leaving them confused and uncertain about the sources of oppression and their own life-molding decisions made in response to that oppression. For this reason, I want to emphasize again that, in every person's life I have studied in any depth, the individual's self-defeating lifestyle could be traced back almost without deviation from adulthood all the way into an oppressive childhood. Usually the degree of oppression has been so great that I marvel at the bravery required to maintain any degree of personal sovereignty.

It is not always possible in therapy to build a cooperative relationship through which the client becomes willing and able to break down childhood amnesia. On the one hand, I have failed to help some of my own clients in this regard, while on the other I have sometimes been successful with clients who have failed with other therapists. Overcoming childhood amnesia may require great courage from the client plus hard work upon the part of both the client and the therapist. Even the failure of several therapists to help a client learn enough about the past to explain his or her current personal failure should not lead anyone to conclude that the explanation for the failure lies outside the life history of the individual.

A most striking illustration is that of a forty-year-old woman who had seen ten or more therapists over fifteen years without relief. She came to me because in her frantic search for a cure she had begun to study research papers on the relationship between psychological and physiological problems. She had read two early papers of mine on the subject of the psychophysiology of anxiety and now wanted me to give her appropriate biological therapy.

I told her on the phone that I did not do this sort of research anymore and that I did not use any drugs or other physical therapies in my practice. Perhaps because I was friendly and took the time to explain myself before her first visit, she expressed a desire to see me anyway. Nonetheless, over the first several weeks in therapy, she continued to talk about her problems in physiological terms and to request medications despite my repeated explanation that I never prescribe medication.*

Her manifold symptoms were chronic and continuous but particularly bad at night. She would suffer from insomnia, night terrors, dread and fear of death, palpitations of her heart, sweating, weakness, breathlessness, and a variety of other truly severe and painful physical and mental experiences. She was convinced she would soon die of both physical and mental anguish and at times became suicidal. She had obtained only partial relief from massive doses of heavy tranquilizers in the past, and this was always fleeting, leaving her with still more symptoms from the side effects.

Her marriage was falling apart and, in addition, she felt barely able to carry out routine duties at her job, which she openly hated.

Despite this severe personal misery, unrelated to any known physical disease, she and her psychiatrists had always failed to come upon any devastating childhood experiences. She had lived with her mother and several relatives in a remote village in France during World War II, allegedly protected from wartime strife, and her relationship with her mother, though vague, was lacking in any rich detail of anguish. Her father had been away in the war the first few years of her life, and she openly disliked him; but again emotional detail was lacking.

One day during the therapy, a passing reference to "sleeping with my

---

*Because my clients are free to run their lives as they wish, I do not object to their obtaining medications from other physicians. Nor do I feel that it is always harmful to take mild tranquilizers under stress. I do feel that I would confuse my role if I dispensed medication as well as insight and understanding and that taking medication is usually an act of self-oppression.

grandmother" opened up the beginning of her childhood recall. It turned out that the mother had been a blind alley for memories because she had proved so helpless and incompetent that she had given over the rearing of my client to two elderly individuals, the client's grandmother and her friend, while the mother languished in another corner of the house.

This client, unbeknown to herself and all her previous therapists, had literally slept on a crack between the beds of these elderly women for the first fifteen years of her life. During this time the grandmother, who ruled the house, had been grossly psychotic and physically ill, often gasping and coughing her way through the night. My client would lie awake in near paralysis next to her, for fear that any false move might precipitate grandmother into a death spasm. Eventually, she was told to sleep alone with grandmother to keep her company during her death throes!

But this was only a part of a long, terrible story of oppression that led to a constant sense that every night was the night of doom. Her family were religious fanatics who terrorized her with stories of everlasting hell, as well as with primitive superstitions about ghosts and people buried alive. Her childhood was also filled with wartime horrors, as she lived in a battle zone, with deprivation and death all around her. All this, too, had been hidden from her earlier therapists, as well as from me, for she had convinced both herself and her doctors that she lived in a peaceful village far from any strife. In reality, the factory near the village had been bombed, local children had been killed playing with discarded weapons, and nearby cities had been seen burning at night.

The story became rich in detail and in terror. I came away with a profound respect for the strength of my client — that she had survived the experience and gone on to have any life at all.

I believe this person would have been lobotomized as a "last resort case" by almost any psychiatrist who uses lobotomy. I am certain that many psychiatrists around the country still think of her as a patient whose profound miseries had such a physical quality and whose childhood was so free of horror that she must have a "mental disease" of genetic origin. But she is just another victim of an oppressive childhood — albeit a very well-concealed one.

Techniques of Parental Oppression

In my experience as a therapist, punishments in the form of severe beatings are far more common than usually suspected, even in the higher socioeconomic classes. Most often, however, the threat of physical force is more heavily veiled. The child must deal with a clenched fist, a twitching hand, a slightly raised palm, or a strap that hangs in a well-publicized place.

But physical assaults and threats are by no means the main or most important methods for implementing parental rule. Maternal suffering is probably the most common technique of all. The mother displays her anguish on a daily basis to her child, blaming it on the child and using it to insist upon unerring obedience. The suffering may be displayed directly, in facial grimaces and a moanful tone of voice, or through complaints about headaches and backaches. The child may be told directly how he or she has been a burden, starting with the awful pregnancy and painful birth.

Some of the most self-hating individuals I have met in therapy have been the victims of chronically depressed mothers. No longer aware that they feel to blame for mother's misery, they go through life feeling that they are to blame for every atrocity in the universe. They spend their lives feeling sorry for other people, or feeling guilty over personal "crimes" they cannot identify because of their hidden origins in childhood.

Withdrawal of parental love rivals parental suffering as a method of control and is, at times, inseparable from it. Sometimes the parent takes this to the extreme of threatening to abandon the child. Occasionally one sees this take place in public, when parents threaten to leave unruly children behind; imagine the frequency and intensity with which it is used in the privacy of these parents' homes. But the withdrawal of love is most often accomplished through more subtle facial expressions and rejecting glances that mother pretends are beyond her control.

Parents also control their children by systematically terrorizing them about the conditions of life outside the family. A young girl is taught to fear all strangers, to distrust her friends, and, in extremes, to scurry back and forth from school in fear of rapists and bullies. Again, the majority of such communications will take place more subtly, as when Mom worries about her children when they venture into the world. All this is done to the child partly in the interest of delaying any attempts to reach for love or for help beyond the family.

Parents frequently suppress their children by manipulating them against each other and against their friends. I have witnessed a mother criticize every boyfriend her daughter brought home, including her fiance; but once the marriage was sealed, the mother began praising the new husband at her daughter's expense. He now became too good for her; she was supposed to treat him better, etc. The daughter became grossly confused and, until therapy, did not grasp that her mother's attitudes always end up badly for her. Her aspirations were always being suppressed — first by Mom's attempts to devalue her boyfriends, then by Mom's attempt to value the chosen husband above her daughter.

Very commonly, parents play children off against each other. Two, three, or more children will grow up, each and every one of them believing that the others are the favored ones. A son will visit his mother only to have her talk about the other son; she does this to all of her sons and to her husband as well.

With her husband, she only talks about her sons. This type of manipulation can span generations: sweet old Grandma is carefully playing up to her grandchildren at the expense of her daughter. Grandma will give little gifts to her granddaughter — a sugar pop, perhaps — which the mother doesn't think are good for the little girl. Or Grandma will question the granddaughter about relations at home: how much Dad is drinking, whether or not Mother goes to church, and so on. All this attention and confidentiality makes the grandchild feel important; but it also harms the child by encouraging her to betray her parents.

Parents can make this kind of self-oppression seem attractive. Mother may tell her son, "She's not good enough for you." This seems to imply that her son is very worthwhile, even while it impugns his judgment and undermines his personal sovereignty by substituting Mom's judgment for his own. Similarly, when Mom acts as if her son's new date is miraculously or unbelievably nice, it makes her son feel good about his choice of a date, but it implies that he is lucky and not quite deserving. Either way, Mom is on top, son is on the bottom, his personal sovereignty compromised — if he puts up with her conduct.

Parents will sometimes split a child in two, manipulating one aspect of the person against another. A young boy comes home all upset because his friends call him "Shortie," and Mom says, "Don't let it bother you, Jimmy. If you were taller, you'd be perfect, and that would be unbearable." She teases him and humiliates him. Though he has suppressed his memory of these humiliations, all his life he seeks health cures to make him tall enough to be perfect in his mother's eyes. Similarly, a mother consoles her daughter on her plain looks, telling her, "You're smart, dear; you'll make it that way." The daughter feels praised — after all, Mom says she's smart — never confronting Mom on this enormous put-down about her appearance.

Very often, people who have been worked over so oppressively by their parents feel very close to their parents. They feel as if Mom or Dad has shared everything with them. There is a seductive sense of feeling intimate with Mom or Dad. Mom or Dad has indeed shared feelings with the child — feelings that suppress the child. As I noted in my discussion of sharing pain, the price of this closeness is submergence of the self. This guilt-ridden exchange becomes the child's model for closeness, so that the child grows up feeling that anyone who is not depressed and depressing is somehow empty or lacking in warmth. Happy couples are seen as shallow. Love is confused with sharing self-defeating misery.

It may turn out that the parent with whom the child felt the least intimacy was the more responsible of the two. That parent at least kept his or her problems separate and out of sight from the child. When a parent is disturbed or confused, judiciously and cautiously maintaining a distance from the child is often a far more ethical posture than intimacy.

The techniques of parental control are as endless and varied as parental imagination. The aims of parental control are also far more encompassing than first meets the eye. Usually we think of parents as focusing most of their attention on the management of obvious areas of conduct, such as toilet habits, eating, dressing, bedtime schedules, study habits, and so on. But in deeply unhappy adults, it is possible to trace back to childhood a history of still more invasive parental control. It is not unusual, for example, to discover a parent who had studied every vocal intonation and every facial expression of the child in an effort to eradicate and suppress any sign of rebellion. A tone of voice that suggested a slight degree of independence or defiance, an intense gleam in the eye, a smile that smacked of pure joy, a head held too high, shoulders thrown back too far — all became the object of attack from an easily provoked, oppressive parent.

The victims of these parents may enforce upon themselves the zombielike demeanor so frequently displayed by young people. Nowadays drugs such as marijuana are used in excess by individuals to self-induce a kind of ambitionless, unaggressive passivity. Like similar zombie behavior in victims of prisons or concentration camps, this robotism is self-oppression — an all-out attempt to stay out of trouble at the hands of a totalitarian tyrant.

Natural Rights and Parental Control

Undermining the child's sense of natural rights is among the most devastating techniques that a parent can use. Much of libertarian philosophy flows from the concept that individuals possess natural rights, or rights inherent in the state of being human. This is what Jefferson meant when he declared that we are endowed by our creator with certain inalienable rights.

Parents who wish to control their children attack their inherent sense of natural rights. When the child acts in his or her own self-interest, the parent may directly assault the child's right to do this by declaring, "What gives you the right?" or simply, "You've got no right." Unlike Jefferson, who believed that God gave each person these rights, these parents imply that they, as parents, are the source of human rights.

When parents don't directly attack the child's sense of natural rights, they may do it indirectly with statements such as, "How dare you!" or "Who do you think you are?" or "Who told you you're so important?" This challenge to the child's basic rights becomes most severe when the parent realizes that he or she has abused the child and thus encouraged the child to feel justified in self-defense. It is not infrequent, for example, for a parent to slap a child around until the child raises a hand in helpless protest, at which time the parent assaults the child still more severely for "daring to raise your hand to me."

Most people surrender much of their sense of natural rights in the face of parental oppression; they remain in doubt about the concept of human rights when they reach adulthood. In therapy or in a close love relationship, these people will confess that they do not feel that they have the right to be happy. At best, these individuals feel that they must work overtime by fawning obediently on others before they will deserve any happiness of their own. This is exactly what their parents wanted them to think — that they must submit to control in order to earn their basic rights.

The political analogy is particularly obvious in the area of natural rights. These parents cloak themselves with a holiness that rivals divine right. They teach their children that they are the source of all rights, and of course they can quote the Ten Commandments to show that God instructs all children to "honor thy father and mother." Like absolute monarchs, these parents will set their own children against each other and build a fear of strangers into their children as well, all to the end of discouraging conspiracy, collusion, and rebellion against their arbitrary rule.

A friend or therapist can quickly spot such a childhood history when the grown child refuses to criticize the mother on the grounds that mother is holy and above all criticism. To talk against her is comparable to blasphemy against God. This was the tactic used by the mother to make sure that the child would not invoke his or her subjectively determined natural right to self-defense against aggression. Needless to say, the child who accepts this viewpoint will be overcome with guilt, shame, and anxiety at the thought of pursuing his or her own self-interest. Even when the parents are long dead, this grown child may conduct his or her life as if still a victim subject to arbitrary and overwhelming parental oppression.

The Very Disturbed Child

Before a child will opt for severe withdrawal in the form of autism — that is, before a child will quit the world of people in favor of the world of objects — that child must have been severely hurt by destructive emotions. The abuse may not have been physical and it may not be obvious to the unloving eye. But a child will not lapse into such a state of withdrawal unless it has been forced to deal with withering rejection. Newspaper accounts, usually laudatory, often describe how the parents of such children have tried everything — spread-eagle bed restraints, screaming, drugging, beating, and so on. You too might have chosen to tell yourself, "Stop the world, I want to get off," had you been born into such a situation.

To some people, it sounds unrealistic to believe that a child might begin withdrawing at age one or two, or even younger, in response to rejection, isolation, or emotional abandonment. But this is not a matter of conjecture; it is an observable fact. Infants removed from their parents and placed in institutions sometimes withdraw to such a degree that they die. Parental love is necessary for physical survival, let alone for spiritual well-being. Emotional tensions in a mother will affect a nursing, week-old infant, compromising its appetite and its digestion, let alone its mood. Pediatricians call this the failure to thrive. Most loving, nursing parents can describe to you the vicissitudes in their moods and the effect of these vicissitudes upon the mental and physical well-being of their children.

As I write this, my wife and I are happily witnessing the truth of these observations with our infant son. He is a full-time job for her, and she needs all the help and attention she can get; the slightest tension within her is reflected in him, while her fundamental joy over him has already given him a solid start. Anyone who doubts a child's responsiveness to love within the first few days of life has never seen a child loved in the first few days of life.

In modern times, those responsible for the care of normal children under stress situations have been forced to face these facts. In World War II London during the blitz, it was found that infants and even older children did better if they remained in London with their parents than if they fled the bombs to the relative safety and tranquillity of well-run nurseries and schools in the remote countryside. Here in the United States, it has been discovered that an emotionally thriving infant or child can deteriorate badly if isolated from its parents while in a hospital. It turns out that separation from the parents is far more traumatic than the surgery and that it behooves the hospital to provide accommodations for parents if the children are to avoid serious emotional scars. This too has been confirmed in my psychotherapy practice, where very early memories of hospitalizations are often experienced as demoralizing abandonments. Those obstetricians who believe in the need to keep mother and newborn infant by each other's side immediately after delivery confirm the importance of maternal warmth and love within the very first days of life.

Conversely, highly disturbed children often benefit enormously from being placed under the care of a truly loving, parent substitute. So-called incurably autistic children have been known to improve dramatically when placed in a general hospital ward in the care of one or two loving nurses or when sent away to more loving relatives. Even the entrance of a decent babysitter into a tense and conflicted household can have a startling and salutary effect upon disturbed children. Similarly, psychotherapy with parents can help young children recover from hyperactivity or withdrawal without directly treating the children. The therapist helps the parent learn to provide unconditional love and a minimal but necessary amount of self-defensive discipline, and the "problem child" quickly responds.

This seldom works out in actual practice for one simple reason — the kind of parent who drives a child toward hyperactivitiy or autism is rarely the kind of parent who makes a dramatic turnabout in therapy and determines to grant liberty and love to the child. On occasions, I have seen such turnabouts in therapy, and children labeled "withdrawn" turn out to be as lovable, bright, and creative as anyone else.

Parental Rationalizations

All parents who seriously abuse their children — and this includes the great majority of parents — tend to deny their true power over their children as well as their abuse of them. They self-righteously portray themselves as helpless victims who suffer mightily at the hands of their children.

It is true that these parents do suffer during conflicts with their children. They suffer in part because they are suppressing their own aspirations to be more loving and more ethical toward their children. Their anguish is also a product of their frustrated inability to dominate their children. It is the response of slave-masters when their allegedly well-loved and well-treated slaves decide to rebel.

Often one child will be singled out as the family scapegoat. He or she is then blamed for all the family tensions and quite often will respond by playing the role. More subtly, severe tensions between the parents will be submerged by the generation of an equally severe conflict with a particular child, much as a political dictator develops a war to distract from his own domestic problems. Either way, the problem between the parents is buried, along with the hapless child.

I rarely treat children in my practice unless they have reached adolescence, and then only if the parents are in therapy. To treat them alone would perpetuate the myth that the child is at the root of the problem. Only as a child prepares to leave home — only when he or she can escape the totalitarian setting — can the therapist safely attempt to help the child to develop his or her own sovereignty and personal freedom, unless the parents are willing to change themselves while the child lives at home.

When one attempts to deal with young clients who live at home, it is common for their attempts to develop personal sovereignty and personal freedom to lead to the severest countermeasures on the part of parents who are not themselves seeking to improve their own self-determination. Again, the analogy is perfect between the totalitarian dictatorship and the individual rebelling within it. Rebels in the family or society risk greater dangers than do the meek and the compliant.

In a family that has been driving one of its children to choose craziness, steps toward recovery within the child sometimes evoke beastlike rage against the child. This happens, of course, only when the parent has abused the child in the extreme: now in the absence of someone to blame, the parent's rage surfaces in all its viciousness. Sometimes this rage may be fanned by jealousy over anyone becoming free. At other times, it is fanned by sheer terror at the prospect of watching anyone stand up for himself or herself. Sometimes it is fanned by guilt, as the parent sees his or her crimes against the child brought to light through the child's resistance to oppression. The dynamics may differ, but the phenomenon is the same — a parent going crazy with rage when a child tries to break free.

The same phenomenon can be seen even when the client is an adult whose parents are aged and living far away. Through phone calls or letters, through another relative, or, indirectly, through the absence of the previously subservient communications, the parents learn that the child is breaking free. Many times the parents will again attempt to stop the individual's growth through suppressive letters, phone calls, or visits.

Parents who have been unethical enough to make a child miserable for eighteen years at home rarely become willing to reverse themselves as they grow older. To do so, they must first choose a self-liberating path of their own; then they must face their past crimes against their children. Parents who have oppressed their children — and only parents who have oppressed their children — often continue to blame their own problems on their children all the way into old age. Unwilling to break the chain of oppression that leads back to their own parents and their own past, they turn instead to blame it all — beyond all justice and rationality — upon their own children.

Often these parents will have friends who share their viewpoint and who circulate stories about how their lives have been ruined by wayward, ungrateful children. There has also been an unfortunate and growing tendency within the professions of psychiatry and psychology to encourage these parents to give up responsibility for the unhappiness of their children by declaring unhappy and frustrated children to be suffering from biological and genetic disorders. These disorders are given a variety of names from "autism" and "hyperactivity" to "behavioral disorder," "minimal brain dysfunction," and "learning disability."

Encouraged by these professionals, many parents have banded together in national organizations to promote the idea that their children have biological and genetic defects. Psychiatrists and psychologists who support these activities sometimes argue that it is counterproductive to blame parents, because their guilt makes them unable to love and to care for their children. To the contrary, nothing would do more for the well-being of children than a concerted effort by these parents to take responsibility for the unhappiness of their children.

In the long run, it is in the interest of the parent to take this responsibility, for it will enable the parent to help determine a better life within the family. Only by facing up to its profound influence on the child can the parent regain pride and self-respect as a responsible and loving parent.

Parents get what they deserve in love and respect from their children, with the one exception that they often get more than they deserve. That these parents themselves suffered at the hands of their parents cannot be used to justify their crimes against their own children. Beware the person who holds his or her parents blameless when they have obviously been oppressive. This person is likely to hold himself or herself blameless as a parent as well. By holding everyone who is unethical toward us responsible for his or her conduct, we are more likely to hold ourselves responsible for any similar conduct toward others.

There is a realistic tension or contradiction between the obvious influence that people have upon each other and the imperative that each person become wholly self-determining. The best practice is to hold oneself responsible, while being aware of the influence of others. No one ever suffered from assuming too much personal responsibility for improving his or her own life, or the lives of his or her own family.

Why Parents Abuse Their Children

Parents abuse their childen because they are able to. They can get away with doing things to their children that they could never do to anyone else in the society. Watch a parent fly off the handle and scream or swear at a child, sometimes in public. There is no way that the same individual could get away with it on the job or with a friend. Similarly, listen to a parent chronically humiliate a child with ridicule and shame. Again, it is hard to imagine any other circumstance in which the parent could so indiscriminately indulge himself or herself. Much of what passes for acceptable parental conduct would be labeled insane or criminal if displayed toward any member of the society other than one's own child.

When confronted with this, parents typically complain, "What else could I do?" or "It's the only thing they understand," or "I tried everything else," or even "I can't help myself when they make me so upset." But this same adult would find many other alternatives in dealing with anyone else, including someone else's child. To make this clear, I suggest to parents that they envision their children as visiting princes or princesses endowed with great wealth that the parents wish to inherit. As an alternative, I suggest that parents deal with their children as if these small, helpless people were, instead, large, well-armed adults, ready to react with force to any insult or abuse. Would the parent not find alternative methods of dealing with such a person?

From a psychological viewpoint, it is unlikely that a father who was beaten as a child will decide to treat his own son more gently, unless he has come to grips with what was done to him as a child. Unless he has had the courage to confront the atrocities committed against himself, he is likely to accept them as normal and perpetrate them on his own child as well.

The parent who wishes to abdicate tyrannical powers over his or her child will not find much encouragement within the society. Witness the Supreme Court's decision that it is all right for authorities to hit schoolchildren. The law of the land now encourages assault and battery, but only if aimed at our smallest, most helpless citizens. I know of no other class of persons against whom physical beating as a punishment is sanctioned. But the ethical parent or teacher will not use this as an excuse. He or she will recall how it felt to be beaten or threatened as a child — how it hurt, and how it had no redeeming value whatsoever.

Chapter Twelve

More Subtle Aspects of the Oppression of Children

For many children, childhood is one unending horror. They grow up using alcohol, cigarettes, and other drugs to keep their daily tension under control. As adults, many become afraid to sleep because of recurring nightmares from childhood. Others become passive and unobtrusive in their efforts to avoid repeating their agonized childhood conflicts with authorities. In the extreme, we have gross personal failure in the form of chronic anxiety, depression, or paranoia. For many of these people, their actual inner experience on a daily basis is more terrifying than the typical person's response to a horror movie.

For many other people, however, the experience of childhood has not been nearly so dreadful. But it has nonetheless undermined their personal sovereignty and self-determination.

Childhood Oppression through Systematic Reward

I have been focusing upon outright deprivation and brutality as methods of control in childhood. These methods certainly produce obvious pain and apparent scars. But if you came from a typical middle-class or upper-class family, you were at least as oppressed through the systematic use of rewards as a means of control.

The theory and practice of behaviorism exemplifies the use of rewards as a means of oppression. As espoused by its originator, John Watson, in the early 1900s, and as currently touted by B. F. Skinner, behaviorism reflects a wholly antilibertarian set of values. It is the psychological embodiment of those principles most thoroughly opposed to self-determination. This is not to say that behaviorism itself is the most important source of oppression in childhood. Of course it isn't. Children were being oppressed long before the term behaviorism was coined. But behaviorism has the honor of being that modern philosophy that most consistently dresses up the same old oppression in a new pseudoscientific language.

Watson and Skinner have carefully spelled out that there is no such thing as free will, personal sovereignty, or personal freedom. They consider the self to be a mirage or myth created to perpetrate chaos and disorder in the psychological, social, and political arena.

A well-planned behavioral program in the school or home fixes the child within a setting rigidly programmed with rewards or punishments, in the hope that specific types of conduct will be produced. The aim is to implement external authority by systematically reducing freedom and thereby convincing the child that he or she can gain nothing from the pursuit of his or her own independent options.

This "benevolent totalitarianism" contrasts markedly with a libertarian environment in which the individual will be unconditionally loved, where reason will be the primary technique of relationship, and where the self-determined conduct of the child will produce new and unexpected results. The goal is a child who considers himself or herself to be his or her own authority.

The effectiveness of systematic reward rather than punishment as a method of control is openly promoted by Skinner. He has declared himself against the use of punishments not only on humanitarian grounds but because punishments fail to achieve their purpose — an obedient child. Skinner reminds us that most rebellion is made against punitive authorities, while benign ones usually go unopposed. Therefore, he advocates the exclusive systematic use of reward for the rearing of children.

Skinner is not wholly correct in his assumption that a home or society fully programmed with rewards would prevent rebellion. People long for self-determination and for freedom, even when authority has been made relatively painless. People long to express themselves in their own way and to seek out new challenges for themselves, even when self-expression and new challenges create pain. The image of robotlike citizens responding automatically to the benign, rewarding authority is a totalitarian dream that cannot be fulfilled.

But Skinner is partly right that people find it more difficult to rebel against or to criticize benign authority. Parental rewards tend to be more binding because children grow up with less awareness of their effects. It is much easier to examine the debilitating effects of chronic punishment, but it is important to grasp the more subtle effects of systematic rewarding as a means of control.

It should also be kept in mind that the distinction between reward and punishment in a thoroughly controlled environment quickly breaks down. A child systematically controlled by parental rewards will soon learn that not being rewarded must be taken as a sign of disapproval or punishment. This is obvious at any children's party where youngsters sometimes scream and weep hysterically because they have not won a prize or at an athletic contest when some of the losers are heartbroken. So bent are the behaviorists upon their simple-minded distinctions that a sophisticated behaviorist like Skinner can disregard the obvious fact that all systematically controlled environments deal out both reward and punishment, if only through withholding the reward under controlled conditions in which the child has no other source of reward.

If you were brought up in an upper-middle-class family, you were probably subjected to systematic reward from a very early age. In its most extreme form, you may have learned to read or play music at a very early age under the influence of a parent who made love conditional upon performance.

Early in the process, you may have been rewarded with a cookie or some other favorite delicacy, much as the behaviorists in modern schools use candy; but soon you were responding to more symbolic reinforcement — attention or feigned love. I do not call this real love, because it little resembled the love that you were capable of sharing — an unconditioned, spontaneous joy in the recognition of another person. But you were told very early that this trade of attention for good behavior was loving on the part of your parents.

From an early age, you were kept in a crib and then in a playpen. When adults are kept in similar confinement, it is referred to as jail or prison, but you were rewarded with praise for staying quietly behind these bars.

Since the house you were in was hardly set up to handle your clumsiness or your inquisitiveness, you seldom were allowed to play, explore, and express yourself. Since everyone had better things to do, you were rarely given hours together with a loving adult whose sole interest lay in having a sweet time with you. You got the idea that people didn't really care about you: your feelings, your wishes, your central importance in your own universe. Most likely the loving spirit within you chronically ran headlong into frustration at the hands of adults who were tired, irritable, or too serious. You learned that getting along with them meant playing their games, and their main game was bringing you up with the aim of reducing any trouble you might cause. Enjoying you and your capacity for life was secondary to keeping order.

As a middle- or upper-class child, your nursery school and kindergarten experience may have been far happier than your homelife. You may have been encouraged to play freely and happily with the other children, even holding hands and sharing hugs with other boys and girls. School projects may have been highly individualized, permitting you to choose your favorite activities from among cutting and pasting, drawing, coloring, or various other educational games. Your restlessness was probably not crushed, and even more formal learning periods may have been spiced with games. You were even encouraged to take breaks and to have cookies or other snacks, followed by a nap or play time. You probably loved school — for the only time in your life.

You probably loved your teacher as well, in a way that would never again be possible. At least there is a chance that kindergarten was a good experience — the nearest thing in your life to a loving, libertarian environment.

By first grade, education became little more than a conditioning process calculated to crush your personal sovereignty and personal freedom, crippling your most natural aspiration for liberty and love. With few exceptions, you did what you were told. Above all else, you made every effort not to look stupid and to avoid being ridiculed by teachers or other children.

You were supposed to work hard in order to earn good grades; in reality, you worked hard from a dread of bad grades. Any joy you got from a good grade was overshadowed by the relief you felt when discovering that it was not a bad grade. Watching the expressions on the faces of other little children receiving their grades, you rarely saw delight. More often you saw nothing, as the child hid his or her ambivalence or misery.

Your teachers wanted you to do well in their terms, and didn't care at all about your terms. Your parents, of course, were mainly concerned about how you looked in the eyes of the teacher and the school. Personal sovereignty was never encouraged and often suppressed by individuals and programs that assaulted your feelings, your thoughts, and your decisions. Personal freedom was limited to moments behind the door in the bathroom, other moments before falling asleep, and occasional escapes with a friend to favorite hiding places.

Conditioning Boys versus Conditioning Girls

If you were a boy, you may have felt you had some areas of personal freedom, but only by comparison to the girls. Girls were a living demonstration of how bad it would have been if you had not been so lucky with the body you were born into. You may have been allowed the luxury of lording it over smaller children and girls, perhaps ridiculing or physically abusing them. This too may have become associated in your mind with liberty. If you thought that girls had it better than you, you as a boy were being oppressed beyond the norm.

If you were a girl, you were subjected much more strenuously to reward than to punishment — although there are many exceptions to this. Your conditioning through rewards was much more rigorous and much more complete than the conditioning to which the boys were subjected. The limits of permitted behavior were much more narrow; and within these limits, you were expected to carry out all your functions with much less gusto. Aggression, as well as sex, was much more carefully channeled out of your life.

You were rewarded for sitting still and looking pretty, for smiling on cue, for speaking in a sweet manner, for walking in a constrained fashion, for running in a helpless fashion, and for looking vacant when in repose. You became docile and often immobile. All this, I want to emphasize, was done largely through rewarding you with approval; but any unfeminine conduct may have been suppressed with humiliating ridicule.

As a girl, you were allowed to express and to share more love than the typical boy. Hugs, kisses, and tender exchanges with your parents and with other little girls were more permissible. But you were hardly allowed to become passionate with anyone. Serious relationships with either sex were ridiculed and disrupted by concerned adults. Besides, most of the tenderness given to you was part of the conditioning process. As the boys traded their freedom for the right to let off steam aggressively and to feel superior to you, you traded your liberty for occasional expressions of affection. Docility and emptiness were so much the approved style, you could have been psychotic in your withdrawal years before anyone in school or at home noticed it.

As a girl, even if you were well treated by comparison to other young girls, you nonetheless grew up certain that the real rewards went to the boys. They had more freedom, they had more opportunity in the world, and they treated you with open condescension, even contempt. This differential rewarding system was as potent as any punishment, and you grew up, almost to a woman, with a feeling of defectiveness, inferiority, and shamefulness. On top of this, you grew up just plain fearful, because no matter how little punishment you were exposed to, you were warned that little girls have much to fear from grown men.

For boys and girls alike, personal sovereignty was so suppressed that when you read about Jefferson's "inalienable rights, among them life, liberty, and the pursuit of happiness," you never once thought they might have anything to do with you and your life as a child. Think about it! You read those words of the Declaration of Independence many times, perhaps at a very young age, and never once applied them to your own existence. If you had, you would have been tempted toward taking dangerous actions.

Adolescent Rebellion

With the coming of adolescence, many of us began a new phase of rebellion against our modifiers. Both liberty and love preoccupied us at least for a time.

No doubt you had been so well conditioned that you never suspected that the battle had already been fought and lost at an earlier age. And because you had no recollection or understanding of your past self-oppression, you had little idea why the renewal of your aspirations for liberty and love stimulated so many painful feelings from within. This is important because, as you began to fight with your parents and other authorities for your right to liberty and love, you quickly realized that something within you was fighting just as hard against you. You couldn't identify this as self-oppression in response to earlier oppression, and so you were hampered in your attempt to fight against the inner sense of guilt, shame, and anxiety. You did not know you had become your own enemy.

A brief scan of your adolescence will remind you that you were routed in your fight for freedom and dignity. Sexually, you came to believe that you were undersexed or oversexed, depending upon how your anguished self-oppression showed itself. You also decided that loving was much too dangerous, if only because love bred rebellion against authorities.

You lost in your attempt to express your passion to fulfillment with your youthful loved one. You may have had sex with someone, and probably it proved to you that adults were right in degrading sex as an expression of tenderness. Or you may not have had sex, giving up the ideal of experiencing a oneness born of combined spiritual and physical passion.

You also found that much of your energy and concern now began to focus on grades. It turned out that your parents and teachers had been right. You should have studied harder to get ahead. Now you had to approach college exams and college applications with renewed terror and dread. Time and again, you wished that you had knuckled under still more, at least enough to guarantee the big reward — the college of your choice — at the end of the scholastic rainbow.

Sometime in the next few years, you completely forgot about your momentary outburst of passion — those few adolescent months when you again aspired toward liberty and love. Thinking back upon it caused you pain. It is the pain of self-betrayal. It can only be overcome with a renewed determination to pursue everything you once wished for yourself at those moments of childhood rebellion.

The Loneliness of Children

Self-hate, guilt, shame, apathy, boredom — all of life's negative personal emotions are first generated in childhood. One emotion, however, may be more characteristic of childhood than any other — loneliness. Children are lonely much of the time. Loneliness is a big contributor to many of the most severe conflicts children have with their parents at very early ages, such as fights over staying upstairs in bed at night and fights over being left behind in the house when Mom and Dad go out.

Loneliness seems endemic to the situation of the child. Consider your own childhood. The odds are great that you were always treated as an appendage to the relationship between your parents and that you had no one to share with you the way Mommy and Daddy shared with each other. You were an outsider looking in on two people who valued their own time together far more than they valued time alone with you. Often you were treated as a pest, a bother, a nuisance, an extra, or, at best, a third party who too often made a crowd.

The little boy (or girl) of five cannot relate to other children with the intimacy required to overcome loneliness. He does not have the verbal skills, the emotional stability, or the maturity to build a lasting, deepening relationship. Usually, he is in keen competition with his brothers and sisters over parental attention and time, and so he cannot freely trust himself to become intimate with them. They may tattle on him or tease him if he makes himself vulnerable by sharing his most private experiences. He has probably been made fun of for being childish so many times that he dares not expose his innermost thoughts to anyone, for fear of being ridiculed. Nothing drives a person into loneliness more thoroughly than this fear of ridicule, and no group of people is as subject to ridicule as children.

Close childhood friends are often so threatening to parental control and authority that parents break them up. Within families, children are set against each other to ease conflict with parents. All this adds to the child's loneliness. Should the child nonetheless seek intimacy with another child, sexual curiosity and even sexual passions may be aroused at a very early age and get the child into trouble with adults. The taboo on sex among children is one of the greatest barriers to the development of spontaneous intimacy among them. It is a major force in keeping them helplessly dependent upon adults for whatever emotional gratifications they can obtain for themselves. After a client has spent some time uncovering childhood, it is not uncommon to discover a forgotten friendship at age four or five that ended traumatically when sexual contacts came to the attention of adults.

Unless a child has been blessed with an older brother or sister, aunt, grandparent, or nursemaid wholly devoted to it, the child endures dreadful loneliness. Even when blessed with companionship, the child almost always must spend night after night alone in bed — a fate few adults would tolerate. He or she seldom has any control over when to visit companions or how they will spend their time together. He or she will feel too helpless to make the most of their relationship. If the parents resent the relationship, the child may also feel guilty about it.

Many children grow into adults who never come out of their loneliness, but who go through life resigned to feeling chronically isolated and disappointed in their human relationships.

The Titanic Complex

The idea that parents often push their children too hard toward success is a common one that is often portrayed in popular literature. Certainly this occurs at times. But far more common and far less appreciated is the tendency of parents and even siblings in families to resent and to suppress any child who shows tendencies to rise above the family's status, ethically, socially, or economically. Even in families in which a child has been pushed to achieve, the same child has very likely been given messages to the effect that his or her success in some way threatens the family. Especially, he or she may be made to feel guilty about the very success the family has supported.

Most people have myriad excuses for why they have not achieved more in life. The various lifestyles of failure are excuses of this kind, and often they specifically focus on economic or professional failure. The individual imagines that *all* successful people are crooks or frauds, or that *all* successful people have social and financial backing from their families, or that *all* successful people come from a particular religious or cultural background. A man may complain that virtues such as honesty and fidelity toward one's family or the need to support children have robbed him of his opportunities in life. A woman may imagine that only women who are willing to sell their bodies really rise socially or professionally. Both may attribute success in others to "lucky breaks." In the obviously imperfect societies in which we all live, enough actual evidence for these views will be found to make them seem realistic, especially to the children of these individuals, who hear these excuses offered on a regular basis by the parent as an explanation for personal failure.

When a child from such a rather typical family begins to make a success of himself or herself, the family members may be pleased or proud, but at the same time, they will be profoundly threatened. After all, if little Joey can grow up to be a loving spouse or parent, a rich lawyer, or a famous person, why did Dad or Mom or little Jimmy not do the same thing? That little Joey has become a more courageous, self-determining adult will not be acceptable, for such an admission holds everyone else up to unhappy comparison.

One of my clients experienced overwhelming loneliness and dread whenever he created a new success for himself during therapy. His first insight came in the form of a memory of the moral lesson his mother drew from the sinking of the Titanic. She told him on frequent occasions that God had punished the owners of the Titanic for their pretentious claim that the ship was unsinkable. That God would destroy such great numbers of people in retaliation against a handful of unrighteous egotists added to the horror of the story and to my client's dread over the implications of his own aspirations to succeed. He named his parentally inspired dread of success, "The Titanic Complex."

As any strong fear, his had been reinforced by much more than an oft repeated story. Under the guise of Christian morality, his mother had continually reminded him how "pride goes before a fall" and how God "strikes down the mighty." Her attitudes toward successful people in the public arena always included hints that they had risen to such heights, in part, through sinful conduct of one kind or another. More important, she made fun of his own attempts to better himself socially in school and became particularly outraged when he made suggestions for the improvement of her own grammar or appearance. She frequently referred to him as "too big for his britches." Ultimately, she would withdraw what little love she gave to him, leaving him with a feeling of desolate loneliness. Ambition and success became antithetical to receiving any love at all, and he chose to suppress his aspirations rather than risk such a fate.

These attitudes can be found in almost any family, usually to lesser degrees, and they are frequently reinforced in schools, in religious institutions, and among peers. Peer resentment of any group members who attempt to better themselves can be very powerful. A young man who grows up in a lower-class community will find that many or most of his friends will snicker at any pretensions he may have to join the class of employers rather than that of employees. As he works his way up in any given organization, he will hear at each level how members at the next higher level have risen on the basis of anything but merit. The idea that successful people are often more responsible and self-determining than unsuccessful people will be anathema to their peers, until they reach a level in which the individuals with whom they typically deal feel successful in their own right.

The popularity of collectivist thinking in our society reinforces the Titanic Complex in its various manifestations. Nearly all collectivist propaganda extols the individual failures of the society as tragic figures suffering from an inevitable fate at the hands of cruel competitive capitalism and, if the issue of personal responsibility is even raised, the successes in the society are identified as the society's most irresponsible members.

It is true that in all the industrialized nations your chances of success are vastly improved if you are born as a son into a rich white family, rather than as a daughter into a poor black one. But it is equally true that individuals from all backgrounds frequently raise their status considerably during their lifetimes. Furthermore, it is true that a major problem faced by any upwardly mobile person will be the fear and helplessness about success that have been engendered by family, by peers, and by religious and political propaganda.

My mind is quickly scanning the ten most successful people among my close friends. All but two or three came from poor and often poverty-stricken families. All had to overcome enormous adversity of one kind or another, including physical handicaps, racial prejudices, and sexism, and could easily have found excuses for failing. None has reached his or her successful stage in life by sheer luck or by unethical activity. All have achieved their positions in life through the persistent exercise of self-determination; and all are aware that, to whatever degree they have not succeeded in meeting their goals, they have been, in part, personally responsible. Nearly all have had to work against self-oppression developed through relationships with parents, and even brothers and sisters who have resented their success and who have made them feel guilty for bettering themselves. Few, if any, feel that their parents are unconditionally delighted with their success.

I do not offer these friends as a statistically valid sample of successful Americans. They are not. But in a day and age when success itself often taints people in the eyes of others, it is important to reaffirm that every successful person has been personally instrumental in holding or improving his or her status, even if the luck of birth originally handed him or her great advantages. Nor am I arguing that any society has ever provided equal opportunity for its members. This can never be achieved without utterly destroying the family. You may or may not believe that greater individual freedom will promote the overall welfare of society. But from the viewpoint of any given individual at any given moment, success will be achieved and maintained through self-determination, and any attitudes of self-oppression will encourage and even guarantee failure.

Overcompensation

It is ironic that people typically fear that they will become precisely the kind of persons that they are least likely to become. The diffident young lady is afraid she might become "violent" if she lets out her feelings. The chronically aggressive, physically powerful male is afraid he will be "pushed around" if he stops aggressing against people. The obsessively perfectionistic clerk is afraid he'll make multiple mistakes if he learns to relax. The conservatively dressed, cautious gentlemen is afraid he will make a fool of himself if he "lets go" at a party. The very imposing and dignified lady, who draws everyone's attention to her as she stands in a room, is afraid she will be ignored if she doesn't perform in some entertaining manner. The impeccably dressed model believes she will "look a mess" if she does not spend hours fixing herself up before going out. The overly conscientious, super-responsible professional man is dreadfully afraid that someone will think him irresponsible. The warm, outgoing, and lively young girl is afraid that everyone will think her dull and boring. The variations are endless and are probably manifested in one form or another in most people.

The fear that motivates the reaction will be deeply embedded in childhood. The diffident young lady who is afraid of becoming violent felt enormous violence toward her parents as a young child and shrank from herself, developing a reactive diffidence. Or perhaps she saw the violence in her parents and was so appalled and frightened by it that she decided never to be like them. Either way, she now is so basically meek that it seems absurd when she says, "If I start letting out my feelings, I might hurt someone." In reality, there is almost no chance of it. Similarly, as a child the super-responsible professional man was clobbered with responsibility at home, at school, and in church. He could loosen up considerably and no one would ever think him irresponsible, but it was precisely this fear — that he would be called irresponsible — that drove him to such excesses of conscientiousness. The impeccably dressed model has such style and carriage that there's little chance that anyone would think ill of her appearance even if she spent little or no time grooming. She grew up in a lower-class, slovenly home and was greatly ashamed of her parents. She has reacted out of fear by developing a carriage no one could fault.

Although originally used by Alfred Adler in a somewhat different manner, overcompensation seems as accurate as any term for describing this phenomenon. It is a compensatory reaction in which the individual attempts to overcome his or her fears by becoming the opposite of what he or she fears she might become. The fear remains, but in reality there is no longer any chance of the individual's becoming what he or she is afraid to become. Indeed, the individual must work hard to overcome this defensive reaction. Often it is the key stumbling block in personal development. It reflects one of the most important decisions in childhood; to devote oneself to being the opposite of what one fears to become.

The Submissiveness of Children to Parents

Despite the myth of the child monster, children are almost always far more submissive to their parents than their parents are to them. Put another way, parents are almost invariably far more monstrous toward their children than their children ever become toward them, even when their children gain physical or economic power over them.

This becomes most obvious when looking at the extremes of oppression committed against children by their parents. Parents often subject their children to outright physical and mental torture — burning their hands with matches, sticking their fingers into hot gas flames, whipping them with straps and sticks, threatening them with loss of limb and life or with abandonment. Parents so frequently beat their children to death or near to death that child abuse has been termed an epidemic by those who prefer to couch moral problems in medical jargon.

Yet it is nearly unheard of to find children who mistreat their parents in kind, even when the parents have become utterly helpless. Instead a grown child who has been beaten, humiliated, and terrorized can frequently be found waiting on his aged mother's or father's every need, at great sacrifice to himself or herself and to loved ones.

The vast majority of suicides are expressions of self-oppressive attitudes learned at the hands of suppressive parents. Anytime anyone I have known has come close to killing himself or herself, a battle has been taking place between parental oppression and the individual's last gasp aspirations for freedom. This battle is always internalized, but sometimes it is going on in the real world as well, as the parent continues actively to oppress the grown child. By contrast, I have never seen or heard of a case wherein a parent chose to commit suicide over conflicts generated by an oppressive child. Sometimes parents try to act as if their children are making them crazy or self-destructive, but invariably the parents had similar conflicts long before the birth of the child and usually these conflicts reach back into their own childhoods. In reality, the parent's anguish over the child rarely has to do with the child's attempts to become oppressive but rather with the child's attempts to get free of the parent by rebelling against its nastiness and lovelessness.

I do not mean to make light of the difficult job of being a parent. Most of us are ill prepared for the job; and if our lives seem to become enormously complicated when our children reach age two or three, it is because we did not anticipate the skill and the wisdom, as well as the love, required of parenthood. Often new parents discover that they had no idea whatsoever of the amount of work and responsibility involved. After all, "Everybody does it." Instead of realizing that everybody does it rather poorly, these frustrated parents are likely to blame the children and to abuse them. They are likely to declare in frustration, "Now I know what my mother went through," when it would serve them far better to determine to act more responsibly than their parents did.

Nearly every client in my practice has been tormented for years by his or her parents, all the while hoping for some crumb of affection from them. Considering the degree of child abuse in the society, it is surprising that we so seldom see a child totally disown a parent. My own clinical experience suggests that children will typically do anything in their power to make their parents happy. Parents, on the other hand, rarely become more loving in response to changes within my clients.

It is worth repeating an earlier theme that guilt over doing harm to one's own parents is one of the greatest barriers to self-liberation. The individual should not self-righteously fool himself or herself into believing that this guilt is a sign of love. Nor is this guilt a sign of decency or humanitarianism. Nor should guilt be confused with respect.

I always doubt protests of respect for one's parents when the grown child is also submitting to abuse from these same parents. Let the individual liberate himself or herself. Once free, the individual can more readily determine if he or she feels loving or respectful toward these former oppressors.

Chapter Thirteen

Parenthood with Minimal Use of Force

By now it may seem that I am a cockeyed idealist who believes that children should be allowed to run wild in the home and to abuse their parents endlessly. To the contrary, I am a great believer in peace and harmony within the home. I enjoy my own children, and they enjoy me. It can be done, and it can be done with minimal force before the age of three or four and with little or no force thereafter. In my own family, occasional force has been necessary to control dangerous or destructive acts, especially around the age of two or three, with a total nonuse of force *or of punishment of any kind* after age six or seven. The problem is to recognize the humanity of children and to treat them according to the same libertarian principles that I advocate in relationships between adults. Parent-child relationships should be made as voluntary as possible, and reason and love should provide the substance that holds adults and children together.

How It Might Have Been for You as a Child

If you are an unhappy person, you probably can recall few times, if any, in your childhood when you were free of oppression. However good or bad your overall childhood experience, focus on the best of your early experiences — perhaps the early mornings by yourself outdoors, or trips to the beach, or visits to a favorite relative, or pursuing your one loved hobby, or playing with your dog or your one human friend, or those moments when Mom and Dad had time for you. Get in touch with yourself when you were loved and when you were permitted the luxury of exploring life more freely. It will tell you a great deal about human nature before it warps itself in compromises with an oppressive world. If you can't remember experiences from your first few years of life, try to imagine your situation from what you've seen of other infants and children.

You were full of energy all your waking moments. You were constantly alert to what was going on around you. Anything that you saw, anything you touched or that touched you, interested you vastly. Your hands and feet and your whole body were alert for contact. If you were held and loved, your body and your eyes cleaved to the one who loved you. You gazed into his or her eyes with adoration. No one had to teach you to love, no one had to teach you to learn, no one had to encourage you to reach out to others and to the world.

You did not get frightened the moment anyone introduced you to something new or strange. You attempted to master it with every means at your command, including mimicry. If someone stroked your body, you did not become frightened by the closeness or the pleasure. You laughed, giggled, got turned on, and had a wonderful time. You did not have periods of misery and depression if you were well loved, but you may at times have become a little tired and irritable. Your worst problem may have been overtiredness — the conflict between wanting to do more and needing some sleep. Probably you also had some difficulty, no matter how sensitive your parents, in adjusting your eating and sleeping rhythms to their predetermined needs and ideas. If you had more grave difficulties, the odds are that you were already in a disturbed relationship with your parents or nurse.

As you became ready to learn to walk and to talk, no one had to give you A's and B's to get you to do either. No one had to push or punish you to make you walk and talk. No one had to tell you it was necessary to learn these things to get ahead or to be appreciated. The world was exciting, challenging, and interesting, and you wanted to learn everything there was to do in the world.

When you were left alone in your room for a few minutes or longer, there was plenty to do and you seldom got upset. On the beach by the ocean, you would play for hours with the sand, shells, stones, and water. You wanted to taste, smell, touch, see, and hear everything that you could. It was the same in the backyard or in a corner of the living room. No one needed to train you to be sensitive.

You found people thoroughly likable, you enjoyed the world, you slept well and looked forward to life each morning. You felt very powerful, generally immortal, as if the good things would go on forever. You assumed all of life would be at least this happy, and you looked forward to starting school on your way toward still more liberty and love as an adult.

You did have to learn not to abuse others. You may have had a tendency, at age two or three, to hit or to throw a temper tantrum now and again. Often this occurred when your parents were too tired or too preoccupied to give you the proper amount of attention. But sometimes you simply had to have your way, when your way was incompatible with important needs of your parents or with your own health. Maybe you screamed when you couldn't get the candy or the toy you wanted, or maybe you wouldn't leave the park when Mom had to go home. At such times you did become difficult, but you responded to firmness and consistency. You rarely got out of control, and you calmed down readily if your parents kept their heads and their determination. All in all, most days went by without any serious conflicts, especially as you passed the age of three or four and developed a broader perspective.

This is how a well-loved and protected child responds. But how dissonant this picture must be with the pictures that most of my readers have retained from early childhood.

If you can remember vivid detail from your childhood — and many of you cannot — you will probably recall considerable pain and loneliness. This is not because we remember personal anguish best. We most certainly do not. It is because most people had a disproportionate share of it in childhood.

Children Have Free Will and Personal Sovereignty

The child starts making decisions at whatever time and at whatever level she (or he) becomes aware of herself and her environment. Probably she is thinking and deciding as she lays upon her back in the crib. As she gets older, toward a year or so of age, her decisions will become better informed and more decisive. She will have more data, and she will have a more mature mind-brain apparatus to organize the data. By the time she reaches one year, her particular character will already be apparent in the degree of self-determination that she shows and the amount of personal impact she has upon her environment. She will be someone to be reckoned with, and the comparison to other children will be apparent. Then, as she grows older, she will bear the burden of the fruits of these decisions. They will accumulate around her. By the time she is four or five, she will be a clearly definable person — someone who has made sufficient decisions about sufficiently weighty problems to be apparent as a person in her own right.

She will be suffering from every decision to cop out on herself; and she will be thriving from every decision to remain personally sovereign.

It makes no sense to recognize the decision-making process in adults but not in children. Even as adults, we are limited by our experience and maturity, as well as by our natural endowment, in how much we perceive, think, and feel. As human beings we may be equal in value or in rights, but our capacities to relate and to express our rational choices depend upon age, health and natural endowment. But one thing is invariable: we make decisions and take actions, whatever the limits of our personal universe.

This does not mean that children can have the same effect as adults do. Relative powerlessness and immaturity do not permit it. But within their spheres, children are as busy making decisions as adults are; and these decisions, for better or for worse, affect their future lives.

The behaviorists would have us believe that conduct is determined by its consequences. A behavior that is rewarded will strengthen; one that is punished or not rewarded will extinguish. To the extent that a child chooses to adhere to this policy, he or she must give up personal sovereignty. If the child defies this policy and refuses to corrupt the inner experience of sovereignty even while losing freedom, he or she can become a vital, effective person.

The child who is being modified must choose how much modification to accept and how many risks to take in defying his or her modifiers. These decisions may be made in a state of terror or confusion, but they will be made. Out of them, the child builds a lifestyle.

It is important to emphasize the child's choices, even in the most terrible circumstances, because choice always exists. As I pointed out in defining personal sovereignty, two individuals will choose to face the most harrowing conditions in entirely different ways, the one facing death while maintaining his or her dignity, the other cowering in fear and compromising to stay alive.

We tend to think that children lack personal sovereignty — or the ability to self-determine their own thinking processes — because of the overwhelming pressures placed upon them, and because of their relative inexperience and immaturity. But there are many times when an adult will also be tempted to feel overwhelmed by circumstances wholly beyond his or her experience and maturity.

People have free will under any and all conditions and at every age. They may vary in their willingness to express that will to their own advantage, but they must always make the choice between helplessness and self-determination, regardless of how difficult it may be to accomplish their aims.

Many of my clients recall vivid fragments of experience from infancy and early childhood. In none of these memories do my clients feel any less of a person than they now feel. They recall no diminished sense of free will or choice making. They were thinking or reasoning as hard as they do now, and sometimes harder. In keeping with this, they had a sense of natural rights and resented interferences with the pursuit of their self-interest.

Some of these early recollections are preverbal, with vivid recall of life in the crib or playpen. There is a recognizable person making recognizable decisions, however unable to verbalize the person may have been. The size of the world was smaller, of course; the breadth of understanding and the strength of mental function was gravely limited. But the opinion-making, choice-making person was alive and active.

Soon after birth, each of my daughters and, more recently, my son communicated to me the existence of a very special person with particular attitudes toward me and toward my wife. Each made decisions about how to respond to us and to the environment. Their character was manifested in their carriage — even as they lay on their backs or bellies — as well as in their gaze and their sounds. When each daughter became verbal, I sensed no great change in the quality of the person herself, but merely the development of new tools to use in communicating about an already real self.

In their lives, as in the lives of most children, "no" was one of the first nonverbal communications. It was made through a vigorous grimace. Later it became one of the first vocabulary words. No single word or concept is more expressive of choice, decision making, and the desire for personal freedom.

The strength of a child's self-assertion was described vividly by one of my clients in recounting his one and only attempt to spank his two-year-old son, who was already able to talk. The father was a very tense young man at the time, fresh out of medical internship, and much of his anxiety was tied up with his role as a doctor. His son had a sore throat and the pediatrician had prescribed oral penicillin, which the boy refused to take. The father had been trained to believe that oral penicillin is much safer than shots, so he told his son he had to swallow the medicine. When the boy refused, he began to spank him. After a few moments he stopped and again insisted that the boy swallow it. When his son still refused, the father got his wife to agree to give the child alternate spankings with him to make him give in. It was a case of a parent determined to win at any cost, and to involve the other parent as well.

The alternate spankings went on for some minutes, when at last, after a spanking by his mother, the boy declared, "I want Mommy to spank me; she hurts less."

In retrospect, my client wished he had broken into tears and begged his son's forgiveness. Instead, he continued this ugly routine of spanking, while demanding that his son take his medicine. The boy finally gave in and swallowed the stuff, held it down for a few seconds, and then threw it up all over his father. That brought an end to the horrible scene.

The morals to be derived from such a story are innumerable; here I want to stress that this child, just age two, was already a very active human being with free will. His personal freedom? That was subject to severe compromise at the hands of his parents, but there could be no question about the strength of his convictions or his determination to make choices despite extreme intimidation at the hands of both parents.

In the story I have told, the boy was under severe stress and stood up to it with dignity and with distinction.

In my practice, I have become increasingly aware of how children maintain their sense of self — a self intimately tied to free will — in the face of brutality. One of my clients was physically tortured at the age of four by his older brother. It was a painful affair in which he was assaulted with pliers, and it left him terrified of going to sleep alone. In therapy, this person was initially unable to recall the details of what had been done to him, but he was well aware of a vow he had made and maintained throughout childhood: "When I get big enough, I'll kill my brother."

He was so adamant about this that he wrote himself notes and put them in hiding places around the house as reminders for when he grew up. Out of moral outrage, he did not suppress his promise and become unconscious of it. If he had, he would have been stuck with a compulsion — a hidden reason pushing him toward murderous conduct for which he would not take responsibility. Because he had the integrity to remember his vow, he was able to reevaluate it as he grew older. Later on when he defeated his older brother in a wrestling match without hurting him, he was able to discard his promise to murder him. He had outgrown such helpless frustration.

Another client of mine, Jenny, showed an equal streak of bravery in her attitude toward her little brother when he was born. There was jealousy, yes, but Jenny quickly found him to be lovable and adorable. She wanted to help her mother feed him, dress him, and play with him, but her unstable alcoholic parent continually warned her that she would hurt her little brother by breaking him like a doll or by being too rough with him. Faced with this constant harassment, Jenny developed the idea that "only Mommy can be a mommy"; but she did not give up loving her little brother.

Several years later, the mother took another step to intervene between her and her little brother. She encouraged Jenny to tattle on him. I have seen this frequently in therapy — parents who turn their children against each other rather than face their own responsibilities for controlling and disciplining their children. But Jenny was different. She turned in her brother once and once only — for she immediately saw the pain that her betrayal caused him. She determined never to do it again and made an agreement with her brother that they would stick by each other.

This same young girl demonstrated her spunk during her potty training. Her ever-oppressive mother would sit her on the toilet at the exact same time every night and insist that she stay there until she had moved her bowels. But this little girl would refuse to comply, day after day, despite harangues and threats from her mother. Instead, she would wait until her mother had given up in frustration, and then she would sneak off to a private corner of her bedroom. There she would deliberately defecate in her pants, after which she would present herself in public to the dismay and outrage of her mother.

Jenny, like other clients who have shown courage, bore the scars of her upbringing. But from early in life she had consciously resisted the malevolent influence of her mother and father and had grown up to be a loving person who managed her life better than most people.

But aren't I opening the way for the abuse of children by suggesting that they have free will and can take responsibility for their own spiritual survival?

The opposite is true. Whether the abuse is expressed through physical assault or through a more subtle negation of the child as a person, the abuse of children is nearly always justified on the grounds that children do not have free will, rationality, or moral capacity. In most instances I have come across, a parent abusing a child declares that he or she is justified because "it's the only thing the kid understands." Questioned on whether this is the only thing adults understand, the answer is that children are different.

Children are not different — at least, not in the way these parents mean. Children are capable of taking responsibility, and many, many times they are more willing to do so than their parents. Children who have been ridiculed, shamed, beaten, and even tortured, often transcend their parents by not losing their sense of empathy, love, and justice. Often while parents are rampaging against children — teaching them to be hateful by example — the children themselves will maintain a sense of love and responsibility toward each other.

I have seen very abused children grow up to forgive their parents — while their parents continue in their attempts to abuse them, even to their deathbeds. By keeping their ethics together despite such wretched early lives, these children maintain their sanity. They suffer from what has been done to them — they have horrible memories to contend with, and many fears — but they do not go crazy; they do not become helpless, irresponsible, hating individuals who deny self-determination.

The Development of Ethics in the Child

Piaget has studied the moral development of the child and has concluded that the child is not capable of developing autonomous ethics until the age of seven or eight, when he or she becomes able to see himself or herself and others as independent actors in a world of mutual cooperation. Piaget has nicely correlated this moral development with the growing ability to reason. I have no dispute with these observations, but I would change the emphasis.

From the very start, the child acts upon an implicit set of ethics: personal growth and survival, and self-assertion toward these goals. Like any living organism, the child must actively seek growth and survival, or it will fail to grow and survive. Thus, the child seeks everything he or she wants in an uninhibited and lusty fashion — until he or she learns to fear the consequences. As the child learns to fear the authority of its parents, it develops what Piaget calls heteronomous ethics, or the internalization of the fear of others. This is very similar to Freud's concept of the superego, but the ethical framework is far superior to Freud's biologizing. I have included heteronomous ethics as an expression of what I call self-oppression. I witnessed it this morning in my son, Benjamin, when I heard him ask to have the volume of the record player turned up higher. I complied, and he became very upset. He wanted Mommy to do it, because Mommy had earlier told him that the volume was too loud. By having Mommy turn up the volume, he protected himself against his fear of her disapproval. In effect, his fear locked him into a heteronomous ethic that established an external, absolute authority that could not be reversed by his own wishes or even by his other parent's actions. When his mother said, "It's OK now, Daddy can turn it up for you," he again expressed upset and said, "No, Mommy do it." His self-protective rules had become more inflexible than the original authority of his parent. Although two months short of being three years old at the time, some of this heteronomous rigidity would undoubtedly persist into adulthood, requiring the analysis of reason before their liquidation.

It is very important not to encourage the child's own self-protective tendencies toward self-oppression. This means that the most subtle forms of force must be avoided as much as possible, including the use of disapproval. Instead, the child's cooperative desires should be encouraged by a loving environment in which all members obviously respect and enjoy each other. The child will then learn to respond to others out of love for them rather than out of fear. The child's self-love will then become the basis for loving others and for respecting their rights.

Love, rather than reason, is the ultimate basis for ethics in everyday life. Young people, uneducated people, and even retarded people, can be very ethical in their conduct when they have grown up in an environment that permits and fosters self-love and a corresponding love for others. Intelligence enables a person to influence his or her environment more readily, and intelligence helps an individual overcome previous influences in the formation of new ideas and approaches. But the more intelligent person is equally able to work out philosophies of evil and to implement them. Brain power is power, for better or for worse. Like a computer's capacity, it can be used for good or bad purposes. What matters most in setting goals is the attitude of the person as a moral agent, rather than the intelligence that the person brings to bear upon life.

The Noncoercive Parent

Just as parents have the power to destroy, so too they have the power to create. Adults can have great influence upon the quality of life within their families. With hard work, judicious restraint, and a great deal of love, any parent can give a happier start to the lives of his or her children. Toward this end, parental commitment to a consistent set of principles can be a great help to both parent and child, especially if the principles foster liberty and love. The nonuse of force is the starting point for such a philosophy.

Libertarian philosophy is based on voluntary association, or noncoercion — the ethical premise that no one has the right to use force or the threat of force, except in self-defense. Voluntary association, or noncoercion, should be the guiding principle of parent-child relationships. If anything, libertarian principles must be adhered to most scrupulously in relating to children, for they are too helpless to stand up for their own rights.

Noncoercion implies that the parent must use the minimal necessary force when defending himself or herself or others against the child. If a slight show of disapproval or a straightforward request will suffice to end aggression, then the parent who uses a sharp word or a hostile gesture has crossed the line from self-defense to outright aggression or coercion. The child's transgression has become an excuse for parental oppression.

Noncoercion also means that you, as the parent, must not administer punishments that far exceed the original crime or act of aggression. If you find it difficult to stop a minor offense with minimal force, you should take care before escalating the conflict. Your three-year-old son has an annoying habit of hitting you with his hand whenever he is peeved. You in turn find yourself using an increasing amount of force to no avail: you ask him to stop, you raise your voice in protest, and finally you command him angrily to stop. If he continues with his bad habit, what should you do? Do you, in turn, hit your child? And if that doesn't stop him, do you pummel him into unconsciousness, on the grounds that this is the only thing he understands? Perhaps this does represent adherence to the principle that one should use the minimal necessary force, yet clearly it is a transgression against the child through the use of force far in excess of the original crime.

Nonetheless, parents frequently escalate their own actions against their children until the children are physically or emotionally overwhelmed and battered. Instead of escalating such a conflict into one in which the child must ultimately feel humiliated or crushed, the parent should back away from the conflict until he or she has sufficiently cooled off to try a fresh approach.

This is a restatement of a principle examined in our initial discussion of self-defense: when you can remove yourself from a situation, you have no right to use any sort of force to change someone else's conduct. Minimal necessary force for self-defense is applied by simply backing off.

The odds are that any do-or-die conflict between a parent and a young child reflects a larger struggle of longer duration, one in which the parent is gravely at fault. The child may feel that his or her back is to the wall because the parent has chronically threatened the child's sense of self-respect. Perhaps the child feels unloved and gains some sense of mattering by struggling with the parent. One could elaborate upon such motives endlessly. The main point is this: no tiny, relatively helpless child will take on a gigantic, all-powerful adult in an out-and-out conflict unless motivated by desperation. Remove yourself from any such struggle until you can get at the source of your child's anguish.

However, in removing yourself, you do not have the right to abandon or to threaten to abandon your child. Because we have brought our children into the world knowing that they must depend upon us as their main source of love, food, and shelter, our children are our prisoners. Since we have brought our children into the world as helpless, dependent captives, we aggress against them if we fail to give them the necessities for personal and physical survival.

We aggress against them if we threaten to withdraw or to limit these provisions. This is a restatement of an earlier principle that the unconditional right to self-defense does not apply to involuntary relationships.

Parents frequently take it upon themselves to manipulate the giving of love, food, and shelter in the interest of controlling their children. They withhold affection or send a child to bed without dinner as forms of punishment. Suppose the parent were in the child's situation — forcibly placed at the mercy of an all-powerful authority who imposes control through the regulation of food and shelter. The parent would consider it highly unjust. But the child's situation is far more vulnerable. This child has literally been brought to life without having any say in the matter, and the child has been subjected to the will of specific parental authorities without any choice on his or her own part. The child is an involuntary dependent. No parent has a right to use this dependency to manipulate or coerce the child.

As a parent, you should avoid resorting to any of the more potent weapons at your disposal. Under no conditions should you use the infliction of pain as a means of control. Even the most benign spanking combines extreme personal humiliation with assault and battery. If you think this is an exaggeration, put yourself in the situation. Imagine that your husband or wife or your boss has pulled down your pants, forced you across his or her lap, and is now slapping your bare behind. Imagine further that you have broken up in shame and outrage and are crying hysterically throughout. Now imagine that your spouse or boss has finished with you and insists that you hang your head and apologize for the original transgression.

If I seem to have disarmed the parent, this has been my intention. When you as a parent have totalitarian control over your child — as you always do — you must never take advantage of your most potent weapons. You must disarm yourself in the interest of a more libertarian relationship. If this seems like a heavy burden to place upon you as a parent, it is a natural consequence of your decision to bring up a helpless and vulnerable human being.

Given that parents must put great limits on the use of force, when is force legitimate? Force is only legitimate when it is exercised in self-defense or in defense of someone else, and only when reason, patience, and love have not prevailed. You have the right to use force to protect yourself and your property from your child, or to protect other people and their property, when all methods short of force have failed. If your son (or daughter) hits another child, you have the right, and the obligation, to prevent the outbreak of violence. If your child begins bashing in your favorite paintings, you have the right to stop him. If he invades your privacy and refuses to leave your bedroom, you have the right to eject him. If he runs about in the communal areas of the house making a racket, you have the right to calm him down. If the noise he generates in his own room threatens the peace of the remainder of the house, you again have the right to stop him. If conditions in his bedroom pose a public health threat to the rest of the house — if he falls asleep with candles burning or if he plays with matches — you have a right to intrude in his space for the sole purpose of preventing the menace to the house. Similarly, if your child messes up communal areas, you have a right to enforce his cleanup of his own messes.

Most parents in therapy who have thoroughly examined their relationships to their children have found that 99 percent of their conflicts with their children have no element of self-defense in them but, instead, involve a constant harping and nagging by the parent about aspects of the daughter's (or son's) conduct that pose no threat at all to the parent — how she eats, when she goes to bed, how much TV she watches, how much she talks on the phone, how much she studies, how she dresses, how often she bathes, whether she will do chores (other than tidy up her own messes), and how neat she keeps her room. Not only have reason and love been thrown to the winds, but the parent, knowing his or her position to be irrational and loveless, defensively assaults the child verbally if the child registers a complaint.

You may not like how sloppily someone dresses, but no court of law would say this gives you the right to harass that person (unless it is your child, of course). You may think his or her eating habits are bad, but there's no chance that your nagging him about it will do anything but give him indigestion for the rest of his life. He may smell bad when he doesn't bathe; but if he disregards his appearance and hygiene, he is probably a severe self-oppressor and his spiritual state, not his bathing, is the issue you need to attend to. He may not want to eat when you want to eat — you probably fight at the table anyway — and his food could be put in the refrigerator to be eaten at his leisure. All this will gall many parents, not because it harms their children, but because it offends their desire to force their children into conformity with their own expectations. They want blind obedience, not respect based on rationality. Parents who submitted to their own parents out of fear and cowardice become indignant when their more independent children resent their attempts to control them.

If it sounds as if you would have to avoid your children a great deal of the time according to my principles, this only means that there is little love being exchanged in your family and that your children, if left to their own devices, would rather watch TV than spend time at dinner with you. Respect for liberty and love dictates that you must make dinner a happy time in order to get your children to eat voluntarily with you. Think about that — dinner as a joyous time. Libertarian principles establish one criterion for human action — voluntary exchange. This means you must offer something to your child when you want him or her to be with you.

There are a few areas in which a child's pursuit of his or her own self-interest might conflict with a parent's needs. Kids who never get off the phone make it hard for the parents to receive phone calls. Children who always watch TV in the family room make it hard for parents to do anything else in the family room. Here the parents have a right to impose schedules. But the parent will have much more luck in convincing the child of his or her rationality if no pretense is made about doing it for the child's own welfare. Instead, the parent's self-interest must be openly acknowledged, and a compromise arrived at.

In my own psychotherapy practice, however, parents who abused their children endlessly about noise from the TV or alleged overuse of the telephone could usually afford an extra TV or an extra phone strictly for the use of the children. Chronic conflict with the child has seemed preferable to letting the child have a small, secondhand TV or a personal telephone.

Curiously, this parent who harasses his or her child about matters that are none of the parent's business is likely to permit the child to instigate severe assaults against the parent and against smaller members of the family. The parent who flies into a rage because Jimmy won't clean up his room is likely to stand by helplessly while Jimmy pummels little June, or while Jimmy makes every car ride a horror by screaming endlessly from the back seat. There appears to be a trade: the parent takes out his or her frustrations on Jimmy, and Jimmy, in turn, takes out his frustrations on everyone. Jimmy gets the worst of it, however, since he not only feels overly controlled in his own private life but also feels guilty about making everyone else miserable.

If you are having trouble with your children, change your principles of discipline. Explain to your children, whatever their age, that you have been abusing them by nagging and harassing them over things that are none of your business but that you have been letting them get away with abusing other people, including yourself. Set down one rule, and only one — that your children not aggress against anyone. Be loving but firm about this — no aggression whatsoever, not even sneers, whines, or wise remarks. You, in turn, promise the same — no aggression. Tell them that all complaints must be presented rationally and that you will respond rationally. Then use force only to stop physical aggression. Use the very minimal amount of force and only after rational, affectionate reminders have failed.

By focusing on such a limited area of restraint and by treating your child with love, rationality, and respect, you will earn respect exactly to the extent that you deserve it.

Children are people — less powerful people. They should be treated with the same respect for their rights, dignity, and individuality that we would demand for ourselves, plus a little extra help in their own self-defense, for they have less power with which to protect themselves. When so treated, young people tend to conduct themselves with respect for the dignity, rights, and individuality of others, even their parents.

All human relationships should start with the minimal expectation that neither party will harm the other. From this minimal expectation, one can work toward the goal of a mutually satisfying and loving relationship. At all times, be prepared to respect the freedom and dignity that is your right and the right of all others, including your children.

What Punishments Are Legitimate?

Here is a good test of whether a punishment is legitimate — can your children use the same punishment on you? If they cannot inflict the same punishment on you, it is an unfair one. It probably depends on your superior size and strength. It probably depends upon an involuntary relationship. Thus, it is unethical to banish children to their room, to refuse to feed them, or to beat them. They have no access to similar punishments.

A parent has one legitimate, effective, and usually sufficient method of punishment — judiciously expressed anger. When a child assaults you or compromises your freedom, show him or her that you are angry. You can do this with an annoyed glance or a voice raised in protest. If the offense is grave, you can state loudly why you are annoyed. If this sort of protest doesn't work with your child, you have probably been so bossy in the past that your anger is now ignored. Your anger nonetheless scorches your child. Even the most apparently unresponsive child suffers the damnation of hell every time his or her parents get very angry. Rein in your anger; use it sparingly and only in self-defense.

Can a parent ever strike a child? Only under conditions in which you would strike the well-armed adult. Only if your safety requires drastic countermeasures. Even then, you must limit yourself to using the least necessary force. I don't suppose such a circumstance arises in one out of a thousand parent-child relationships.

Rethink what I have said; it has obvious, important implications. Your child should love and respect you so much that he or she responds immediately to your anger. If you do not have this kind of relationship with your child, forget about all forms of punishment and start from scratch, building a decent, loving family.

I have ruled out all the most commonly used punishments. In concluding, I want to focus on an extreme measure frequently used against children — refusing to let them leave the house.

Making a child stay at home, or "grounding," in current slang, is one of the most contradictory, absurd, and self-destructive actions a parent can take. It makes a clear statement to the child — your home is a prison. What is a person's natural response to a prison? The response is resentment and escape. If you want to turn your home into a place that your child hates and wishes to escape from, force the child to stay in it.

Home should be a refuge, not a reformatory. Home should be a place in which a child finds companionship, not solitary confinement. Always keep your home open to your child. Always make it the best possible place to live or to visit. But never communicate that you think home is a bad place by making your child stay home as a punishment.

Even if making a child stay at home were not self-defeating, it would still be unethical. It is the imposition of an involuntary relationship. It is imprisonment, and imprisonment should be illegal except as established by law for serious crimes, such as physical violence and theft. It should only be imposed by objective bodies called courts, and never by friends or family. Don't corrupt your relationship to your child by trying to become prosecuting attorney, judge, jury, and jailer, all wrapped up in one role called parent.

Good Reasons to Coerce Children

There are, of course, a few good reasons and a few important times to use force on very young children, especially infants. One of my clients, who is a physician, reminded me that I would find it hard to be a pediatrician because pediatricians frequently have to use force on children. If a child under age one or two is brought in with a fever, the doctor may have to use restraint to perform a variety of painful diagnostic procedures. The treatments may also inflict pain, and force may be needed to implement them at times. The parent who takes the child home may have to carry out prescribed orders, again against the will of the child.

In Benjamin's life, mild force is occasionally used on him. When he was six months old, for example, he was very upset about some hard mucus in his nostrils but refused to let me remove it with tissue. Discussion would have gotten us nowhere. So I gently but quickly cleaned his nose, after which he felt much better. The matter, hopefully, was forgotten in minutes.

Benjamin, like many children, becomes quite confused about his exact wishes when he gets very tired. He may be very eager to go to sleep, and yet he may be equally eager to stay awake. He yawns, frets, and tries to stay awake. Finally, he breaks into confused crying. If his mother or I then put him to bed, we are acting against some of his wishes. He shows his confusion and resistance by crying for a minute or two in the crib before he drops off into a long and happy sleep. There is no doubt, however, that force has been used on him.

I feel great fear and trepidation as I point out these examples of the need to coerce a small, preverbal child in order to give it medical or health-related care, or in order to act in its obvious best interest. I am afraid my readers will think of still other justifications for using force. I am afraid they will mount up and up, and open the way for justifying ordinary child-rearing practices. I want instead to reaffirm that such occasions are relatively few, and that, as the child becomes verbal, they become fewer and fewer. By the time a child is six or seven, the need for coercion should seldom, if ever, arise in a happy, rational relationship between parent and child.

I also want to reaffirm that when a parent finds himself or herself using force on a child, even on an infant, it is important for the parent to hesitate long enough to think the process through very carefully. I was very cautious about restraining Ben before cleaning his nose. I did it only because I was sure in my own mind that he would be immediately more comfortable. I would not have done it for cosmetic purposes, and I would not have done it "again and again" if it became obvious it gave him no relief. My wife and I are careful not to put Benjamin in his crib against his protests unless we are sure he is tired and ready to drop off to sleep.

Is there any rule of thumb for using force on very small children? Yes, only if it is very important, and only if there is no other way. And *very important* should usually refer to the child's needs, not to the parent's needs.

When I asked my wife, Phyllis, about using force on Benjamin, she said "I think about avoiding force all the time." She spends a great deal of her day trying to make Benjamin's routines of living as enjoyable as possible for him, and whenever he resists one of the routines she takes it as a sign that he is unhappy about it. She then tries to modify it or to put it off to another time, when he may be more willing to go along with it.

To illustrate the point I am making, Phyllis reminds me about her experiences diapering Benjamin. In the first two weeks, he sometimes cried loudly when she changed him. Instead of blundering ahead with this procedure on the grounds that it was an obvious necessity, she began to experiment and to pay careful attention to when he began to cry. It turned out that Benjamin did not mind being diapered, but that he hated being placed upon his back on a firm surface. Apparently it made him feel uncomfortable or awkward (or whatever the equivalent of such feelings might be in a two-week-old). Phyllis instead developed a method of changing him on his belly, and now he hardly ever complains.

I have already been through bowel training and a variety of other allegedly traumatic experiences with my older children. The trauma is almost always the result of conflict generated by the parent. Children like to do adult things as soon as they are able. They will "toilet train" themselves through mimicry, in the context of a happy, loving relationship. If they continue to soil themselves beyond the age when they are physically able to control their bowels, they are in self-oppressive conflict with an adult.

Before using force on a child, *stop, look,* and *listen*. The odds are that your reason for imposing force is hardly as important as the maintenance of a happy, loving relationship.

Chapter Fourteen

How Parents Can Live with Free and Happy Children

In the past I gave lectures on "How to Raise Free and Happy Children," but when I invited my own children to join me in my speeches on "raising children," they told me they did not like the concept. "How Parents Can Live with Free and Happy Children" appealed much more to them. Parents do have the determining influence on the outcome of child-parent relationships. Their task, however, is not to "raise" children but to learn to live with them. Anything else is oppression.

Permissiveness and Parental Self-defense

A libertarian upbringing need not be permissive in the negative sense. I do not advocate giving a child anything he or she wants. I advocate giving a child anything that is feasible within the circumstances of the family. There is a considerable difference between giving a child more than the adults have and giving a child an equal share in family opportunities.

More important, I am not in favor of letting the child assault the adult's personal sovereignty or personal freedom, any more than I favor the adult oppressing the child. I am talking about mutual respect and a very firm rule of conduct — that neither the big nor the small are allowed to assault each other. I am applying the unconditional right to self-defense — each person's right to protect himself from harm — to all people, including children.

Permissive families seem bent upon crippling a child by removing his or her opportunities for independent judgment and action. They "spoil" the child by denying him the right of self-determination. Permissiveness has again become a concern in recent years. Largely as a part of the growing cynicism about human nature and the concern over drug use and rebellion within the younger generation, a reaction against permissiveness is now justifying renewed disregard for the rights of young human beings.

In preparing a child for adulthood, this is the main ethical principle that he or she needs to know — aggression against others is illegal and punishable. But punishment will hardly ever be needed if the child has been respected all along by the adults. A child whose sovereignty is never assaulted and whose personal freedom is limited only by the most careful considerations will not frequently abuse his or her parents. Unlike those who seem to grow more cynical with age, my own experience has led me to an increasing trust in the inherent worth, beauty, and purity of the human spirit.

There is never any reason to attack or deny a child's absolute personal sovereignty, even if a parent feels constrained to limit the child's personal freedom. If a mother feels that certain of her five-year-old son's actions must be prohibited for the safety of others, she should focus only upon her own desire to limit the child's freedom. She should tell a child, "I will not allow you to do this," rather than, "You don't want to do this." As the child grows into adulthood, he will still know his own mind and be free to expand his conduct as he develops greater rights within the society.

Unhappily, too many parents feel compelled to attack their children's natural desires to know their own feelings and thoughts and to make choices. This crippling of sovereignty makes most people thoroughly confused about their own minds as they reach adulthood.

"But don't children have to respect the human rights of their parents?" Of course they do. To be free of coercion is a human right, and you have the right to be free of any force at the hands of your own child.

If you stand firm and refuse to let your child abuse you physically or verbally, you have solved almost the entirety of the problem of permissiveness. But remember — the best way to encourage your child to treat you well is to always treat him or her well. You will then rarely find the need to resort to force or to a harsh word. If your seven-year-old daughter whines or screams at you, you will only need to remind her that you never treat her in the manner in which she has begun to treat you. This, of course, requires that you never nag or shout at your daughter.

Parents have the right to protect themselves — their security, their privacy, and their property. You have a right to a safe and peaceful space in your own home, one in which you can keep your child away from you. Usually this will be the bedroom, or perhaps a study if there is space available. Sometimes it will be the living room at special times of the day. And your son (or daughter) has the same rights. You must never intrude in his bedroom without asking, and there are times of the day when he too may need privacy in other parts of the house. He should be able to exclude you from any area in which he is playing with his friends, just as you can exclude him from your entertainment.

You have a right to keep your thoughts to yourself; and when you do not feel like answering a question, you have the right to say so. So does your daughter (or son). She has the right not to tell you anything that she chooses not to tell you, and she has the right to demand that you stop asking her questions. You have the right to have her leave your personal property alone, and you have the right to insist that your daughter not damage any of the communal property, such as furniture. With a young child, under age three, for example, this is best handled by putting away easily injured property for the duration of babyhood and early childhood. But also remember that your child has a right to protect her property, too. Unless you really do believe in sharing, so that you frequently lend out your favorite toys — your watch, your wallet, your gun or fishing rod, your sewing machine, your car — then do not expect your daughter to willy-nilly share her toys with anyone who comes into the house. Respect her property exactly as you want her to respect yours, and you will probably have little trouble in this area.

You have the right never to be assaulted by your children. They must never threaten you with raised hands, and they must never strike you. You may restrain your son if you catch him assaulting someone — indeed, you should restrain him — but unless there is violence in the family emanating from you, there is little likelihood that your child will spontaneously choose violence as a way of life.

As a parent, I have always been extremely hard line in defending my dignity, as well as my property and my body. I developed the habit of protesting to my children whenever they showed the slightest sign of disrespect for me. Whining, a very common form of aggression among children, has never been tolerated in my home. Smart remarks, ridicule, even a cross tone have usually led me to express my dissatisfaction. But this has put an equal burden on me. I try never to whine at my children — something parents do far more frequently than they realize. It is called nagging. I avoid using even a cross tone of voice, for it implies that the child has really done something seriously wrong. The result of this is an unusually peaceful relationship in which my children and I can spend whole days together without being disagreeable with each other. The result is a relationship in which a great deal of time is spent having fun.

It is a truism that love and understanding are the essence of any good family relationship. It is less understood that love and understanding can only thrive to the degree that a relationship is free of coercion. Involuntary association is the greatest enemy of love, and freedom is its greatest ally. You will find that love and esteem for your child are the best inducement you can give for treating you well.

Compulsory Education and Other Coercive Institutions

School provides one of the most common sources of conflict between parents and children, for here the state itself intervenes to tell parents that they must coerce their children.

Most libertarians do not believe in compulsory education. Those few who do usually advocate a system in which parents and children have a greater variety of choices available to them. As one alternative, some libertarians would have the state finance compulsory education by giving educational rebates or credits to parents to purchase education in nongovernment or private schools. While the education of children would be assured, parents would be able to pick the school of their choice from among a variety of freely competing alternatives. Other libertarians would simply do away with tax-supported schools.

Unhappily, none of this would do away with parental power over children. Children would still be forced to obey their parents' wishes regarding schooling. Should schooling be treated as a medical or health-related need in which parental discretion must outweigh the very young child's own decision-making? I do not have an easy solution in regard to this, though I think that allowing children to choose their own parents would go a long way toward ameliorating the problem. A ten-year-old who disliked his parents' attitudes could seek others more compatible with him. More important, creating a context of rational, loving communication between parent and child would lead to the solution of such problems between the parent and child.

For our purposes, it is not necessary to get into the pros and cons of compulsory education and its alternatives. Even most libertarians obey the law and send their children to school and, therefore, must deal with compelling their children to attend. This is how I have handled the issue.

First, I have never lied to my children about school. I told them from first grade on that the government made me send them to school. I told them that, if they did not enjoy the particular school to which they were going, I would talk it over with them and try to improve on the situation at school through my own interventions or try to find a better alternative. I told them I'd do everything I could in my power to find as happy a school setting as possible and to back them up personally when in conflict with authorities but that I had decided to obey the law and send them to school.

Second, I told them that they must not take their teachers too seriously. I explained that many of their teachers would be bullies and worse. I urged them to view their teachers not as "authorities" but as "other people" and that they should learn to remove themselves emotionally from emotionally upsetting people. I explained to them how I had learned the art of thinking my own thoughts in boring classes, while maintaining a studious look on my face.

When they came home with stories about nastiness and stupidity in their teachers, I generally accepted their viewpoint as rational (it almost always was). I tried to figure out ways to help them get along in the situation. Usually this involved their seeing the teacher as a person whose ethics should neither be applauded nor taken seriously. Sometimes it was necessary for my wife or me to go to school to back up the child. Usually this amounted to nothing more than reassuring some wretched bully of a teacher that my children had real parents. With such bullies, threats are hardly ever necessary — only a parental presence.

Third, I tried to explain to my children that most of what they would learn in school would be poorly taught, unnecessary, and irrelevant, but that any bright person could master it easily enough to enjoy some of the day's events. I assured them that most of their education would come from within themselves, from their friends, and from the pursuit of knowledge on their own.

Finally, I told them not to take the grading system seriously as a reflection of their worth. I also told them that getting good grades had nothing whatsoever to do with "learning" or with "being educated" and that getting good grades was mostly a reflection on the individual's willingness to spew back material in an acceptable fashion. I made it very clear that their report cards meant nothing at all to me, but that their daily happiness meant a great deal to me.

Over the years, my children have received fairly high grades with very little studying, but neither of them has tried to be at the top of the class. Looking back over the years, my children agree that they have largely enjoyed school. They have accommodated to the coercive situation by turning it into a social get-together with their friends, against the background of a largely humdrum class-schedule interspersed with occasionally interesting educational experiences. Sometimes, they find school-related activities genuinely exciting, such as a relationship with a good teacher, a special study project of some interest, sports, cheerleading, or the school newspaper. I believe that their happiness at school has a lot to do with being loved at home and with not taking school and their teachers too seriously.

The view I am suggesting may seem very radical, but my own experience suggests that many people share it with me. In my private practice, many parents who have no notion of "libertarianism" or "anti-statism" realize that public education is largely oppressive and boring. They recall day after day stuck in the doldrums of a classroom. Yet they have tried to "motivate" their children to "take school more seriously." They feel like hypocrites and they fail to achieve their ends.

I have frequently seen the same phenomenon in regard to religious training. Nearly all of my clients have looked upon their religious education as fundamentally suppressive and irrational. And yet many have gone on making their children go to church and to Sunday school. It strikes them as a "revelation" — albeit a revelation of a whole new kind — when I suggest that they follow their own judgment and liberate their children from institutional religion.

As a parent, you will develop a much happier and fuller relationship with your children if you stop hypocritically forcing on them the very institutions that tormented you and made you miserable as a child. In regard to religious education, you can put an end to it if you wish. In regard to compulsory education, you can try to find the happiest solution for your children, and you can teach them the art of maintaining personal sovereignty in the face of external compulsion. You can help them take themselves more seriously and their "formal education" less seriously.

John Holt, an educator who does not align himself with libertarianism, nonetheless urges parents to keep their children out of school and to educate them at home. This could be one libertarian alternative, but most parents will find it hard to adopt in the near future. Whether or not you have the energy, the time, or the inclination to follow Holt's policy, as a parent you must recognize that school will not provide your children with an education in becoming free and independent. Instead, your children will be taught to accept the authority of others in matters where individual reason and individual conscience should prevail. Unless your children are to discover and sustain the truth on their own, you must provide the most important aspect of their education — confirmation of their capacity and their right to think and to feel as independent persons.

In general, I have tried to dissuade my children from the idea that authorities or laws are sacred. There is a superstition that people are morally obliged to obey laws and even to worship laws. I do not think so. Along with Thoreau and a variety of other heroes, I personally believe that the individual is, instead, obliged to listen to his or her own conscience. Neither you nor I asked to be born into this particular nation, nor even onto this particular earth. I see no reason to hold sacred the particular compulsions laid upon us by our ancestors or by our contemporaries in this or any other society. I happen to like America better than other nations because it permits more freedom and diversity. I especially approve of the Bill of Rights. But, in general, I find most of the laws of the land to be coercive and unjust.

On the other hand, overtly breaking laws is rarely in anyone's interest. It leads to all manner of aggravation. Even the most radical anti-statist tries not to get into trouble with the government over minor issues, even though he or she has determined to rebel actively, as through tax resistance or draft resistance. Whether my children wish to be rebels in adulthood will be their own business. As far as I am concerned, I want them to grow up with a healthy, happy disregard for all forms of authority and coercion. If they eventually choose to rebel more actively against authority and coercion, that will be their own business.

Teaching Good Habits

"But isn't a parent obligated to make his or her child develop good habits?" This question most frequently comes up around eating and sleeping habits in young children. By nagging or threatening a child in an attempt to enforce certain habits, the parent corrupts the child's natural inclination to do what is in his or her own best interest. This parental interference encourages the child to rebel to maintain a sense of independence, even if this rebellion costs dearly in terms of his or her own health or well-being. In my therapy practice, it is commonplace to see a young adult who would like to lose weight, study harder, or get a better job, but who refuses to do so precisely because a parent vehemently demanded such actions. So reluctant is the young adult to conform to parental orders, he or she may fail to pursue otherwise desirable ends.

Most attempts to make a child learn one or another good habit turn out to be cases of parental bullying. The parent has a fixed idea that children are supposed to listen, and he takes any independent thinking as a personal affront. Often the bullying is aimed at making life easier for the parent, without regard for the actual needs of the child.

Eating provides a typical illustration. Children often go through long periods of time when they want to eat specific foods and nothing else. Parents, on the other hand, tend to insist that children eat whatever is put on the table. Such parents argue that the child's health will be impaired or that the parent's own energy will be drained by making special menus for the child. In every instance I have thus far come across, there have always been one or two foods that the child dearly loved, typically hamburgers, hot dogs, or chicken, each of which can be highly nutritious if properly selected and cooked. Usually the child also likes at least one vegetable. In no case I have heard of has the child's favorite food required much culinary skill or effort. Children like simple things. Almost invariably, the time consumed in cooking such a special menu involves no more than a few minutes; and almost without exception, if served such a menu on a regular basis, the child will soon enough find himself or herself growing interested in other foods. Why don't parents accept this? Because they have too much power and insist upon implementing it, even if the end result is more hassle than it is worth.

Is there any time that you as a parent should use coercion concerning something like an eating habit? Yes, but only in self-defense. You should not let a child throw food at you. But what child would throw food at a parent who always cooked his or her favorite meal?

The best way to help a child develop good habits is to have good habits of your own and to know how to explain them to your child in a reasonable fashion. Out of love for you and out of self-interest, the child will mimic you.

But if you try to force good habits on your child while you yourself pursue bad ones, you will only further alienate him or her with your hypocrisy. Because of resentment against you, he or she may pursue bad habits in order to make you angry.

Protecting the Child

Confronted with such narrow limitations on the use of coercion, the parent is likely to exclaim, "What if your daughter wants to have sex at age ten? Or what if she is taking drugs?"

Whether my children have sex or take drugs should be no concern of mine unless I can really argue it is causing them harm. Even then, I have to prove my viewpoint to them, since I cannot use force.

Promiscuous sex? The ingestion of obviously harmful drugs? Certainly I consider promiscuity a sign of unhappiness within a person. Certainly I hope my children will not take dangerous drugs. But, in my own opinion, these are pseudo-issues that need never come up in a happy family. Children who chronically do things to harm themselves are always in flight from a wretched home situation. Drugs, loveless or promiscuous sex, and other self-destructive activities reflect self-oppression. If I saw such a problem with one of my daughters, I would spend my time examining my own conduct toward her. I would attempt to find out what I was doing wrong. If I decided I was doing nothing wrong, I would be stuck with tolerating my daughter's own decision-making.

What about the two-year-old who tries to toddle across the street? What about the two-year-old who touches the hot stove?

That's easy to answer: a child of that age can get into trouble only while being actively neglected by a parent. A two-year-old walking hand in hand with a parent by a street is not likely to pull her hand away, knock the parent down, and throw herself in front of a truck. Watch a parent who is screaming at or spanking a child who goes into the street; you will see a parent who would rather do something else than keep a loving, playful eye on the child.

As soon as children are old enough to understand hot stoves and cars, they will stay away from them — unless they are already in a struggle with an oppressive parent. If a struggle has already developed over "don't go in the street" at age two, then the child — being naturally independent — may carry out the struggle still further, even at the risk of getting beaten up by a parent or killed by a car.

The parent must share responsibility with the child for the child's situation. When the situation is going sour, the parent needs to look mostly at himself or herself, for the parent holds the greater power and hence has the greater influence.

In the case of a child who does reach an older age with a tendency toward self-destructiveness, even if coercive interventions were ethical they would be likely to fail. It is impossible to imprison and isolate a young person in today's society. Coercive measures are also likely to backfire by giving the child more reason for self-hate, as well as for hatred of his or her parents and all life. The parent who is in conflict with a child bent on self-defeating actions can often do little more than pull back from the conflict, admit his or her own past contributions to the problem, and beg forgiveness. Once over that hump, the parent may begin relating to the child through reason and through love, to whatever extent the child may be willing to extend trust. This means that the parent may have to suffer in apparent helplessness while his or her child takes drugs, stays out late, or consorts with bad companions. But the parent who admits past errors and who tries to change is likely to be surprised by the rapidity with which the child responds, while the parent who continues to resort to coercion is likely to worsen the situation.

When a parent discovers that a teenage son or daughter has already developed a self-destructive lifestyle, the parent is entitled to refuse to cooperate in this conduct. Refusing to cooperate is very different from actively interfering or imposing force. A parent may refuse to allow drugs in the house, especially if he or she feels legally jeopardized by the presence of illegal substances. A parent may refuse to lend out the car or to support another car for a child who gets in repeated accidents. The parent has especially good grounds for this, because his or her own insurance policy is at stake. But if a child uses illegal drugs outside the home, or legal ones within his or her own room, parental intervention is on shaky ground. Similarly, if a child buys a car out of personal funds and manages to obtain auto insurance, a parent is overstepping his or her authority in intervening.

Too often I have seen allegedly concerned parents indirectly encourage their children to commit crimes and to take self-destructive actions. Some parents give their children no attention unless they are in trouble. Other parents get vicarious satisfaction out of watching their children fight authority. Therefore, I do make clear that a parent can and should refuse to cooperate in a child's self-destructive activities. As an issue, it is always secondary to building love, trust, and respect with a child.

There is another form of protection that children do need and yet too seldom receive — protection from other adults. Most adults grow up believing that children must take great care not to insult, embarrass, or disappoint adults. As children, they were taught to be good, thoughtful, courteous, and so on, in their contacts with adults. Adults, on the other hand, took little care to be good, thoughtful, or courteous toward them. These grown adults now enforce the same code of submissive ethics upon their own children.

Recently, one of my clients was examining how he was still obedient and diffident before his elderly parents, often to the detriment of his own new family. As he was describing this, he began to see parallels with the raising of his own little boy, who was becoming shy and timid around adults.

My client explained how his son would look down and refuse to shake hands and how he would try to escape from the living room and the visitors to play by himself. Before and after these incidents, the father would take his son aside and explain to him his duty to be courteous to guests, but it did no good.

I encouraged him to imagine himself in the body of a small, shy child, looking up at an enormous adult, towering several body-lengths above him, with an enormous hand extending down toward him. The father immediately got my point, but asked, "Shouldn't I be teaching him to treat our guests with respect? After all, they are our guests!"

"And he is your son," I replied. "And it's supposed to be his home. Is your first duty to make adults feel comfortable while visiting, or is it to make your son feel secure within his own home?"

It may be necessary to insist that visiting adults be courteous to your children, but with well-loved children it should rarely, if ever, be necessary to insist that they be courteous to visiting adults. Children have the right to be shy when four, and shy again when fourteen. According to the principle of voluntary association, parents have no right whatsoever to insist that children relate to anyone who comes into the house; but they have the obligation to protect them from abuse from anyone who comes into the house. Children treated with this kind of concern will usually feel so secure around their home and their parents that they will be delightful to associate with — when they feel like it.

I am writing this shortly after Christmastime, and I have fresh in my memory several stories about my clients' taking their children to visit grandparents. Parents will come up with all sorts of excuses to justify submitting their children to the oppression of their grandparents. "Grandma will miss Jane if I don't bring her over"; "Grandpa only has a few more years to live"; "How much harm can they do to her in only a week?"; "Don't we owe it to them to leave Billy with them when we go away?" Sometimes the excuses are more clearly self-serving, such as, "We'd never get out at night if Grandma didn't babysit," or "Grandpa pays for all her clothes."

However one examines the morality of encouraging this submission, it comes down to the involuntary subjugation of the child to the needs of others. The parent is unwilling to protect the child because the parent is unwilling to stand up to his or her own parents.

Honesty Is Not Always Your Child's Best Policy

The right to privacy and to personal sovereignty includes the right to remain silent or to refuse to answer questions. This right in personal affairs is broader than taking the Fifth Amendment or refusing to incriminate oneself. In personal relationships, an individual should have the right to withhold information for any reason whatsoever, other than to commit fraud or to cheat upon an agreement.

Parents insist, "Tell the truth," when they have no intention whatsoever of reciprocating by "telling all" about themselves. Often the parents have little interest in the truth itself; they are seeking to enforce free access to the child's mind. They want to crack the child's sense of privacy by convincing the child that he or she cannot withhold thoughts from the parents. These parents want to dominate and control the child.

When stuck in an unfree exchange — one enforced by guns or by superior size and strength — it is often self-defeating to tell the truth. It is almost always self-defeating for a child to "fess up" under pressure. These children grow into adulthood unwilling to lie, even if their lives or the lives of their loved ones depend upon it.

Lying is not an absolute evil. Telling the truth becomes unethical when it allows an oppressor to hurt us or other innocent persons. Under such conditions, we tell the truth out of cowardice. Honesty by itself, then, is not an ethic. It is a necessity if you want to create voluntary relationships, but it is a liability if someone has already imposed an involuntary one upon you. You have the right to lie, exactly as you have the right to use force, in order to escape oppression. So does your child.

I have never pressured my children to tell the truth. Instead I try to build a noncoercive, voluntary atmosphere in which they will feel free to tell me what they freely choose to tell me — and nothing more. I feel the same way about my relationship to my wife, friends, and clients. Even in psychotherapy, it is unethical to pressure the individual to say anything he or she does not wish to say.

On the other hand, dishonesty or lying can be used unethically to impose an involuntary relationship upon someone. If you agree to deliver certain materials to a person and you take money for it, knowing you will never carry out your end of the contract, you have forced an involuntary loss on the other person. This is fraud.

Fraud is a common method of imposing an involuntary relationship upon children. It frequently takes the form of a hidden agenda lurking in the mind of the parent who claims to have the child's best interest at heart. A mother, for example, pretends to bring up a child to be an independent adult, while undermining the child's self-esteem, hoping to keep him or her at home forever. A father pretends to love his son, when he really wants to manipulate him into taking orders.

Parents should be very careful about defrauding children, but they should rarely worry about their children defrauding them. If your child lies to you, your child is afraid of you. He or she *learned* to distrust you. Look to yourself first, before you come down hard on your children for lying.

What Children Owe Their Parents

The child did not bring the parent into the world and is therefore not responsible for the parent's life. Even when the parent becomes helpless in sickness or old age, the child cannot be held responsible in the same sense that the parent was once responsible for him or her in childhood. The child may wish to help the parent out of love or out of a desire to return kindness, but there is no absolute or immutable obligation to do so.

"But I brought him into the world. I fed and clothed him and sent him to school. Doesn't he owe me anything?" Let us suppose you find a semi-stuporous drunk lying in the street and you decide to bring him into your home, to feed him, and to put a new set of clothes on him. When he wakes up, does he owe you anything? You have done all this for him without his consent. He owes you nothing other than that which he wishes to give you. If he is pleased with your conduct he may decide for himself that he wants to repay you. If he decides that you have kidnapped him, he may want to bring charges against you. So, too, your own child owes you only what your child personally determines.

Parents don't have a right to bring children into the world unless the child's happiness is their sole reward. To bring a child into life for purposes other than the joy of parenthood is unfair to the child.

In my own home, my refusal to use my children to take care of my own needs means that they have no chores whatsoever other than those that they choose for themselves. They do not have to help clean up the dishes and they do not have to help clean up the house, although they often lend a hand. They do not mow the lawn or take out the garbage.

There may be some rationality in requiring children to help with meals and with household chores, since they share in the benefits. But, personally, I do not think that children should be required to do such things. If parents cannot handle the financial or energy requirements of bringing up children, then they should not have children. If they have mistakenly had children before being able to afford the cost or the energy expenditure of feeding and housing them, the children should not pay for the mistake. I can imagine some rational disagreement on this limited question of children helping with household chores; but children themselves universally resent chores aimed at keeping up their parents' homes, and I have accepted this opinion as having sufficient merit to let it stand. My conclusion is that I should not have brought children into the world if I were not prepared to take care of their basic needs for them.

Only in households with many children, and hence many beds to make and many dishes to be washed, are parents able to force sufficient work from their children to justify the hassle. Most parents are seldom able to extract a worthwhile work contribution from their children. Since the enforcement of this work as a "principle" to "teach responsibility" is only likely to make the children resent all household chores all their lives, it often becomes purposeless.

This concept of child-parent relationships runs completely counter to the traditional notion of bringing children into the world to add to the security of the family, to earn money, or to take care of the farm. The extreme is the traditional agrarian community where children are born and raised as free labor for the parents. I don't believe in the use of children for slave labor, even if the slave-masters are their own parents. We should bring children into the world for their own sake and for the pursuit of their own self-interest.

The ethics I am proposing became more feasible during the industrial age. Few families within a modern economy need their children to help with survival needs. Should an atomic war or some unforeseen horror befall our civilization, a parent might be compelled to insist that children help with mending clothes, cooking meals, or other survival needs. It might be necessary for the children's own survival, and that would justify their working in joint family ventures. But it would be immoral to bring new babies into the world at such a time with the intention of using them as slave labor for the support of the parents or other children. Similarly, it would be wrong for the parents to sit back while the children produced more work than was necessary for their own survival. Parents should always encourage their children to fulfill their own destinies.

Will this breed irresponsible children? It depends on what you mean by irresponsible. It will encourage your children to defy conventional oppressive morality, and it will encourage them to determine their own lives in their own freely chosen directions. It will encourage their inherent belief in the pursuit of self-interest and their own freely chosen ideals. It will also encourage your children to love you.

Does this mean that you as a parent have no claim upon your child — not even upon his or her time? Yes, this is exactly what it means. As your child grows up, you don't have the right to demand that he or she live near you or devote any energy to you. Your child may find a lover in Japan or may decide to colonize another planet.

You must have no claims upon your grown child's life. If you in your old age become helpless, dependent, and in need, you probably made a dreadful mistake in the conduct of your own life. Do not impose it upon your child. Do not pass it on to another generation.

But shouldn't a child feel obliged to take care of a parent who has come upon chronic illness or accident? If the child has such obligations, he or she would be a slave, forever tied to whatever bad luck or bad planning the parent endured. A grown child may wish to take care of a parent out of love, respect, or genuine gratitude, but this must be the grown child's own decision.

Enjoy your children by identifying with their happiness. This is your sole reward for parenthood — and it is a great one.

What Parents Owe Their Children

Parents bring their children into life, and they owe it to them to do everything in their power to give them a high quality of life while they require parental care.

Standards for the quality of this care will depend upon the parent's own standard of living. So will the duration of care. Poor parents make a grave mistake in sacrificing their own security or happiness by draining the family's resources for the benefit of their children. These parents will resent their children, and the children will grow up feeling so indebted to the parents that they will have difficulty leading lives of their own. Similarly, rich parents should not withhold things from their children for fear of spoiling them. This suppresses the parents' natural desires to give everything they can to their children, and it will make the children rightfully resentful.

Should a parent sacrifice his life for a child? Knowing that your son may die, do you consciously give your life to save his? Do you cut out your heart or your last kidney to save him from death? Your child has the right to get everything out of life he can — including everything you can give him — but not at the expense of your own survival. Self-love and the pursuit of self-interest is a basic human right. If you believe that you should sacrifice your life for another person, even your child, you have made yourself of less importance than that other person; you have made yourself into his slave.

I occasionally hear a mother protest that she loves her children so much that she would sacrifice her life for them. There is encouragement within society for viewing the maternal role as a form of martyrdom; and in addition to the maternal guilt that motivates the assumption of such a role, these mothers are able to use their martyrdom to manipulate their children with guilt. Usually these parents in actual practice fail to provide the children with those few things they should supply, such as unconditional love and a basic respect for their rights. When a parent protests that he or she will do anything to save poor Jimmy from the clutches of drugs or from failing at school, check to see if the parent is also willing to restrain his or her own temper or to give up a few hours on weekends for Jimmy's undivided attention. A parent who advocates extreme self-sacrifice for the alleged sake of his or her children is a parent who suffers from guilt. This parent is probably a self-oppressor as well as an oppressor.

A parent obviously owes it to a child to be rational and to be ethical. A parent also owes it to a child to learn how to be loving. This issue comes up with surprising frequency in therapy, for many parents feel as if a child should be stuck with whatever craziness a parent manifests. They take their hapless children to psychiatrists, while they themselves continue on their crazy path.

Nowhere is the principle of justice in our personal lives more apparent: sanity, ethics, and lovingness are their own rewards. The parent should become sane, ethical, and loving for his or her own sake. Confused and resentful parents often overlook this obvious truth. This illustrates how muddled ethics have become within our society. Some people actually consider it a sacrifice to love their children, and they find lots of other parents who agree with them.

Terminating the Parent-Child Relationship

Parents often terminate their relationships to their children. They leave them with other members of the family, they abandon them, they drive them away, and sometimes they commit them to oppressive institutions for the retarded or the mentally disturbed. Often parents terminate the relationship while the children remain at home. They do this by withdrawing attention from the children, leaving them virtually on their own. Several of my clients and friends raised themselves for most of their childhood.

Children, by contrast, have very little ability to terminate their relationship to their parents. Until they are teenagers, they have almost no capacity to run away. Relatives, neighbors, and the police are legally obligated to return them home. They cannot be taken in by someone else they may prefer, even if these hand-picked parents desire the task and can prove themselves competent and loving. When older children run away, they must become fugitives from the law — hardly an attractive alternative for a fifteen-year-old. That so many children nonetheless run away indicates how oppressive family life can become.

For children to maintain voluntary relationships with their parents, they must have the right to "run away" — to seek out more advantageous homes for themselves. If society recognized this right, a major step would be taken toward reforming the family. Each parent would have to offer his or her children a good home or risk losing them to a better offer.

There can be little hope for this concept receiving serious moral or legal attention in our present society; we are too far away from considering or implementing basic rights for children. But you, as a parent, can personally convey this attitude toward your children. You can make it clear to them that you want to win their affection and to earn their allegiance with all the energy and care you would devote to winning over someone who was not forced to stay with you. You can treat them as if they are honored guests in your home — guests whom you hope will stay for years and years, literally until they grow up. Think how good this will make your children feel. Will it spoil them? Yes, in a sense. It will encourage them to believe that they deserve such treatment from others as well. They will grow up and seek out friends and mates who will treat them as you have treated them. They will make happy friends and families for themselves.

Unconditional Love for Children

I have defined love as joy in the recognition, understanding, and awareness of the humanity of another person or living creature. I have called it a positive response of one life force to another. Love is the placement of value upon life in general and upon a specific life. Love feels so good because it affirms life. By loving someone else, we affirm the value of all life, including our own, and we affirm our own value as a loving person. No harm can ever come from loving, and no good can ever come from withdrawing love. Unconditional love is the single most important gift you can give to your child.

Parent and child thrive when they affirm, through each other, the inherent value of life and, more specifically, the inherent value of each other's lives. This is an aspect of any relationship made intimate through close and continued contact, but it is an even more important aspect of parent-child relationships, because children who go unloved may suffer the effects of it for their entire lives.

As a parent you must at all times make clear to your child that love for the child is without strings. The strength of the love must be kept constant throughout conflict and disappointment. This means that no matter how angry or disappointed you feel with your child — no matter how little you esteem his or her conduct — you must not withdraw love. Even in the act of defending yourself from attack, love must not be withdrawn. Treat your child in this fashion and you never need worry about whether your child will love you in return.

Unconditional love is not only a necessity for the child, it becomes a boon to the parent. If you know that nothing your child does can prevent you from loving him or her, you will also know that no circumstance can ever cause you to make very gross or damaging mistakes as a parent. Such errors can only take place when you have withdrawn your love and begun to act in a loveless manner. Vindictiveness, vengeance, over-reactions, protracted rages — all this will drop from your repertoire, for it is incompatible with love.

A parent's lack of love is usually in direct proportion to the abuse that he or she heaps upon the children. Love is the main restraint against abusing others, for love says, "I recognize your human quality," and hence grants equal human rights to the individual, whatever his or her age. For the parent locked in conflict with a child, it is vastly important to distinguish between this unconditional love and the more conditional feeling of esteem. The parent may not respect the child's conduct, but the parent can find within himself or herself the capacity to love the child — to reach out to the child with the recognition of his or her inherent value.

It is not a parental duty to esteem or respect a child. Esteem has to be earned by the child. But it is a parent's duty to love a child. Love is recognition of life. It says, "You are alive and the life within me reaches out to you." Love requires that you make an effort to discover another person's humanity. You have the duty as a parent to create conditions within the family in which love has a maximum chance to thrive, and you will suffer if you fail to do it. Your child will suffer equally as much, if not more, and will rightfully resent you.

On a few occasions, parents, especially men, in therapy claim that they no longer miss their estranged children or that they had known them so little before the divorce that they have no feeling toward them. Usually, this is an unethical attempt by fathers to avoid continued responsibility for children who have been left behind and who obviously miss and need the father. The parent suffers from this unethical denial of his own inherent tendency to reach with love toward his children, and, of course, the children suffer from knowing that the parent displays no interest or affection for them.

It is hard for me to imagine how a father (or mother) could achieve an ethical and happy life without taking responsibility for developing and maintaining a relationship conducive to love between himself and his children — however far away circumstance and his own irresponsibility have carried them. Similarly, an expression of love — even long delayed — can mean a great deal to a child. Even a grown child in his twenties or thirties who has not seen an irresponsible parent in decades may respond happily to an extension of genuine love. It is never too late for a child to benefit from a reformed parent. Parental love is like sunshine to a plant — it provides the light and the warmth necessary for optimal happiness.

No Utopian Solutions

I do not want to leave the reader with the impression that I foresee utopian solutions to the problem of childhood oppression. Giving children the right to select their own parents, for example, will be sharply limited by the relative inability of these small, immature, and helpless beings to exercise such an option. Not only do they lack sufficient experience with the outer world to choose among better alternatives, they have a natural attachment to the people with whom they have shared their early years. Children are also subject to so much oppression and are so likely to choose self-oppression in response that it is hard to imagine a society in which children freely leave one family in favor of another. The right to seek out one's own family would establish an important right for children, but far more important is the establishment of new attitudes on the part of parents in general.

State intervention does not offer any hope in this arena either. Others who have noted the abusiveness of typical family life have gone on the record in favor of government child-rearing institutions. Before experience and reason changed my philosophy, I was a full-time consultant with the government in the area of mental health and education and helped plan government-funded preschool programs. From a practical viewpoint, there is no reason to assume that these will provide the needed love and rationality any more than the typical family would, and they will certainly be lacking in diversity. From a libertarian viewpoint, increasing government intervention into the lives of its citizens is a danger as grave or graver than that of the individual oppressive family.

I am, therefore, not urging radical reform of the family on the political level as much as I am urging radical reform of parental attitudes and values. With time I hope that our laws will also recognize that children are people and that they should have most or all the rights accorded to adults, especially the right to defend themselves and to be defended against physical and mental abuse, and ultimately the right to choose parents for themselves.

Chapter Fifteen

How to Love Freely and Happily

Liberty and love often seem at odds with each other. Many individuals believe that the two are incompatible and that love leads to the loss of liberty.

Romantic love is the most intense and the most binding. But passionate sexual attachment to an individual is not unique in its qualities. Profound attachment to any person or place or to any creative activity presents all the paradoxes of liberty and love.

Love and Self-sacrifice

When people truly love each other, they may become willing to risk death for each other out of self-interest. The other has become of such value that it seems worth the risk of life to keep the person in one's life. In loving relationships, the risk of death is related to self-interest; the man who risks himself defending his loved one gains so much from his loved one that the quality of his own life depends on the life of the other. He values that person almost as much as he values himself, because his loved one brings so much happiness to him. The nearer this equation is reached — valuing oneself as much as one values another — the nearer one is to pure love.

I do not believe, however, that people should feel morally compelled to give their lives to save the lives of others. Risk is one thing; outright sacrifice is another. Outright sacrifice implies that the other's life is more valuable than one's own. This is usually a self-oppressive, guilt-ridden decision.

It is imaginable to me that one person might give up his or her life for another in a very rational manner. An aged grandmother, for example, might sacrifice her life for her young grandchild, or for anyone else whom she loves and whom she wishes to have as full a life as she has had. A man employed as a bodyguard, such as a president's secret agent, might rationally decide that his contractual agreement includes the possible sacrifice of his life for that of the president. I might disagree with his decision to enter such a contract, but I can accept its rationality and ethics.

I bring up these exceptions with great hesitancy and concern. In my practice of psychotherapy, I have found that a preoccupation with sacrificial conduct *always* derives from self-oppression rather than from love or from freely chosen contractual agreements.

I do not wish my wife or children to give up their lives in order to spare mine, and I do not plan to give up mine in order to spare theirs. I will take grave risks because I value them very much and because I have based my life upon sharing the risks of living together "for better or for worse" as a part of our love relationship. But I want all of us to believe in our own self-worth as individuals and to place the highest priority on our own individual lives.

I want to reemphasize that self-love is the starting point of a rational, happy life and that love does not generate sacrifice as much as it obliterates the concept by creating mutual and shared interests. In contrast, parents teach their children to equate love with sacrifice in order to dominate and control their children.

One of my clients vividly recalled how a neighbor's child had been burned nearly to death in a horrible accident. My client was only ten years old at the time, but in therapy he relived the stench of burning flesh as if it were in the room. He also vividly recalled how the burned child was murmuring under his gasping breath, "Don't tell my mother; don't tell my mother."

Years later, my client got to know the permanently crippled boy better and to understand the enormous guilt that motivated his deathbed plea to be spared his mother's recriminations; but of more direct importance to my client, his own mother heard about the incident secondhand on the day it occurred. One of the neighbors had described to her how the boy had been "thinking of his mother to the end" by pleading for her to be "spared the sight of his burned body." When my client returned home that day, overcome with anguish over what he had witnessed, his own mother took him aside and said "Would you think of your mother at a time like that?"

For years afterward, my client would lie in bed at night envisioning horrible tortures during which he would become a perfect child by hiding the details of his agony from his mother. Beneath this awful self-oppression lay paralyzing resentment of her constant oppression of him. He had but three alternatives in his own mind: submit to her cannibalistic abuse of him, fight her in what seemed to be a kill-or-be-killed conflict, or leave home. At the age of ten, he chose to submit and to rationalize his self-oppression as love for his mother. This established a pattern that would persist with women until his therapy.

Many individuals walk through life amid fantasies of sacrificing themselves in glorious attempts to prove their worthiness to live. It is an awful irony, this desire to prove one's worthiness to live by destroying oneself in the interest of another. One of my clients could not walk near a playground without imagining the successful rescue of a child from the clutches of a mad dog, a falling object, or a violent criminal. Another imagined that he would meet a woman and prove his love by giving up his own pleasure and his own aspirations in her interest. Still another was preoccupied with what he would do if presented with a situation in which he must choose between himself and his loved one, as in a life-raft that will hold only one person. Sometimes such fantasies are brought to fruition as individuals throw their lives away in futile attempts to rescue others for whom they feel no love.

Giving Love Outweighs Getting Love

Much of the guilt individuals feel in an allegedly loving relationship is generated by the failure to love or by the self-denial of loving feelings. This came up when one of my clients began to feel very indebted to me. Therapy had been going well, and nearly every aspect of his life was freer and more filled with love. Then he began to tell me that I did not charge a high enough fee. He constantly reassured me about what a good therapist I was and how I should make more money.

I scrutinized my own conduct but could find nothing guilt-provoking in my behavior toward him. I was satisfied with my fee; I wanted nothing more from my client. But I was very fond of him, and when it was time for his session I would look forward to it. I especially loved the joy he felt as he worked through one or another barrier to his own happiness.

I asked my client if he felt that I was doing anything to make him feel guilty, and he could think of nothing. He had not even identified his remarks about my fee as a form of guilt. But, over several sessions, other manifestations of guilt became apparent. He had solved a difficult sexual problem with his girlfriend and now felt he should share the details of his happier love-making with me, since I had allegedly been forced to sit through all the more unpleasant details. The man felt obligated or indebted to me, and it was becoming a major block to the therapy and to his growth. Because he owed me so much for the progress he had already made, he was afraid to become still more indebted through any future gains he might make.

I now realized he was treating his girlfriend in the same fashion. She brought him more happiness than he had ever known with a woman, but he wanted to back off. He already owed her too much. He was getting so much from me and from her that he feared he would owe us his life in return.

What was his debt? Did he owe anything to me or his girl?

First, we talked objectively about what one owes a therapist who has helped one find happiness. He himself was involved in the safety inspection of dangerous equipment. If he found a defect that saved lives, did his clients owe their lives to him or did they owe him a reasonable fee for his normal service? He realized he had been looking at me in a distorted light, that he thought he owed me happiness in return for the happiness he had found through therapy. We reached agreement that this made no sense, but he gained little relief from his guilt or indebtedness.

Then I thought about how much affection I felt for him, but how little he let himself feel for me. From his many remarks, I could tell my feelings toward him were reciprocated. Sometimes he would burst with pleasure over our exchanges during the therapy. But he had never admitted even to feeling fond of me.

I told him: "We've agreed that you've been feeling guilty and indebted toward me. But if a person were at ease with his feelings, what would he feel toward someone who helped bring happiness into his life?" This was obviously a leading question, but it had quite an effect. He hemmed and hawed, blushed heavily, and then blurted out, "Love! I'd feel love and I do feel love for you." He broke into a grin and beamed his bright smile at me.

"When you first asked me that, I started getting more worried," he told me. "I thought that now I owed you love, or some other kind of self-sacrifice. I got very confused. And then I just let myself feel good about you, really good, and for those few seconds I didn't feel as if I owed you anything."

Through his oppressive upbringing, and through the subsequent unethical demands he had made upon others, this man had rarely known love as joy in the presence of another human being. Love had become sacrifice: beginning with his mother, he had sacrificed for others, and then he had demanded sacrifice from his girlfriends, all in the name of love. In reality he had shared very little love. Now he was drastically afraid. If the weak and distorted positive feelings that he used to call love had become excuses for mutual enslavement, what new enslavement would be required by these more intense feelings toward me? He therefore suppressed his feeling of love for me, despite the great value and joy he found in our relationship. Guilt signaled his self-oppression.

I do not denigrate the desire to be loved. Instead, I want to put it in perspective. I have seen many clients drive themselves to distraction seeking love from the people in their lives. It has gained them little. At times, being loved has actually thrown them into a state of panic, for they feared the consequences, such as vulnerability to others. But to love is a wholly different matter. The moment one loves, life becomes better. A person has a right to seek out people who will love him or her. But a preoccupation with getting love is self-defeating. It puts one into constant worry over what others think of oneself. A person should focus upon his or her evaluations of, and feelings toward, other people.

Often, when people are too afraid of becoming dependent, they have been self-destructively focused upon getting love. This has made them demanding rather than giving. It has made them helpless rather than strong. It has made them other-determined rather than self-determined. The more you desire to love rather than to be loved, the better off you will be.

When most people think about loving someone or something else, they immediately run smack into guilt, shame, or anxiety. As in all other cases resulting in such responses, outright fear lies at the heart of the negative emotion. Most people are terrified of love.

Why this fear of being loving or loved? Throughout the oppressive childhood of most people, being loved has been directly associated with being oppressed. Parents, teachers, and religious functionaries alike speak of "love" for the individual when they mean control, manipulation, self-sacrifice, and outright bullying. Love becomes a cover story for every oppressive act taken by parents and authorities of every stripe. "Mom loves you" means Mom can do anything she wants to you.

Typically, "God loves you" also means that God or his self-appointed priests can demand tortured self-sacrifice from you, in the form of an agonizing self-denial of your sexual drives or total subservience to irrational and oppressive religious ideologies. "God loves you," but he's got hell and everlasting torment to back him up, just in case you don't love him in return. It is surprising how an otherwise sophisticated person can reach adulthood with an unshaken association between love and torment, as a result of the combined influences of parents and priests. It is "surprising" only until the person's life story unfolds. After years of religious indoctrination, associated with parental enforcement of religious attendance, it is no surprise at all that many people run from "love" as they would run from burning napalm or the fires of everlasting hell.

Every aspect of oppression that I have described in my examination of childhood can become linked with "love." "Love relationships," in the minds of many people, are relationships of mutual self-sacrifice, torment, manipulation, and destruction.

The inhibition of the desire to love is one of the most self-destructive forms of self-oppression. Love is connectedness to life; to suppress love is to disconnect from life. Many people go through life feeling "disconnected"; they call it "alienation," a "sense of meaninglessness," or simply "boredom." Often it is a fear of loving or being loved.

Desperate Need and Love Are Not the Same

Love is the placement of value upon another person; it brings joy. Need is a sense of missing something; and it brings pain. It is an emptiness that requires filling. Love is a fullness that overflows and replenishes itself. Need controls the person, and the person must often struggle against it. Love is created by the individual; he or she can flow happily along with it.

A need is similar to what psychologists call a drive. It is reduced by fulfillment. A person who is hungry can eat and feel satisfied. A person who is sexually aroused can have an orgasm and feel a reduction in his or her physical tension. But a person who loves feels no sense of "tension" and no corresponding sense of "relief."

The person who has experienced himself or herself as loving wants to expand upon this experience as a more and more loving person. He or she becomes loving most of the time and feels good about it, unlike the person who feels sexually aroused or hungry all the time and feels frustrated.

The comparison to sex makes the difference obvious. After having a good sexual experience, two partners will feel complete bodily satisfaction. But, if their sex is integrated into their love for each other, they will continue to feel loving after their sexual needs have been fulfilled. They may continue to hold each other, feeling more and more love in each other's presence. Sex is a need; it gets gratified. Love is a creation; it grows boundlessly.

There is often a direct opposition between love and need. The less a parent loves a child, the more the parent is likely to need the child and to take actions that make it difficult for the child to grow up and leave home. I have seen parents fall apart ethically or psychologically when their children leave home, yet these parents are motivated by personal emptiness rather than by love.

Similarly, I have seen many children so in need of their parents that they could not function without them, even after they reached adulthood. These grown children have suffered grave oppression, and as grownup self-oppressors, they are afraid to leave home. They "need" Mom and Dad, but it has nothing to do with love.

Often in the very first hour of therapy, the confusion between need and love will become apparent, and my client will be vastly relieved by discovering that the two are not the same. Typically, the client comes in stating that he deeply loves a woman who has recently broken up a romantic relationship with him. His alleged love for this woman is manifested by such things as extreme anxiety, agonizing sexual needs, excruciating loneliness, profound jealousy over the woman's new life and successful bid for freedom, and a desire to do everything to force the woman to return to the fold.

Usually it turns out that all this is taking place as the reenactment of childhood threats or losses that my client has shoved into unconsciousness. My client neither esteems nor loves the person whom he cannot bear to lose.

It is hoped that in therapy my client will decide he must face himself and stop trying to force a reunion upon the alleged loved one. Once my client stops emotionall bullying the other person, he must face his own enormous fears about himself, including his lifelong failures to be self-determining in his romantic relationships.

Nondependence and the Fear of Needing Too Much

Many people express desperate needs and make believe that these needs are equivalent to love, while other people are afraid to feel or to express any needs at all and make believe they don't wish to love anyone. Again, the confusion between intense need and love is key. The confusion leads the person to bully others into fulfilling his or her needs on the grounds that he or she loves them or to refuse to relate to other people in a loving manner on the grounds that it reflects a dangerous and unethical need. Often a person vacillates from one position to the other, the consistent principle being the confusion between need and love.

The fear of needing too much is often expressed as the fear of becoming too dependent. To love someone is interpreted as becoming too dependent upon the person. Love and dependence are seen as forms of enslavement. Independence is confused with doing without others.

In reality, all successful people depend upon others for help and emotional support. True independence is the capacity to *choose* whom you will depend upon in a self-interested, rational manner. In contrast, unchosen dependence is healthy only for small children.

Dependence exists in any mutually self-fulfilling relationship with another person. I depend every day upon my wife for helping me to renew my love for life. Her smile or the touch of her hand can change a bleak moment into a happy one. I am dependent upon her for everything good in our relationship, but the dependence is freely chosen.

What about the frequently expressed notion in psychiatry that psychotics and other disturbed individuals are too dependent because they have allegedly insatiable needs for attention or love? Such people are not dependent, even in comparison to normal children, for they do not make satisfying use of other human beings. Failing to get what they want from anyone, they make a racket, cause trouble, and generally constitute a pain in the neck; but this reflects on their *helpless inability* to be dependent. Some are so afraid of becoming dependent that they will die of hunger or disease before submitting themselves to the care of others. They flee in panic from offers of love, attention, or help. Using a word I coined in my second novel, *After the Good War,* I define these people as *nondependent* rather than dependent.

Nondependence is the unwillingness to depend upon others. It is nonrelationship. In its extreme form, nondependence goes hand in hand with the most irresponsible of lifestyles, such as psychotic intensities of paranoia, depression, or anxiety. It is an extreme form of self-denial or self-oppression.

People also confuse nondependence and independence. People who are afraid to love rationalize that they want to be independent. Actually, they are terrified of admitting a desire for intimate human contact.

Next time you excuse a failure to love on the grounds that you need your independence, it may help to ask yourself if you are feeling truly free and self-determining. Ask yourself if you are truly pursuing your own self-interest in an independent fashion or if, instead, you are too frightened to reach out toward another person and are rationalizing nondependence.

It is commonplace to see a previously nondependent person collapse into helpless, childish dependence after forming a romantic relationship or upon getting married. This person has done relatively well on his or her own, despite a lurking desire to hold someone else responsible for his or her unhappiness. He or she has managed a "single" household, gotten up in the morning on time, found things to do when bored, and watched his or her own diet. Similarly, this person has managed to avoid the pitfalls of extreme self-hate or rage. But his or her apparent independence has reflected nondependence, or the inability to choose a satisfying, dependent relationship. Once in proximity to a new loved one, the old desires to surrender personal sovereignty are given full play. The focus is no longer on "making it on my own" but on getting the other person to "help." The help may vary from getting awakened on time in the morning to receiving pep talks when feeling down. When the help is not forthcoming, the previously meek person may vacillate between self-hate and rage at the loved one.

Often there is an apparent improvement in this person's self-esteem when he or she decides "to hell with the other person." This renewed sense of well-being is fraudulently based on a sense of "independence," when in reality the individual has returned to nondependence. The individual lacks the ability to relate to another person while maintaining personal autonomy. The only way to have a flourishing love relationship is never to use the relationship as an excuse for giving up any degree of personal sovereignty, self-determination, or responsibility for oneself.

Needing People

The subject of needing people perplexes the modern individual. While I have distinguished need from love and warned against using need as an excuse to coerce others, I do not want to cast doubt upon the reality that people have great needs for the presence and companionship of other human beings. I do not know exactly how to categorize or describe this craving, but there is no doubt that human beings desire the companionship of others, and that the absence of this companionship breeds loneliness and emptiness.

A surprising number of people have started out their first therapy session with me by explaining that they know it is *not* good to need people. Sometimes, they will bolster their position by citing previous therapists who have told them that people must be able to do without other people. My clients are often happily surprised when I point out that human beings have always lived in societies and that, within societies, they almost always live in couples and in families. I may also point out that isolation from human beings is one of the most severe punishments that can be inflicted, and further, that people typically remain in very unhappy relationships partly because they feel so desperately in need of any kind of companionship.

This need for people seems more primitive and fundamental than love. However poorly understood this need may be, it nonetheless exists and must be satisfied for most people to have a start on personal happiness. I therefore urge people to admit openly their need for others. Once acknowledged, it can be dealt with in a rational and self-fulfilling manner. The need must not be allowed to overrule other equally important requirements for the good life — including the right to self-defense against aggressors — and it must not be allowed to imprison people in unsatisfying relationships. While we "need" people, we are at times best off managing the need to some degree on our own, while we seek out better friends and lovers. Recognize the depth of your need for companionship, and set out to fulfill it in a deliberate, conscious manner.

Love Can Be Painful

As people fall in love, they realize that there is something irrevocable in what they are feeling. Therefore, in the beginning of passionate relationships, before each partner becomes sure of the other's love, there is often a great deal of fear.

I have often had the experience of watching a client fall in love amid a storm of anxiety. Adolescents and old people alike have marched into my office brimming over with a brightness that almost always means, "I have met someone," only to collapse into anxiety within a few minutes. At that moment of anxiety, we are able to see exactly why their prior love affairs deteriorated and collapsed; they were too afraid to pursue them. Now we are able to identify the reasons behind the fear. Some of these reasons go back to childhood oppression at the hands of parents, and some go back to betrayals of the opposite sex committed by my client. My client fears repeating the same self-destructive conduct. But some of the fear is what I would call objective. My client has picked out someone to love and cannot be certain if the other person will return the love and establish an intimate relationship.

I make clear to my client that every attempt to make this passionate attachment conditional upon guarantees may doom the relationship. Two people refusing to take a step without reassurances means that no forward steps will be taken.

To fall in love is frightening and dangerous. People often deny their love in order to deny their fear.

Must the equation between love and fear continue?

Yes and no. It can become more moderate with time, as you learn to trust your own ability not to wreck or to betray the relationship, and as you learn to trust the same qualities in your loved one. But you cannot be protected from the knowledge that many things can interfere at any time in a love relationship, including enforced separation or physical death. A man or woman who does not experience great fear when a loved one is threatened with serious illness or separation is a man or woman who does not dare to love. It's that simple: you can't have love without facing the threat of loss.

To be committed to anything is to risk losing it or failing at it. A woman (or man) afraid to commit herself is a person who has her own reasons for being afraid; she must become brave enough to learn about her reasons and to overcome them, even in the face of continuing, realistic fear. She especially must overcome her own unethical, self-oppressive tendency to handle life by denying its importance to her. This is true whether we are talking about commitment to work, to play, or to love.

The potential pain involved in unconditional love increases the need for self-defense and toughness. It is futile to kid yourself into thinking that you can be a loving person without becoming a very tough person. By loving, you create new self-interests that must be defended, including the well-being of your loved one and of any children you may bring onto earth. You also make yourself vulnerable to your loved one, should he or she betray you. You must then be prepared to defend yourself from the person most close to you.

I cannot exaggerate the importance of personal strength and a dedication to one's own self-defense as a prerequisite for loving. Time and again I have watched clients glimpse the meaning of love, only to retreat from it in panic because they lack a firm sense of the right to self-defense. Their personal vulnerability overwhelms them at the moment of loving. Utmost toughness is required before anyone can dare to love with all of his or her heart.

Love Can't Make You Crazy

It is a common, everyday misperception that passionate, romantic love can drive a person mad. This is because love often brings out or exaggerates an already unethical style of life.

When people fall in love, they often do everything in their power to deny it. They become frightened, even terrorized, by the realization that they have assigned such importance to another human being. Their love challenges all the crazy ideas with which they have degraded themselves and the opposite sex. Their cover story that they don't care is shattered.

Conversely, a decision to love can uplift a collapsed individual. It can be seen to happen in seconds, literally in seconds, and it is only a lack of courage and honesty that causes a relapse.

On many occasions I have had clients walk into my office stuck in the midst of anxiety, depression, or paranoia. When I am able to break through to make a relationship with my client or when my client risks perceiving me as a safe and worthwhile person, the client's craziness dissipates on the spot. This demonstrates how the smallest ray of love, friendship, or trust can banish madness.

Of course, no one can solve a lifetime of problems in minutes. There will be relapses. I will fail; my client will fail. We will both have to do a lot of work to find out how and why my client gave up the courage to love. All this, of course, requires enormous responsibility on the client's part; it cannot succeed without a courageous client. There are no cures given out by any therapists — only opportunities for those who are daring.

Nothing affects a person so much as the placement of value upon another human being. To those who do not dare place such a high value on another person, this seems irrational. To me this placement of so high a value on another person is the height of rationality.

Chapter Sixteen

Love and Sexuality

I am sure that many readers will glance through this book and immediately turn to this chapter; given an unfamiliar book, I might do the same thing. I can only hope that you'll take my advice and back up at least to the preceding chapter on "How to Love Freely and Happily." Better yet, begin the book at the beginning. Sexuality can become one of the most interesting, exciting, and rewarding expressions of love, but only after liberty and love are thoroughly understood.

An Affirmation of Sexual Possessiveness

We live in a society that has come to denigrate individualism, individual rights, and private contractual agreements. This has undermined love as the most passionate expression of individualism. It has also made sexual possessiveness a dirty word.

Nowadays, a common form of self-oppression is the denial of one's own desire to possess an exclusive relationship with a loved one. Allegedly liberated individuals claim not to desire sexual exclusiveness in their romantic attachments. This is pure hypocrisy. When a person is truly prized in a loving relationship, that relationship takes on such importance that both partners guard against any interference.

I have never in my personal or my clinical experience known a person who romantically loved another person without wishing to possess that person exclusively. Invariably, denials of possessiveness are either self-oppressive or reflect an actual lack of love. If happily married or committed people seem not at all concerned with possessiveness, it is only because their commitment is so thorough and unconditional that neither partner threatens the relationship with outside flirtations.

Jealousy is different from possessiveness. As a negative personal emotion, or a loss of self-esteem, it reflects a failure to pursue one's self-interest or sexual possessiveness in regard to a loved one. If a man sees another man making a pass at his wife, anger is a positive response because it constitutes a direct response to the threat. Jealousy sets in the moment the individual doubts the validity of his feelings. Jealousy is possessiveness and anger rendered impotent by self-doubt. The chronically jealous man is a man who doubts his right or ability to take care of his own interest within a love relationship.

The desire to have an exclusive relationship with another human being is no different from any other ambition; it can be sought after ethically or unethically. Because an exclusive sexual relationship is so fervently desired by so many people, it has become a model for destructiveness between people; but it can also be a model for one of life's most creative adventures — romantic love.

There is a difference between wanting to possess someone and forcing possession upon someone. There is a difference between having a wish and forcing someone else to fulfill your wish. It is the difference between voluntary exchange and rape.

In affirming "sexual possessiveness," I am not affirming the use of emotional or physical force in attaining it. People commonly confuse sexual possessiveness with expressions of jealousy and with guilt-provoking attempts to bully the partner into becoming "faithful." Any time any kind of pressure is put by one person upon another, the entire validity of the relationship falls into doubt. If you truly love your sexual partner, you recognize that person's right to determine whether or not to be exclusively yours. I doubt the genuineness of any love in which the allegedly loving person submits to a sexually exclusive relationship out of fear of hurting or disappointing the other person. These principles have been already elaborated in chapter ten, "Guilt Is an Unethical Emotion."

Nor does "sexual possessiveness" imply an abrogation of self-ownership. It means that most self-owning persons desire sexually exclusive relationships with loved ones and are willing and eager to make agreements to give each other exclusive sexual rights.

That sexual love is possessive and that love can only thrive in a wholly voluntary setting presents the individual with a most difficult ethical challenge. The individual who loves must be prepared to feel a great desire for an exclusive sexual relationship with his or her loved one, all the while refraining from making any coercive communications. This means that you as a lover are stuck with making an offering of yourself, and if that offer is refused you must bear the pain. I will go so far as to say that you should not even communicate your pain to your loved one unless you are sure your intention is not to create guilt. A love relationship should be kept free of all emotional oppression. It is that simple, and that difficult. Most love relationships fail because one or both individuals refuse to grant separateness to the other person, making it difficult for the other person to determine freely whether or not he or she wishes to love in return.

Romantic Love and Bodily Sex

People live in bodies, and frequently they love through their bodies. Sexual love — or love through bodies — is romantic love, and it is considered the ultimate expression of love by many persons. It is one of the most intense human experiences.

Bodies are also among the most frequently used excuses for not loving. Men and women refuse to commit themselves responsibly to love because they still want other bodies, allegedly for sexual variety. Men and women also excuse their failure to love each other on defects in bodily beauty — "His body turns me off," or "I don't like the shape of her nose" "... her breasts," "... her ankles." Many sexually driven persons also use sexual passion as a distraction from being with each other. They preoccupy themselves with bodies and with climaxes instead of with each other.

For many people, the ideal of romantic love is dominated by sex. But even in passionate love, nearness to a body is most important because it brings nearness to the person within the body. All love, sexual or not, is essentially spiritual — it involves one person loving another person.

The body is a vehicle for loving. It can express love. But the body cannot create love. When a man feels that his body is driving him sexually and emotionally, he has lost track of himself as the center of his existence. He has shifted responsibility away from himself toward the mechanics or biology of his physical structure. When he attempts to satisfy himself by multiple orgasms or other sexual acrobatics, he misses the true source of his passion — his desire for companionship, intimacy, or love. Such a person can end up feeling estranged not only from himself but also from his own skin and sexual organs, for he has made them into something they cannot be, a substitute for true intimacy with another person.

You will feel more in touch with your body when you recognize it for what it is: a flesh and bone structure, no different in essence from anyone else's body, not even much different from any other mammalian body. You can feel more loving and attentive to your body when you recognize that it cannot create or satisfy your desires to be loved and to love but that it *can* help you express and accept love.

You can enjoy the people you love by looking, touching, hugging, smelling, and otherwise sensing their physical existence. You can communicate with them through, and by means of, their bodies. But when you confuse the person with the current state of his or her anatomy, you have begun to estrange yourself from that person.

Men and Sex

The body hunt that preoccupies so many males, as well as some women, is a self-destructive lifestyle. It can only end in disappointment and alienation as the hunter continues to miss out on the true joy that people can give to each other. The focus that so many women put upon themselves as bodies to attract such men can only build a legacy of future disappointment, for they too are playing in a game without lasting value. Preoccupation with sex and with bodies provides escape from life's most difficult challenge — the development of a mutually satisfying relationship between loving sexual partners.

The starting point for solving any sexual problem is to redefine it in terms of self-determination, esteem, and love. This in itself can liberate the individual from his or her self-defeating obsession with bodily function.

A middle-aged man, Rob, came to see me suffering from impotence of several years duration. He had been in therapy with an analyst for several months and had gained insight into his difficulties with his mother and his unresolved anger toward his former wife; this had brought him no relief from his inability to have an erection while having sex with the woman he loved.

He had not dared think of his erection as an extension of his love. Going to bed to have sexual relations was tied to performing, being manly, giving pleasure, and getting pleasure, but not to sharing love. These ideas had been reinforced by many years in the armed services where his companions frequently treated sex in this manner.

Once Rob shifted attention from bodily performance to sharing love, he became more able to confront the last vestiges of fear and resentment in regard to women. But he still panicked over what would happen if he continually failed to "get it up." I suggested that a man can make love to a woman without using his body at all. Having decided to use his body, a man can find many ways to share love without using an erect penis.

I also pointed out to Rob that he would undoubtedly become sexually erect one day or another, some time or another, if he lay in bed with the woman of his choice, sharing his affection for her. There is no way to avoid it! The only issue is to let the love out — to have the courage to feel intimate, close, warm, and loving.

The true goal of love is a union that transcends bodies: a coming together of individuals so close in their awareness of each other that bodies tend to become one and then to disappear. What sort of techniques can you practice on a body that has disappeared? A person's inner self cannot be manipulated. With this realization, problems with sex disappear; but problems with love appear.

My client Rob was in love, and he had gained some analytic insights from his previous therapy. Now unlocked from his misidentification of the problem as a physical or sexual one, he was able, with a session or two, to overcome his impotence, and his body at last became an avenue for expressing love.

Another middle-aged man, Phillip, turned out to have the opposite problem. He tried so frantically to enjoy his sexual partners that he would persist in repeated sexual relations until his body became sore and exhausted. He tried for bigger and better orgasms and even multiple orgasms with more than one woman in an evening.

When alone, Phillip would suffer from sexual frustration. Self-assurances that it was harmless to masturbate did not assuage his sense that something was the matter. Even if he wanted to, this forty-three-year-old man could not go through an evening alone without becoming sexually excited. He felt that he could not control his body, but that his body controlled him.

Phillip was fond of two or three women he was involved with, and they obviously liked him. Sometimes he thought he was in love with one or another of them. But having terminated two unsatisfactory marriages, and having failed to find any peace in love-making, he began to doubt that he could ever be fully satisfied sexually. Projections into the future left him wondering anxiously what would happen when age caught up with him and rendered him less energetic in bed. Yet the projected decline of his sexuality also appealed to him. Perhaps he could find tranquility through the sexual quiescence of old age.

Much like Rob, Phillip had mistakenly identified his problem as sexual. It was helpful to trace his sexual preoccupations back to an early and very precocious adolescence fraught with anxiety and depression. As a youngster, he could never relax with himself or his family. The development of early sexuality made him feel more alone and yet more in need of human contact. His mother added to the strain of his precocious biological development by making subtle sexual gestures toward him, by hugging him more tightly than he wished, by trying to kiss him on the lips, by staring with too much fascination at his face. She also hinted that her husband — his father — left her unsatisfied. She made references to women who allegedly began to enjoy life only after old age reduced their sexual drives. Thus, she reinforced his preoccupation and his hopelessness in regard to sex.

He in turn would stimulate himself to masturbate to the point of exhaustion every night. Yet masturbation would never satisfy him or give him rest. He did not dare acknowledge that his problem reached far beyond the realm of the body into the world of alienation, loneliness, and despair.

Shortly after coming for therapy, Phillip met a woman with whom he immediately shared a new personal closeness, and his sexual difficulties abruptly took a new and ironic turn. Instead of desperately trying to satisfy himself with this woman, he found contact with her so inviting and so exciting that it frightened him. When this girl touched him or when he touched her, there was no question about reaching new peaks of excitement — there was, instead, the fright of feeling overwhelmed with passion.

It now became more apparent to Phillip that this was not a sexual problem. Throughout his life, he had not felt truly close to a woman. During his upbringing, he had handled his mother's excessive sexual preoccupation by denying the reality of women as people and by withdrawing his love from them. Instead of patiently awaiting a woman whom he could love, he then pushed himself to love women for whom he felt nothing more than friendship or a mild attraction. When with these women, he would, in his words, "rev up my sexual engine" to hide from his anxiety, guilt, and loneliness. Now that he had found a woman he really loved, he had to face both the intensity of his personal emptiness and his fear of women. Gradually, as he let himself feel more loving, love-making became more fulfilling. Gentleness, patience, and personal sharing made holding hands with this woman more satisfying than making love with anyone else, while actual sexual relations took on a spiritual beauty to him.

Phillip was astonished to find that his previous lust for women hid his great fear of them as well as his enormous need to find a single woman with whom he could share his more intimate thoughts and feelings. Instead of being drawn to her by his bodily need, he was now motivated by a desire to share his life with her. He found himself more interested in her as a person than as a body and was delighted to discover she too loved him for himself.

We cannot treat ourselves or our loved ones as bodies or as machines and get away with it. Impotence, frigidity, premature ejaculation, hypersexuality, insatiability, a vague sense of disappointment over sex, and so-called postcoital depression are all expressions of difficulties in loving. Not to communicate this to a person is to cheat him or her of the meaning of love. Most of the volumes written about sexual problems and sexual techniques therefore mislead the individual.

But what about the boy who masturbates by himself or gives himself gratification while staring into a magazine centerfold?

What about the woman who uses a vibrator to find satisfaction?

Obviously there is something bodily in these activities; but when they are mainly bodily, the experience will often be one of relief, similar to a good scratch. If the person is able to let off great quantities of tension or even anxiety, there may be a high degree of excitement and subsequent release. But it will be followed by other, less fulfilling feelings: loneliness and disappointment.

Women and Sex

While the split between sexuality and love seems frequent and debilitating among men, it rarely manifests itself so blatantly in women. Instead, women seem to suffer from the opposite — a sacrifice of sex for allegedly spiritual values. Women very frequently say such things as, "I don't climax, but it really doesn't matter; I love my husband and I like to make him happy." But it is unheard of for a man to say, "I don't climax, but I satisfy my wife and that's what really matters to me." A cursory examination of these statements made by women shows that they are pursuing lifestyles of self-sacrifice and personal failure.

Many authoritarian institutions, including most religions, inhibit sexuality as a means of enforcing submission of the individual to authority. Since greater submissiveness is demanded of women, it is not surprising that greater sexual inhibition is also demanded.

Among women, the inability to climax during sexual relations is probably the most common complaint. Often, they are more able to satisfy themselves by masturbating or by using a vibrator in the presence of a man or while alone. Some of these problems at first glance seem purely sexual in origin. Women in our society are more coerced to postpone, hide, or lie about their sexual needs. If a woman is very attractive sexually, she can become so good at fighting off insensitive males that she cannot relax and enjoy the man she cares about.

Nonetheless, it is rare to find a woman — or a man — whose most important sexual problem relates directly to feelings about the sexual act or even to religious morality. Instead, we again find conflicts and failures with men that reach back into childhood relationships within the family, including submissiveness to male members of the family. Women become convinced that they must service their men in bed; and since it is possible for them to lie about having orgasms, they become accustomed to dramatizing fake climaxes and phony satisfactions to please their men. This can become so deeply ingrained that the woman only confronts her problem when a man who truly cares about her lets her know that he is not fooled and that he wishes he could truly satisfy her. Even at that point, the woman may still be so oriented to the needs of the man that she comes to the therapy session motivated to enjoy sex so that her man will be happier about himself as a man.

The woman who subjects herself to so unsatisfying a sexual orientation has usually subjected herself to self-denial and subjugation in many other aspects of her relationships with men. She must reassess all her rights.

There is so much male brutality associated with sex in our society that it is not infrequent to find women who have been suppressed physically as well as psychologically by men. It is astonishing how frequently female children are beaten. Where a woman has already been treated badly by her father and where she has chosen to continue submitting to ill treatment from her male peers, the occurrence of a rape can be devastating.

Male domination and female submission are so much a part of our social standards that acts that border on rape are often passed off as "natural" by males and females alike. If the man is "drunk," assault, battery, and attempted rape have been excused as a "date" at the fraternity party. If the woman is married to the man, rape may even lose its legal meaning, and the woman may have no claim against the man. From the woman's viewpoint these realities may confirm that men are too dangerous to trust in a loving relationship.

Given the rampant sexual oppression of women, it is not surprising that so many women lose interest in sex. In therapy they declare that they would be "just as happy" if their husbands never sought sex with them. My first advice to such women is to say no to their husbands. They must establish their basic rights in regard to sex; and as in everything else in life, the first and most crucial right is the right to refuse.

Once a woman has learned to say no to men, she has taken the first step to establishing her own sexuality. She may come to the conclusion that she does not love her husband, and that this is the basis of her aversion. Or she may come to the conclusion that she does love him but that he must give up abusing and using her before she can dare to feel the love. Or she may come to the conclusion that she herself became such a self-oppressor that the problem is largely her own and that she must learn to enjoy sex with a man who is truly sensitive and loving toward her. The outcomes are multiple and unpredictable. What is predictable is this: a woman who cannot say no also cannot say yes. She must learn to take complete charge of her body and her sexual activities. She must become self-determining in regard to sex. She must pursue it wholly out of self-interest and not to "service" a man. Only then will she be able to make choices based upon her honest evaluation of her true feelings toward her sexual partner.

Never have sex unless you feel like it. Never have sex unless it reflects a warm and at least friendly contact. Sex is as good as the love it expresses.

Often the self-oppressive woman has been encouraged into the viewpoint as much by watching the oppression of her mother and other adult women as by any direct aggression against her. Frequently my female clients will describe the appalling submissiveness of their mothers, combined with an understandable lack of interest in all sexual contact with the fathers. Sometimes my clients report the opposite, an aggressive, frustrated mother and a withdrawn, asexual father. Either way, the young child will draw important conclusions from what she witnesses, and among them is likely to be a fear that women cannot and should not enjoy their sexuality.

Children and Sex

I have worried a great deal over giving my opinion on the matter of sexual freedom for children, because I am afraid of losing many otherwise sympathetic readers. But this is not a book aimed at winning converts; it is aimed at communicating the truth, as I see it. The truth is that sex between consenting equals is as harmless among children as among adults.

In my practice, I have frequently come across a variety of sexual encounters between small children, typically aged four or five, which are recalled as purely enjoyable experiences between friendly and sometimes loving partners. In a few instances, I have known people who "played house" at age five, complete with sexual relations. It caused them no harm and appeared to have been genuinely happy and fulfilling as an act of intimacy. In recent years, especially, I have known adults who had rather extensive sexual experiences from the start of early adolescence, including longterm sexual relationships.

I do not wish to suggest that children, or even adolescents, are capable of having the fullest and richest sexual experiences, which I have characterized as romantic love. But, then, neither are most adults. Most adults are blocked in part by their preoccupation with making up for years of sexual frustration; sexual experiences earlier in life can go a long way toward liberating individuals in adulthood to give up the body hunt in favor of looking for romantic love.

I have, of course, come across instances in which children have been harmed in the context of sexual relationships. This has taken place when an involuntary relationship has been imposed upon a child by a stronger, older, or nastier individual. Some of my clients have harmed themselves as well as others by taking advantage of younger or more helpless children in their own childhoods, and some have been harmed as the victims of such abuse. Sex between an adult and a child is almost always harmful to the child. It cannot take place on the child's terms. Almost invariably, the young child is being taken advantage of. Besides, any adult who seeks out sex with a child is obviously in search of something other than a relationship between consenting equals.

While my ideas may seem very radical, in actuality they reflect a rather commonplace reality. Children frequently do have sexual experiences among themselves. Often these experiences are unique successes as forms of exploratory communication — exploratory about feelings as well as bodies. Sometimes they turn into disasters, when adults discover these activities and punish the children with extreme cruelty. But this cannot be an argument against childhood sex. It is one more argument against the oppression of children.

Children must be protected, not from sex but from sexual aggressors. If two little children are fond of each other, and if they have learned to treat each other with respect, do not worry about what they are doing behind closed doors. They may be having more fun than you do when you get behind closed doors.

There is a myth created by Freud that children typically or naturally lust after their parents. I have done a great deal of in-depth psychotherapy and cannot confirm Freud's finding. More often, parents lust after their children; almost all incestuous relationships are initiated by and maintained by the parent. When children do lust after their parents, it is out of frustration. Because they are cut off from seeking intimacy with their peers, they become unduly dependent upon physical intimacy with their parents. This may express itself in fantasies of having sex with the parent, but the fantasy is rooted in helplessness and frustration, and the individual would far prefer sex with a peer.

Fantasies of sex with a parent are often rooted in seductive hints from the parent. The child's sexual fantasy is then a last ditch effort to please the parent and to gain some attention.

As I dramatized in *After the Good War,* permitting children to have sex among themselves would go a long way toward liberating them from oppressive parental authority. This is the main reason that parents fight so hard to prevent sex between children. Sexual freedom would allow their children to become truly independent of them.

Masturbation

Even the more "liberal" popular books on psychology and children still hint at dire results from masturbating, and so it seems necessary to hold that old bugaboo up to the bright light of reason. Having let go of the old myth about masturbation causing "insanity" as well as "moral degeneration," we now hear that masturbation is "antisocial" and reflects an unhealthy turning inward by the child. This viewpoint suggests that playing with one's own body is so inherently more interesting than playing with other people and their bodies that it must be prohibited lest it take over the individual. It also implies that parents and even peers have so little to offer children that the average child, given a chance, would prefer to sit around touching his or her genitals.

At the heart of these fears about masturbation is the threat it presents to the authority of the adults. One best-selling authority on sex states: "Self-gratification may make the child less accessible to the influence of parents and peers."

Of course, a continued preoccupation with masturbation to the exclusion of other activities is a sign of unhappiness in a child, just as a continued preoccupation with any activity may suggest unhappiness. What should a parent do about a child's masturbating? Nothing. Indeed, if you know that your child is masturbating, you are probably spying on him or her. Stop meddling. Since most parents have so much anxiety about sexual activity in their children, the best advice on the whole subject is probably "Mind your own business." Those few parents who have a lusty, joyful attitude toward sex should communicate that to their children.

For most people, masturbation remains a taboo even into adulthood and even as a part of mutual sexual satisfaction. Although most people masturbate, few seem to take much joy in it. This in no way encourages them to take *more* joy in sexual relations. Overall, masturbation fits into lifestyles of failure in much the same way as the more socially acceptable forms of sex do. Few people get as much out of it as they can.

Homosexuality

One of the most striking examples of a child fighting back against sexual oppression was shared with me by a young woman who, at the age of eleven, had come upon her drunk father and an equally drunk male companion tormenting her mother. While her mother made helpless attempts to free herself from a corner, her father was egging on his friend to fondle her body. The young girl, witnessing this aggression against her mother, first thought to pick up an iron from the kitchen table to bash in her father's head, but then experienced an instantaneous feeling, "He's not worth it." Instead, she cocked her fist back and threw her small but lithe body into a furious punch that knocked her father to the floor. He and his companion then slouched from the room in humiliation. The child wanted to call the police as well, but her mother prevented her.

The incident was never again spoken of in the house; but from that moment on, this young woman regarded her father as unworthy of her attention. In the years that followed, she began a homosexual relationship. That relationship has been going on for many years since the end of therapy and is one of the most loving and mutually satisfying relationships with which I am familiar.

This brings me to a question that I am so often asked, "Is homosexuality a perversion? Is it wrong?"

As Thomas Szasz has pointed out so well, any attempt to evaluate human conduct as bad or wrong must ultimately rest upon the values and the intentions of the individual doing the evaluating. Many homosexuals consider that they are satisfied with their love relationships and are justified in pointing out that their successes were achieved despite hostility from society.

"But can't homosexual lifestyles be traced to childhood trauma, as in your young patient with the brutal father?" Yes, we can sometimes (but not always) find influences in a person's childhood that will help us understand why he or she chose one or another sexual attitude. But that doesn't prove a great deal. Perhaps heterosexuality is merely a common response to pervasive propaganda.

I am heterosexual in my own conduct, and my preferences are in that direction. But most homosexuals who have come to me for therapy have expressed as strong a preference for their own sexual orientation, and few have desired to change. They have wanted to improve their sexual relationships in much the same way as heterosexuals, while maintaining their original orientation.

But what about the biological function of sex?

Sex long ago ceased to have a primarily progenerative function in our society. How many times in your life have you had sex with the actual intention of having a baby? More often, you probably had sex *despite* your fear of having a child. The overwhelming majority of sexual acts are done for personal reasons other than the creation of a child. In my own opinion, the best reason for having sex is the sharing of friendship, companionship, and love. By these standards, the criteria for success or failure in homosexuality differ not at all from those in heterosexuality.

Sexual Appearance

There is probably as much misplaced anguish over sexual appearance as there is over sexual function and sexual orientation. Most of us at one time or another have been concerned or obsessed with real or imagined defects in our sexual organs, skin, height, weight, hair, or other aspects of our sexual image.

People so obsessed with sexual defects feel hurt, cheated, or otherwise unfairly treated by fate, and their bodies become symbols of this misfortune. The hope for large sexual organs or a more beautiful body — or the desire to possess someone else with these qualities — then becomes a means of getting restitution. All this denies their own personal participation in their unhappy lives.

Because women are more often subjected to operations on their sexual organs, they more frequently face the consequences of sexual disfigurement. Although this may surprise many readers, the response to surgical mutilation, such as mastectomy, varies enormously from person to person. I have known women who were very much ashamed of their figures after mastectomy, and who used their disfigurement as an excuse for not pursuing love relationships. But I have also known women who have taken the loss of one or even both breasts more in stride, especially if their lovers have shown little or no negative reaction. Much depends on whether or not the woman or her lover treats the mutilation as a personal failure. This will reflect attitudes they have had long before the surgery.

Sex as Loving Communication

The most common sexual failure is expressed as a vague disappointment or sadness about sex, which the individual has come to accept as inevitable and even normal. When I describe how satisfying sex can be, this individual admits that he or she thinks of such gratification as mythical or unattainable.

There are many ways to conceptualize the acceptance of this vague yet chronic dissatisfaction, but sexual alienation is as good a phrase as any. The sexually alienated person is alienated from himself or herself and from other people. He or she is unwilling to love.

People usually benefit from sex only when they feel like sharing closeness, friendship, or love. When I find someone protesting against this as idealistic, moralistic, or old-fashioned, I usually find someone who is desperately trying to avoid meaningful contact with other human beings. Even married people who believe they love each other may be dismayed over my equation between sex and intimacy. They often find themselves more loving before they begin the sexual act or when sex is not involved at all.

Whether or not a person thinks that sex is communication, he or she will nonetheless communicate feelings with every expression, touch, and movement made during sexual contact. Frequently a woman will complain that her husband shows no feeling during love-making. A careful review of her experience with him during sexual intercourse will show that he communicates a great many feelings during sex, but she wishes these particular feelings were not present. She may sense that he is distracted and thinking about someone or something else; or she may find that he is too rough and aggressive, as if trying to dominate her, or that he's just interested in relieving his sexual tensions and doesn't really care what she gets out of it.

Further review of this woman's own feelings will show that she too is making many negative communications during sex. She may act as if "I'm doing you a favor," or "I resent your wanting to have sex with me," or "Get it over with quickly," or "I'm tired," or "I hate it when you touch me like that," or more frequently, "I've given up hoping for gratification."

Trying to make sex more communicative under such conditions is self-defeating, for the communications will be destructive. Instead, the entire relationship must be questioned and evaluated by each partner. Does the person want to be married or involved in a love relationship, or is he or she merely too afraid or too guilt-ridden to separate? Having reached a decision to work on the relationship, the person can then begin to investigate the quality of feeling toward the partner. By the time strides have been made in improving the overall relationship, sex will often begin to improve without any special attention from the therapist, beyond a reminder that sex is personal sharing and communication. If this does not turn out to be the case, then a more intensive investigation of sexual attitudes and experiences is necessary.

When confronted with the relationship between love and sex, many people immediately respond, "Then why did I enjoy sex with partners I didn't like, or with partners I'd never see again?"

There are occasional times when a gratifying sexual adventure occurs as a result of long abstinence, or drug intoxication, or the excitement of an illicit meeting, or the lack of personal conflict in a one-night stand. But despite the prevalence of fantasies about this kind of sex producing great fireworks, sexual satisfaction in such encounters is very rare, unless it turns out that a strong personal attraction is also present.

When people tell me that they are sure that their own best sexual experiences have not been associated with love, I ask them to describe these experiences in detail. One middle-aged woman replied, "John was good at sex. You know, he had a lot of good techniques. I'm sure he didn't love me, but it was the best sex I've ever had."

"Did you love John?"

"John wasn't right for me. He was not the marrying kind. He didn't love me."

"But did you love him?"

"There was something very special about him. I was glad he wanted to make love to me, even if he didn't seem to love me. Yes, I cared about him. I felt very romantic toward him. But I knew it couldn't work."

As it turned out, she felt more love toward John than toward any other man she'd gone to bed with.

Occasionally people do seem to find that love-making is only satisfactory when they do not love the individuals with whom they are having sex. This can result from making a split between sex and love to avoid meaningful and threatening personal relationships. But this is not as common as people would like to believe. It often turns out that the partner who enjoys the sex *does* care for the person whom he or she is allegedly indifferent toward. It may also turn out that the purely sexual partner is very attentive and sensitive to the person, showing a great deal of caring and even love in the way he or she conducts love-making.

There is a more dismal reason why some people feel that they enjoy sex with partners toward whom they are indifferent. Let's say a woman claims to love her husband, while she enjoys having sex with a man toward whom she feels very little. When she looks more honestly at herself, it turns out that she prefers the relatively bland relationship. The person who enjoys sex with a relatively indifferent partner may find indifference preferable to the hate she feels toward her regular partner.

If you think that you enjoy sex with people for whom you feel relatively little, take a good look at your relationship with every one of your sexual partners, past and present. Ask yourself what you have really felt about each person — not what the person felt toward you, not what you were supposed to have felt, and not what you kidded yourself into feeling. You may find that the fling you have dismissed over the years was really the most romantic few hours of your life, spent with a person who interested and attracted you. Reconsider your current attitudes, including the unhappy compromise that puts you into bed with a person or persons toward whom you do not feel romantic love.

Sex has little or no meaning in itself, and attempts to think of sex as separate from love lead to anguish, shame, failure, and frustration. Sex without love requires a great deal of phony propaganda to keep it afloat. The best way to overcome sexual problems is to prepare oneself for romantic love and, especially, to understand sex as loving communication.

Manipulative versus Honest Communication

If I may tease some of my friends and clients, the fact that many of them are lawyers has made me realize that there are two wholly different kinds of communications: lawyerly ones calculated to convince, and honest ones calculated to communicate the truth. The first type has as its goal a specific effect upon the listener. Its sole or overriding aim is to influence, change, or modify the person at whom it is directed. It might be labeled "manipulative communication," and it often involves force or fraud. The second type has as its main goal the most accurate representation of the truth from the viewpoint of the communicator. It may be labeled "honest communication." (Wonder of wonders, I have turned everyday language into a technical one!)

There are two different kinds of honest communication. In the most common type, which I call *informative communication,* we already think we know the truth and we wish to tell someone else about it. Thus, I wish to get across my ideas about the psychology of self-determination. But there is another kind of honest communication with the purpose of self-discovery or discovery of the truth. This is *exploratory communication* in which the individual develops a cooperative effort with another person, for the purpose of exploring or developing ideas and feelings.

In talking with ourselves in the privacy of our own minds, we can also employ each of the communication styles. We can be manipulative or honest with ourselves, and, if honest, we can be informative or exploratory. Creative thinking is largely exploratory thinking and takes the most courage.

Most of us have a great deal of difficulty giving up manipulative communication in favor of honest communication, and some of us never do. Even having determined on honest communication, we have difficulty putting aside the impulse to speak about what we already know, in favor of talking about what we do not know. Conversation aimed at self-discovery or at the discovery of new ideas and new aspects of our friends is often very frightening. Especially, it can undermine our defensive styles of thinking and acting.

In our society — indeed, in all societies — we are taught manipulative communication. It is the only way to survive childhood and the educational system. As we grow stronger and learn more, we may then attempt to make honest, informative communications about what we already know. But to communicate about that which we do not know is a great and new step. Therapy, friendships, and love relationships should aim at creating sufficient trust and safety for the partners to communicate with each other as a means of exploring and discovering each other.

Typically, romantic relationships begin with manipulative communication aimed at impressing, seducing, warding off, or otherwise controlling the other person. If progress is made, manipulation is then replaced by informative communication, in which each person attempts to give an honest picture of himself or herself and to learn about the other person. If the relationship succeeds, informative communication is joined by exploratory communication in which each person discovers unexplored, exciting realities about himself or herself, as well as about the other person.

This growth through manipulative, informative, and exploratory communication takes place in bed as well as across the table. Sex as loving communication and sex as honest communication can be informative or exploratory. Most loving sexual communication is of the first kind; the individual tries to communicate his or her love to a partner. This is the safer kind of communication. But love-making and love relationships become far more interesting and exciting when self-discovery and discovery of the other person become more important. For men and women alike, a more robust and exciting sexual experience becomes possible as each person reaches within himself or herself to discover and express new heights of feeling.

Keeping Lost Love Alive

A young woman in her early twenties came to see me for the first time. She had been in traditional psychoanalysis for a year some time ago without success. Now she came into my office looking shy, inhibited, and very uncertain about what to say. She told me that she had dropped out of school and was working part-time. Nothing much appealed to her or motivated her.

I asked her how far back she could recall such feelings, and she said rather quickly, "To about eighth or ninth grade. It got worse again in my junior year of high school."

This took us no more than four minutes into our first interview when I asked her, "What happened in eighth or ninth grade and in your junior year?"

She immediately broke into tears about a man she had loved. With deep embarrassment over her own tenderness and romanticism, and with considerable surprise, she went on for an hour to talk about him and her wish to love. By the time her first session was over, she already looked more radiant and happier. She had gotten in touch with her capacity to love.

In most lives, there has been at least one loved person — a parent, a nursemaid, a childhood friend, a brother or sister, often a grandparent, uncle, or aunt. Typically, when a person comes into therapy, he is feeling alienated and has forgotten that he ever loved anyone. He may even deny that he has ever possessed the capacity to love. When at last the love is rediscovered, even if it is only a moment from the far past — the entire experience of loving can be regained in full force. The person again loves.

216 Love and Sexuality

The rediscovery of love can be one of the most crucial experiences in self-liberation, and it often startles my clients: "I can't believe it. I had forgotten her entirely and now I'm having those feelings all over again." Once a person loves, that love is forever real. It can be tapped, reexperienced, and used as a stepping stone to still more love in the future. By keeping love in awareness, an individual maintains a sense of what is truly valuable in life. Love becomes an ideal with which to measure his or her attitudes toward life and toward his or her fellow humans. It gives continuity and even a sense of the eternal to life.

Love is like gold in a world where paper money has no fixed or enduring value; it provides a standard of beauty and permanence against which to measure the quality of one's life.

One client, a professional man in his thirties, often wondered why he felt as sane as he did — and, in particular, why he felt at all able to love — since he could not recall sharing any good feelings with his parents or his brothers or sister. He also wondered why he was panic-stricken when he dared express his feelings of love toward his lover.

Although he was white and had little contact with black people, he had especially warm feelings toward black people whom he met, and that gave us a clue to look in his early history toward a dim memory of a teenage maid. After enormous efforts to focus on his early childhood, it unfolded that he had slept in the same room with her, often in the same bed with her, and had been her constant companion from his first weeks of life until he had reached school age. Then she had left his household to marry, and he had fallen into a profound depression. As far as he was concerned, this woman had been his real mother, as well as an ally in an otherwise loveless and hostile family.

How could he have forgotten all about her for thirty years? His biological mother had been so resentful over his love for the "nigger girl" that all evidence of her existence had been eradicated from family history, including photo albums and discussions. The child had been made to believe he must forget her or suffer increasing hostility from his biological mother. Gradually, he gave up the memories of singing and playing with his spiritual mother, of sleeping on her breast, of chatting with her late into the night. He had forgotten how she sometimes stood between him and his parents when they would attempt to spank him.

When all of this came back to him, he was overcome with both painful and beautiful feelings. He had to go through the agony of recalling her departure from the home and his subsequent hunger strikes and vicious conflicts with his parents. He had to recall his pain as he cried with his spiritual mother the night she left the family; and he had to recall her tears as she begged him not to cry so hard. It was one of the deepest experiences of grieving I have ever witnessed. But it was also a glorious experience; he was getting in touch with a part of himself that he had lost, and he was learning why he was so afraid to let out all the love that lived within him.

Of interest to those unfamiliar with the exactness with which early childhood memories can sometimes be recalled after long periods of blankness, this man was able to locate and visit his spiritual mother. She was astonished to discover that he could remember back to the details of their relationship, and she was embarrassed. She felt she had perhaps been wrong in treating him like her own child and was relieved to know that he considered her four years with him to be the saving grace of his childhood.

One of my clients listened to a tape of a speech in which I spoke about the individual discovering long-forgotten childhood love. To his surprise, he remembered that he had fallen in love at first sight in the fourth grade with a little girl who lived down the block from him. Over several months they had spent much of their free time together, sometimes sitting and reading silently, sometimes playing tomboy games, often walking back and forth to school together.

While my client came from a lower-class home, this girl came from a still lower one — and he became acutely aware of her inferior social status when his classmates would make fun of her dirty neck or country ways. His own family ridiculed the idea that he would have a girlfriend, and he picked up a vague but significant sense of disapproval from his mother, who lived a joyless and loveless life of her own. Toward the end of the relationship, his girlfriend endured an embarrassing incident in class, and he abandoned her rather than identify himself with her. He has a poignant memory of her little brother walking near him on the way home from school, urging him to no avail to at least talk with her.

By giving her up, he bought more security among his classmates and his family, but he never again would let himself love a girl so sweetly, genuinely, or fully. He could distinctly remember the decision that this kind of love was wrong and that he'd never do it again. He suppressed himself so thoroughly that he did not date with any seriousness until after high school graduation.

My client's recognition of this spontaneous, romantic love and his abandonment of it permitted him a much better look at the contrasting bleakness, heaviness, and guiltiness that characterized his relationship with his mother, as well as with subsequent women. In that therapy session, he got a glimpse of the joy associated with loving.

My client frequently works with children. The memory of his little girlfriend helped him liberate still more of his feeling for these children, and even more for adults, whom he had placed in a joyless category.

It is not uncommon for clients to rediscover moments of great importance, frequently times when they were able to love their parents or siblings despite the anguish in the family. One of my clients was distressed over her difficulty loving men, and it was an important step when she could recall the period of time, at age seven, before her father left for a long tour of duty in the army. She had worshipped him up to that moment — and then had repressed her feelings during his long absence.

Often the experience recalled may have to do with a little brother or sister who was loved. My client may come to realize that she had been able to love her little brother or sister before the hate and competition engendered by the parents turned the early love into rivalry. The recall of this love can rekindle the sense of self as a loving person.

Sometimes the experiences recalled do not have to do with people but with pets, places, or activities. A person who finds school boring wonders if he ever had any interest in learning. Then he remembers the many games and artistic activities he loved as a small child, before a divorce wrecked his childhood by leaving him in the care of a malicious mother. He now retaps his love for art. Another person remembers a series of vacations in which he discovered the outdoors and now begins to orient his life more around these activities.

Sometimes the memory blocking is for recent events, as the person rediscovers his love for a person he has lost. Most dramatically, this can be seen when a depressed person has dealt with the loss of a loved one by denying the person's importance. As soon as the pain of loss is faced with a decision never again to deny the love, the depression begins to lift, and the craziness falls away. The pain lingers, but not the helpless irresponsibility and despair. The person mourns and gradually recovers.

One such story ended very happily. A man came to me feeling very depressed and despairing about his forthcoming marriage. While his marriage approached, he would periodically drink and party too much, desperately trying to have a good time before "tying the knot." At times he was manic to the point of craziness.

It turned out that he had been very much in love, and was still in love, with a woman whom he had driven out of his life several months earlier. His new engagement was a rebound of the most cowardly kind, and he called it off. After hard work in therapy uncovering the reasons for his ill treatment of the woman he really loved, he was able to get in touch with her; and eventually they were married.

Even when the loss is permanent, as through death, it is important to keep the feelings of love alive. If the love is denied, the individual ends up denying his or her own aspirations for love; if the love is kept alive, the individual confirms himself or herself as a loving person and keeps alive the potential to love others.

The Paradox of Liberty and Love

Just when we begin to feel that we have discovered personal freedom and personal sovereignty, we begin to love. Love then attaches us to people, to places, to objects, to animals, to work, and to ideals. Freedom becomes the right and the capacity to express what we discover within ourselves — our love for others and for life.

Often a person begins to fall in love and then asks what has happened to his or her freedom. My answer is this: you are free to deny or to accept your love, but if you deny it, you crush yourself. You may decide that a love relationship cannot work out to your own self-interest, and so you may choose not to pursue it to fulfillment; but do not kid yourself into thinking you can obliterate the love you feel within yourself. Each love you feel becomes a part of your reality — your capacity to appreciate and value life.

Love is the light that shines on reality; it is the infusion of life into a lifeless world. Love makes existence worthwhile. The ultimate of personal sovereignty is the awareness of one's capacity to love, and the ultimate in personal freedom is the opportunity to express and to share this love. To be a free person is not to be lonely and isolated but to be deeply involved in life.

Love can only be experienced by a person who is in touch with personal sovereignty. Only the person who is internally free can know his or her true capacity for love. Every trace of guilt, shame, anxiety — and every other manifestation of self-oppression — will inhibit the experiencing of love.

To know love within oneself, one must be personally sovereign. To express love in the world, one must have a degree of personal freedom. The capacity to know love and to express love will be proportional to the amount of personal sovereignty and personal freedom that one experiences. In this manner, liberty becomes the liberty to love.

Love is an unconditional, unmodified, uncoerced, untrained, inherently human affirmation of life. This affirmation of life is experienced as a vital, energizing, liberating, happy sense of self and others! We get free to discover that we are attached all over again. But now the quality of the attachment is different. It is self-determined or freely chosen in our own self-interest. It brings joy! No harm can come from loving others, but only from submitting to them. Liberate yourself to be free to love and to pursue your ideals.

Chapter Seventeen

The Individual in the World

Throughout this book I have focused upon intimate aspects of our relationship to ourselves and to our loved ones. But self-determination will profoundly affect every aspect of our lives. It may lead us to change careers or to reevaluate our politics. It may even affect how we view reality.

Self-determination brings us into conflict with any irrational authority that attempts to impose itself on us. No authority is more important in this regard than our parents. How we deal with them will vastly influence how we deal with all other forms of authority and with life itself.

Confronting One's Parents

For most people, confronting their parents about past and present mistreatment at their hands is the most difficult task in life. Nothing threatens grown people more than telling their parents how abusive, loveless, inconsiderate, insensitive, or irresponsible they have been. As I have pointed out in many ways throughout this book, most people will abuse themselves or other guiltless persons rather than confront the true source of frustration in their relationship with their parents. All lifestyles of failure reflect an unwillingness even to recognize and understand parental oppression, let alone to confront it directly in the person of the parents.

Most authoritarian therapies advocate reconciliation with parents. A person who reconciles with oppressive parents before they have reformed themselves will also be willing to remain under the suppressive influence of the authoritarian therapy. Conversely, a person who faces his or her parents in a forthright manner is not likely to knuckle under to other forms of authoritarianism.

If you are like the vast majority of persons, you have limped through life without ever dealing honestly, forthrightly, or courageously with your parents. You may be too quick to confront others with imagined insults or transgressions against you, but you will be as slow as possible in saying anything to your parents, regardless of their mistreatment of you or your loved ones. Similarly, you are likely to blame your husband or your wife, or even your children, for causing all your personal problems, but you will go to any length to excuse your parents, though they are far more responsible for any long-lasting problems you may have.

Two observations have been reconfirmed time and again in my personal and therapeutic experience: first, I have rarely if ever seen a person develop a happy love relationship while remaining under the negative influence of living or deceased parents; second, confronting one's parents is often the single most self-liberating experience in life. In clients who have seen other therapists before me, a common cause of failure has been the previous therapist's refusal to hold parents responsible for their treatment of children and, especially, the previous therapist's refusal to encourage or support the client's desire to confront his or her parents with their abusive, unloving ways.

A book could be written about the various rationalizations made in our society for not holding one's parents personally responsible: "They didn't know any better," "They were from a different generation," "It's too late now," "All it would do is upset them," "They'd never understand," "All my friends have worse parents," "They meant well," "They tried their best," "They wouldn't take me seriously." Sometimes the rationalizations disclose obvious fears: "Everyone in the family already thinks I'm irrational, strange, or crazy," "My mother would start crying and screaming," "My mother would look so hurt," "My father would throw me out of the house," "They wouldn't lend me any more money or take care of the kids on weekends," "They'd tell all the relatives."

Often fears are expressed that the confrontation might kill the parents; and in a surprising number of cases, grown adults fear that their aged and even feeble parents might try to kill them. Always there is a sense of futility and guilt. Often these feelings are wrapped up with various homilies about respecting or not hurting parents no matter how much harm these parents may continue to inflict on everyone in the family. It is not unusual to see an old man or woman make miserable the lives of a dozen children and grandchildren, while everyone treats the old tyrant as if his or her feelings are inviolable and sacrosanct.

True love for parents is never at the root of the fear of confronting them. Among those people I know who rationalize their failures to stand up to their parents, I have rarely heard of any of the following: "Thanksgiving and

Christmas with them will be such a joy, I hate to spoil it by bringing up the past," "They're such wonderful old people, good as gold, there seems little purpose in stirring up the past," "There's no point to it because they will honestly admit their faults, take responsibility for their failures, and ask forgiveness," "They'll show genuine concern that their attitudes have hurt me, and they might offer to seek counseling in an effort to help themselves relate better to me," "They'd be the first to admit that they were bad parents and that they now wish to show me renewed respect and love," or "It will end beautifully with all of us feeling more close." Parents who have unhappy children are rarely parents who are willing to change, to grow, or to take responsibility for their relationship to the now grown children. If they were this responsible, their children would most likely not be unhappy enough to desire a confrontation or to seek the help of a therapist.

Why is it so hard to confront parents? Precisely because *fear of parents is the most dreadful fear in human experience.* Upon it is built most other debilitating fears, including the fear of God and political authorities, as well as more ill-defined fears of life and death. A knowledge and understanding of this fact of life is crucial to self-liberation.

In therapy, it may take weeks or months or longer for the individual to come to grips with the true intensity of the fear of his or her parents. First the individual needs to acknowledge his or her self-defeating lifestyles. Once these are recognized and partially dealt with, the underlying fear may become more apparent. Or the individual may discover the depth of the fear when asked by the therapist why he or she puts up with so much abuse from the parents.

Given that confronting parents is such a hard task, why do it? That it is such a hard task suggests why it should be done. By finally standing up to your parents as an equal demanding respect, you cut to the core of your worst and oldest fears. In the act of making this confrontation, you will learn more about your own fears as they surface before and during the encounter. You will see more clearly the great resistance that your parents have always shown to taking any responsibility for their past or current ill treatment of you. You will witness their willingness to sacrifice your dignity, well-being, and happiness to their emotional needs. The parental source of your self-oppression will become blatantly obvious. Ultimately, you will learn that you can become self-determining and proud of yourself in the face of your worst oppressors. It will go a long way toward helping you feel independent and mature.

By no means do I wish to suggest that there is anything magical or easy about changing your life through confronting your parents as an equal. The work leading up to the confrontation is more important. The understanding of its purpose is crucial. Everything you can do in preparation to understand your relationship to them will stand you in good stead.

If your own personal inner work were not most important, then you would have no hope of self-liberation if your parents are deceased or otherwise unavailable. When parents are dead, the work can be conducted within the realm of imagination. It may be helpful to dramatize an encounter using friends or a therapist as a stand-in for your parents. You may find it useful to recall crucial moments, such as holidays that were unhappy, or times when your parents abused you or your children or spouse. You may wish to look at old photographs, visit your childhood homes, talk to relatives (especially brothers and sisters), or take any other action that will make your childhood more vivid, and your imagined encounter more real. When these experiences are vivid again, you can reenter them in your imagination as a self-respecting, self-determining person and reenact them in a new and more satisfying manner.

People vary enormously in the kind or degree of confrontation they desire with a parent. While I make clear in therapy the importance of dealing with one's parents, I never push anyone into a real-life encounter. Any attempt to "motivate" a person in this direction merely replaces the authority of the parents with the authority of the therapist. The client ends up confronting the parents not with his or her own authority but with the therapist's authority. This is in no way a liberation for the individual. In general, if you are trying to help people professionally or as a friend, you will do them no service if you try to push them into anything, even into receiving help. Therapists who pressure their clients to change their lives are compromising the personal sovereignty of their clients.

In making the most of finally confronting your parents, it is very important to conduct yourself according to the principles of self-determination:

First and foremost, the purpose of the confrontation is to establish yourself as an equal capable of holding your parents responsible for their past mistreatment or current lack of respect or outright abuse. The object is to become free of guilt, shame, and anxiety or self-hate in the presence of your parents. The purpose is not to "get love" as much as it is to "demand respect." Whether or not your parents wish to give you love is their own business now that you are a grown person. If they are not willing to love you, you will value yourself more if you look upon it as their loss. Now that you are grown you can give and get love in other contexts. The main purpose of the encounter is to overcome your *fear* and your *helplessness* in dealing with your parents. If they in turn wish to become more loving after being confronted with their oppressiveness, then it might be worthwhile to reopen that possibility.

Second, your emphasis should be on changing your own conduct rather than your parents' conduct. If you handle yourself in an ethical, self-determining, and self-respecting manner in their presence, you will feel better regardless of what they do or say. A confrontation is not an excuse for "losing control" but an opportunity for gaining control. If you plan to fly off the handle or to become hysterical, you will not benefit from the experience.

The unconditional right to self-defense also suggests principles for dealing directly with your parents:

First, you will gain no longterm gratification from abusing your parents in retaliation for their abuse of you. Your gratification can best be achieved by protecting yourself against their aggression while using the minimal necessary force. In the extreme, you will do better to declare your disrespect for their conduct and to leave their presence than to become involved in an emotional or physical brawl.

Second, if your parents refuse to take responsibility for any of the abuse they have given you, the encounter will be very painful for them. Their pain is not your responsibility. You have the right to be self-determining in their presence, and you have the right to demand an explanation and even an apology in regard to their lifetime oppression of you. If your parents are ethical and if they have reformed over the years, they will welcome the opportunity to set things straight.

Third, if you keep in mind that the object is to change yourself, not them, you will not succumb to bitterness and hate. You can make the most of the encounter even if they refuse to listen, to care, to act rationally, or to admit to a single fault. If you conduct yourself as you determine, you may have your first experience of adult separateness from your parents.

Fourth, do not permit any parental attacks on you, however slight, to go unnoticed. Any hints about your childishness, craziness, badness, etc., must be encountered. Any attempts at ridicule or humiliation must be pointed out and rejected. All attempts to ignore you or to make you feel guilty must be brought out in the open. All threats against you must be met. You will probably have to express anger. Ultimately, you may find it necessary to make clear that you will have nothing more to do with them unless they treat you with dignity and respect. These are legitimate standards and actions if you want to be treated with respect.

It is important for you to take full responsibility for all encounters with your parents. Out of guilt and fear, most people want to wait for a new provocation before confronting their parents. If you have been abused all your life by your parents, you don't have to wait for one more abusive act before you react. Instead, you will be much more in control of the situation and much more self-determining if you establish a formal time, in advance, when you plan to discuss your relationship, past and present, with your parents.

In taking responsibilty for the encounter, make sure you really want to do it and that you feel ready to do it. Don't justify the confrontation on the grounds that this book, your therapist, or any other third party thinks that it is a good idea. If *you* don't think it's a good idea, don't do it. Fighting one authority with another will not build your self-esteem.

Reading this section of the book may especially bring out your guilt, shame, and anxiety about your parents and give you excuses for feeling paranoid, anxious, or depressed. If you are having these painful feelings, do not kid yourself into believing that they result from "love" for your parents. You may love them, perhaps, but these painful feelings are the product of *fear* and *helplessness* learned at their hands in childhood and reinforced at their hands in adulthood. If you fear that an encounter may lead to some dreadful but undefined doom for you or for them, work harder to understand their effects on you. When you finally encounter them successfully, you may find that you are freed of this vague dread for the first time in your life. You will find that neither God nor your parents will strike you down for standing up for your own human rights.

Parental confrontations are frightening, guilt-provoking occasions. Don't rush into them, and don't act as if you have to make up for a lifetime in one day. Bring up what you feel capable of bringing up, and no more.

It is very dangerous to confront your parents unless you are or wish to be physically independent of them. Any adolescent who tries to implement a confrontation with his or her parents is likely to be met with an overwhelmingly hostile reaction. Since the adolescent is not in much of a position to leave home and will have no moral support from anyone in his or her attempted confrontation, it is likely to be a disaster. The young person reading this book is probably best advised to store up his or her ideas and perceptions, awaiting a later day of relative safety before directly pursuing a confrontation.

Obviously, it is dangerous to resist parental aggression if your parents are in a position to beat you up. Parents who wish to control their children will sometimes go to any extreme in order to implement their desire, including the infliction of physical injury. Until you are out of the home and willing and able to support yourself, confront them with grave discretion, if at all. On the other hand, many young people have been regularly beaten by their parents until at last they have stood their ground and fought back.

As an adult, most of your bouts with severe losses in self-love, self-esteem, and self-determination will follow contacts with your parents or reminders about them. A letter, a phone call, or merely a recollection about your parents may be exactly what threw you into that state of anxiety, depression, or paranoia for which you thought you had no explanation. The next time you feel unexpectedly and inexplicably upset, look to the recent past for contacts with your parents or reminders of past oppression at their hands. If the contact seemed "good" or "uneventful," ask yourself if it left you feeling happy and loved and respected. Especially look for a hidden or subtle reminder that you are supposed to put the interest of your parents ahead of your own welfare or well-being.

Nothing is more important in life than being able to stand up for yourself with your parents. Nothing is more disastrous in adulthood than allowing your parents to reinforce the oppression you experienced as a child.

If you are a parent, and if you have oppressed your children and failed to give them respect and love, it will not do you or them any good if you sit around feeling guilty and self-oppressive. Determine to change your ways, regardless of how bad you have been and regardless of how old or distant your children have grown. Decide to treat your children with the respect and love that should be accorded to the lives that you brought forth on earth. The odds are overwhelming that your children will welcome the change; and it is absolutely certain that you will feel better about yourself. If you become consistently respectful and loving toward your offspring, they will probably forgive all your past transgressions and show a surprising willingness to establish a happy relationship. But even if your children do not respond to the changes in you, you will certainly find it easier to forgive and to respect yourself.

Confronting Oneself as a Child

At many points in this book, I have reiterated the importance of recognizing free will in children as well as in others whose minds have been handicapped by physical damage or mental stresses. Here I want to reaffirm the importance of the grown adult's understanding that he or she had free will as a child.

In any successful psychotherapy or in personal liberation, the adult must face the choices he or she made as a child that now persist in the form of self-destructive, outmoded actions. The failure to appreciate free will in children is one reason why some psychotherapies are endless and why people so often gain so little from so much "insight" into childhood. They continue to think and to act as if their childhood responses to life were mechanically or behavioristically determined and that their own self-oppressive choices or decision making had nothing to do with the guilt, shame, and anxiety from which they suffer. They may even use their alleged insight into childhood misfortunes to justify continued helplessness. All their insight comes to nothing, for it lacks the one insight that matters: that individuals can only grow by learning about the responsibility that they have for their lives. It is disastrous to excuse any conduct on the grounds that it was determined before the age of free will. If you didn't have free will as a child, when did it start? When you were fifteen, eighteen, or twenty-one? Why then? Why ever? If you deny free will in yourself as a child, you end up with a good excuse for denying it in yourself as an adult. You can maintain that you never grew up.

The idea that you had free will as a child can be very liberating. It means you were always a person, as far back as you can recall. You can actually track yourself back in time and find out what you were thinking and doing. You can have a sense of yourself as a moral agent throughout your entire lifetime, and you can come closer to understanding the decisions that created step-by-step the person that you now identify as you. If you were relatively more free of oppression during some of your earliest years, the experience of yourself as a self-determining, self-aware person may become stronger the farther back you go into your past personal history. This can be a great revelation. You may rediscover the person you tried to abandon as you grew up under oppression.

Consider the possibility that you possessed free will from the start. If so, you are real — you have an inherent nature characterized by decision making. This will not only change your historical perspective on yourself; if you are trying to be a good parent or teacher, it will increase your appreciation of the personhood of children. You will be more willing to respect their rights.

Most people opt for a relatively high degree of irresponsibility or unconsciousness throughout their lives, from childhood on through adulthood. They do not want to confront the atrocities committed against them; but even more so, they do not want to confront their cowardly submission to their oppressors. This is the main reason for childhood amnesia. The most difficult experience to recall is our own participation in making ourselves helpless. But in every area in which you deny that you made choices, you will remain imprisoned by the choices that you did make for which you now refuse responsibility.

Since childhood puts all children at such a disadvantage, most or all children come out with a great many cowardly and self-destructive decisions that they do not wish to face.

Young girls decide that all men are bad and that they will get even with them when they grow up; or they decide that men are better than women and must be submitted to. Young boys decide the same things about women. Children decide that it is better to lie than to take the consequences; or they decide to always tell the truth, even if it threatens their survival. They decide to avoid hard work for fear of failure, or they decide to work at things they hate to please their parents. They decide to hide their feelings from themselves, or they decide to flaunt their feelings to everyone. They decide never to give love to anyone, or to give love to people who cannot love them back. They decide to wantonly hurt people whom they feel have hurt them, or they decide never to hurt anyone, even in self-defense. They choose lifestyles of personal failure in which helplessness replaces self-determination and self-hate replaces self-love. Almost every destructive lifestyle can be traced from adulthood back to crucial decisions made in childhood.

In evaluating a person's denial of personal participation in his or her growth and development, it is important to distinguish between the person who says, "I had very few alternatives to choose among, given my circumstances," and the person who says, "I didn't make choices." The first person accurately describes the situation of the typical child — choice in the face of limited alternatives and frequent cruel oppression. When this individual grows older, he or she may then be able to take advantage of increasing liberty. But the person who denies the existence of any choices in childhood has denied himself or herself as a human being and will be inflexibly unable to take advantage of increasing power and freedom as an adult.

Adult life, as well as childhood, holds many threats, including loss of love, loss of job, and death; the grown adult can always feel justified in continuing to claim, "I have no choice." You will always have excuses for not making a choice — should you look for those excuses. At no point does life become easy as we grow up, and sometimes it becomes more difficult.

"So I could have confronted my parents and risked going unfed or unloved?" That was your choice, and choices as difficult as this abound in adulthood if you try to live your life to the fullest. There will always be threats against your survival and your integrity as you stand up for your principles. In this, adulthood differs little from childhood. For some who have been blessed with decent childhoods, adulthood may offer even less security. Bravery is always required to achieve liberty and love within one's own life.

Most of us who have survived childhood have a lot to learn about being brave in the pursuit of liberty and love. We have much to learn about our self-betrayals and our betrayers; we have to throw off an enormous legacy of childhood fear and helplessness.

Choosing a Career You Love

Because we have free will and make choices in every aspect of our lives, we inevitably bring forth our own special contribution to life. This is true in our jobs as well as our family and love lives. Some of us create order and sanity; some bring chaos and craziness. Some of us add to life; and some detract. Some create beauty; and some make a mess.

If you find yourself denying that you are creative in your work, instead give your attention to how disappointed you are with your creations. If your job appears devoid of creativity, take an honest look at how you are contributing to the bleakness, sterility, or boredom. If you discover the situation really lacks what you're looking for, you must face the challenge of seeking a new job or a better profession. Find one that you love!

Commitment to work or to one's profession is identical in most respects to commitment to another person or unconditional love. In therapy, I have often watched the individual struggle with a major decision regarding his or her career in much the same fashion as a person struggles with a decision to love a man or a woman. Often the two crises are faced at the same moment by a person eager to transform his or her life for the better, and it is not uncommon to see a person find romantic love and a happier career during the same period of time.

Career choice is often as frightening as falling in love. A successful lawyer with a large firm decides to strike out on his own. A student with proven accomplishments in many fields decides to opt for a very risky future as a musician. A woman gives up the safer gratifications of family life to venture into the business world. Another woman decides to give up a professional career to become a housewife and must face calumny from her "liberated" friends. A young man who has been told he is stupid decides to apply to college. A person from the lower class decides to throw off his self-image of poor boy as he gives up a secure job in favor of a risky business opportunity. A government bureaucrat decides to take a stand that threatens his career but promotes his values.

Professional choices often remind me of the old dilemma: whether to marry the safe and dependable person or to opt for the one who really excites you. Most people seek safety rather than love in their families and in their careers. It is no wonder they become mired down in badly compromised and boring family and professional relationships.

Young people on the threshold of choosing whether or not to pursue their true professional aspirations must fight the threat of family disapproval, the fear of competition, and the prevailing cynicism that says a person cannot love his or her work. Older men and women who yearn to change their professions must overcome the fear that it is too late. Some adults must face the dilemma of depriving their families in the pursuit of a financially uncertain future.

Financial insecurity is by no means the major psychological barrier that the person of any age must confront in pursuing his or her career. This becomes obvious when my client will be receiving a government pension, with enormous security in the form of a guaranteed salary, and yet feels afraid to spend his or her next twenty "retirement" years developing a long-lost occupational dream. Often an older woman with a successful husband faces the same situation as her children grow up and leave home. She still lacks the courage to pursue her latent ambitions, even though she no longer needs to fear financial insecurity. Before you dismiss your professional aspirations on the grounds that you can't afford the financial risk or loss, make sure you are being honest.

Failures in personal and family relationships seem to play a far more important role in psychological collapse than do failures in the career world, at least among middle- and upper-class people. This is probably because our entire character and outlook on the world has begun to form long before we develop any ideas about work. We develop our personalities in relation to our mothers, fathers, and siblings, not in relation to our teachers, bosses, or coworkers in later life. We bring disturbed personal relationships into our educational and professional lives, rather than the reverse.

Nonetheless, there are many times when career issues are extremely important and seem to play a major role in the development of personal failure. Usually there are special circumstances to account for it. A young man who grows up in poverty has a great deal of trouble changing his expectations for himself. Or having changed his expectations, he has a great deal of difficulty getting any enjoyment out of his work because he so greatly fears that failure will land him in the lower classes again. Or perhaps he has grown up in an upper-class family that put a high priority on certain kinds of business or professional work, while he wants to do something more personally satisfying but below his family's financial or social standards. Or perhaps a woman wants to pursue a career in defiance of what she has been taught about women both in her family and in school. Perhaps a black person wants to compete in an arena previously closed to his or her race.

Many of these conflicts originate in the social and political system, but the most oppressive impact is often transmitted to the child by the parents in an almost indelible fashion during the impressionable first years of life. The victim of poverty, racism, or sexism must come to grips with the fearful, cautious, and self-demeaning attitudes of his or her own parents, or political consciousness by itself may not free this person from a lifelong sense of fear and helplessness. Experience has led me to conclude that even when there are great social pressures acting against the person — as the woman or the black who seeks success in a restricted profession — the major psychological or personal struggle will take place between the individual and inhibitions enforced by his or her parents. The major internal struggle will not come in confrontation with the teachers who taught that women or blacks were inferior or limited; nor will it come in facing the propaganda seen on TV. The conflict will be fought over attitudes he or she learned as a small child from the people most important in his or her life — the parents.

Romantic Love and Rebellion against Authority

The pursuit of romantic love reflects a commitment to individuality, choice, and personal freedom. For this reason, the decision to love is among the most revolutionary decisions that two people can make. They become a twosome devoted to personal liberation. Cowardice in facing this revolution leads many people directly into personal failure.

I have already written a great deal about inner struggle in overcoming the fear of loving. In romantic love, the individual must often struggle directly against external authorities. As in *Romeo and Juliet,* parents, church, and state may become involved in manipulating passionate lovers. Often the lovers betray themselves and each other.

Not everyone knuckles under to those forces that would turn us into faceless, nameless, and loveless robots. Some people find the courage to fulfill romantic love. In the most rebellious and self-assertive action of their lives, they marry someone of their own choice — daring to defy their upbringing, their schooling, and every other warning that romantic love is an adolescent phase or a form of insanity.

Romantic love is an ultimate expression of individualism. It declares that life really matters and that one's own wishes and those of another person take precedent over tradition, parents, fears of loss, personal problems of all kinds, and death itself. I say death itself, because to love one person so intensely is to defy the threat of loss through death.

Because romantic love so fully expresses our desires for personal freedom and individual choice, romantic love is the enemy of all totalitarian religions and governments. China, the last word in totalitarianism, exemplifies this. Personal relationships take a back seat to the requirements of government control, and romantic love is discouraged.

The literature of romantic love recognizes its antiestablishment and rebellious nature. The star-crossed lovers cannot get together because of parental resistance, conflicting nationalities, racial or social distinctions, prearranged marriages, or other external forces or establishment values that seek to control the individual.

Knowing Human Reality

Our view of reality is heavily influenced by childhood. Our ability to achieve new and more accurate perceptions and understandings will depend upon how much or how little we have compromised our ability to reason and to love as we have grown from childhood to adulthood.

When we speak of an individual losing touch with reality or becoming crazy, we are usually referring to a very specific aspect of reality — human relationships. We do not become alienated, crazy, or unreal in our feelings as a result of encounters with mountains, trees, or automobiles. All disturbances that we label "out of touch with reality" involve persons, or *human* reality.

In the psychology of self-determination, *knowledge of human reality* is defined as follows:

> knowledge of the actual or true nature of people, including human nature or the shared qualities of people, as well as the unique qualities of individuals; knowledge of the subjective experience of oneself and others.

Both liberty and love play key roles in providing an opportunity to gain knowledge of reality. In the absence of liberty, or in the presence of coercion and oppression, individuals tend to hide from each other. Victims of oppression must hide their feelings and thoughts in order to protect themselves. They must give the impression required by their oppressors — they must be good prisoners, good mental patients, or good children — or risk serious consequences.

The oppressors as well must hide many of their own feelings. They do not wish to "give away" any information that might help the victims undermine their authority, and they must hide from themselves their own more sympathetic feelings toward their victims. Oppressors also try to categorize their victims as "prisoners" or "mental patients" or "children," without giving them the full range of human qualities. This in part explains why jailers, institutional psychiatrists, and authoritarian parents alike know so little about those over whom they have power. The exercise of coercive authority excludes knowledge of the inner experience of those over whom the power is exercised.

An entire book could be written on this theme — involuntary relationships breed a lack of knowledge about the reality of the human beings within the relationships. Oppressors and the victims alike develop strange and inaccurate perceptions of each other and of themselves. This is as true between parents and children or between lovers as it is between citizens and their totalitarian rulers.

Love is also very important in understanding reality. In its absence, a great gap is left in one's knowledge of other people. Love fails to flourish in an authoritarian or coercive setting, and this compounds the ignorance of human reality generated within such settings. Love enables people to open up to each other more and increases their understanding of the inherent or potential goodness of human beings.

Understanding reality at its most basic level involves recognizing the existence of other human beings. The failure to recognize the existence of other human beings is closely related to the unwillingness to love others or to grant them liberty. It manifests itself subtly in denials, devaluations, or distortions of another person's inner experience and natural rights. There is a tendency to discount or demean the importance of what another person feels or thinks. In the extreme, there develops a conviction that other people do not exist. A surprising number of people have a profound sense that they are the only ones alive or the only ones who have feelings or moral sensitivity.

People who fail to perceive reality may exclude either good or evil from their knowledge. Often they see only evil, malevolent, destructive intentions in themselves and others. Often they see only emptiness. But sometimes they go to the other extreme and see only "love" and "goodness" all around them.

There is an important place for a knowledge of evil in anyone's perception of reality, if only for the person to be able to protect himself or herself from force and fraud. Women who grow up "overprotected," denying the nature of evil, become easy pickings for con men when their paternalistic parents or husbands are no longer there to protect them.

The challenge is to recognize evil without succumbing to it and without becoming frustrated, bitter, depressed, or otherwise morally helpless.

Freedom from Authority

By now it must be obvious that I have a seldom expressed view of authority

— I don't believe in it. I say "seldom expressed" because I believe that, deep within every individual, a libertarian heart beats to its own rhythm and resents the imposition of any arbitrary, irrational authority.

By "arbitrary, irrational authority" I mean any authority, except one whose purpose is limited to *the enforcement of liberty and the protection of the individual from force and fraud.* Very, very few authorities limit themselves to such a narrow spectrum as the defense of the individual from aggression. In reality, most authorities actively transgress against individual freedom, and most perpetrate fraud of one kind or another.

There are many different kinds of authority, but for my purposes I shall distinguish between the authority of expertise, moral authority, and political authority. The authority of expertise has nothing to do with the other two. It is authority based upon knowledge or skill, it has no inherent capacity to control or to abuse anyone, and it may be accepted or rejected by every individual. I may think I am an "authority" on a given subject, but you do not have to accept my viewpoint.

Moral authority is always oppressive. A moral authority is any individual, group, or institution that seeks to control others by means of emotional, psychological, or spiritual pressure and manipulation. Most forms of psychotherapy, most aspects of psychiatry in general, nearly all religions, and most parents are moral authorities. Moral authorities do not appeal to the individual's capacity to reason or to love, or they do so merely for propaganda purposes. Beneath their veneer they rely upon guilt, shame, and anxiety, as well as outright fear, to control the individual. A moral authority thrives not by offering something rational but by threatening something terrible, such as everlasting hell, ostracism, hopelessness, or a guilty conscience.

When moral authority gains the power to coerce through the legitimized use of force, it becomes political authority. In many parts of the world, the moral authority of religion is backed up by state laws. In all parts of the world, psychiatry's moral authority is enforced by its capacity to lock up and to treat people against their will. But the ultimate political authority is, of course, the state itself. Every human being on earth is born into a state that assumes that it can exercise part or even whole ownership of the individual through various laws controlling his or her life and property. That nearly all people, including most establishment philosophers and political scientists, have assumed the rightness of this situation in no way obscures its foundation of force.*

---

*For a philosophic justification of libertarianism and the limited state, see Robert Nozick, *Anarchy, State and Utopia* (1974), and for less technical, general introductions to libertarian politics, see Murray Rothbard, *For a New Liberty* (1973), David Friedman, *The Machinery of Freedom* (1973), or Roger MacBride, *A New Dawn for America* (1976). None of these excellent books completely reflects my own focus on bringing more humanistic attitudes into political libertarianism. (See Breggin, "Why Libertarians Need Humanists" (1979), and "Libertarianism and the Liberal Ethos" (1979) in the bibliography.) Many of my colleagues, friends, and clients have found my psychology of self-determination useful in their personal lives without necessarily

There is another kind of authority so rare that it must be examined as a separate category, and that is freely contracted libertarian authority. You or I may choose to subject ourselves to a system of authority out of our own self-interest. For example, if you and I disagree about the terms of a contract to which we are parties, we might subject ourselves to the binding arbitration of a trusted third party. Freely contracted libertarian authority is the *only* authority that I choose to recognize as legitimate in my own life. I do not even recognize freely chosen nonlibertarian authorities, for I do not believe that a person who contracts to be a slave should feel obliged to fulfill the contract.

These obviously are very complex questions with many ethical and political ramifications. I am not attempting to develop a coherent political philosophy in these brief pages but to establish some guidelines with vast practical implications in everyday life. Neither you nor I should feel bound to obey any authority, except as it reflects our own freely chosen commitment to the ideals of liberty. This means that you and I are in no way bound to obey *any* of the major authorities on earth today — all of whom maintain themselves by means of emotional and physical force.

I am not advocating continuous open rebellion against all the authorities on earth. This would be foolhardy and self-destructive. I *am* encouraging each of us as individuals to see with clear eyes the reality of the oppressive institutions that surround us and, whenever possible, to act on our own behalf to avoid the worst influences of these institutions. I am speaking out for *reason* and *individual conscience* instead of blind compliance.

Many people fear that such an attitude will lead to disastrous social consequences. Authority, it is thought, protects us from our baser instincts and desires, but instead it encourages our basest desires to be helpless and fearful. State authority, for example, has for centuries played on fear and helplessness in order to encourage submissiveness among its citizens.

Psychological freedom is freedom from the influence of irrational or oppressive authority—both external authority as it exists in the real world and internalized authority as it exists within the person's mind as self-oppression learned at the hands of childhood authorities. Self-liberation is liberation from all authority except the authority of one's own rationality.

Some people fear that this viewpoint will lead children to grow up unprepared for the realities of life. Actually, this philosophy prepares children to deal with the reality of oppressive authority. A child who understands

---

agreeing with my libertarian politics. I have been able to carry out libertarian principles in my own life and in my psychotherapy practice and know from direct experience that these principles encourage a maximally productive and happy life for the individual and for those who depend upon the individual. It has never been possible to test libertarian political principles in so complete a manner, and so I remain a political libertarian who advocates a general thrust toward limiting state power, while awaiting future results before determining with any finality how far or in what manner the principles may be extended.

authority can deal with it more rationally and effectively. There is no greater risk on earth than to grow up with blind obedience and trust in the authority of religion, the state, or a charismatic leader.

These are topics about which much has been written; and, again, I do not wish to defend an overall political ideology but rather to remind us as individuals that we did not choose the religions and the states into which we were born and that these institutions should be evaluated against the standards of liberty and love. When authorities fail to meet our standards, and when we realize that we did not freely choose them in the first place, these authorities lose their moral hold over us. We no longer feel bound to them by guilt, shame, and anxiety. We recognize them for what they are and allow them only as great a hold on us as they are able to maintain through outright force. We maintain our personal sovereignty, even though we find our personal freedom vastly compromised. We can then choose to relate to these authorities when we desire to, or when we must, while we reserve within ourselves the right to escape from their oppressive influences whenever possible.

To live life fully and rationally, the individual must recognize his or her own rationality as the final authority in all matters of personal importance.

The Personal and the Political

Human action is governed by the same principles, whether in the arena of personal life or political life. The twin principles of libertarianism are a belief in free will and a belief in the individual's right to express free will through personal freedom. This means that the individual must be free to create voluntary relationships, to pursue self-interest, and to advocate personal ideals. He or she must be limited only by the injunction against the use of force or fraud in achieving his or her own ends. This philosophy has obvious political applications and, in fact, has been much more extensively applied to the world of politics.

Although I have been a stern critic of many American institutions, especially my own profession of psychiatry, I believe that America today provides one of the last arenas for whatever freedom exists in the world today. The Declaration of Independence and the Bill of Rights are still the highest expressions of political freedom in the world today; and though America rushes headlong toward increasing totalitarianism through the burgeoning of bureaucratic government control, America still remains among the freest nations on earth. My hope is that we may yet reverse our growing betrayal of liberty and individualism.

The personal and the political are inextricably intertwined. If the government of the United States suddenly began to reaffirm the principles of "life, liberty, and the pursuit of happiness," sending Big Brother into retreat, many of our citizens would find themselves hopelessly mired in personal helplessness. Before long, we would be moving again toward big, paternalistic government and the erosion of our liberties. So self-oppressed are most of our citizens that they would seek a return to oppression as their only "safe" way of life.

Oppression must be simultaneously attacked within both the personal and the political arenas. We must develop a renewed commitment to political freedom, and at the same time we must develop a better understanding of personal sovereignty and personal freedom.

True political freedom may not come for hundreds of years. Perhaps it will never come in the history of the earth and humankind. But the individual can nonetheless keep his or her ideals alive and can make the most of whatever freedom can be maintained or created during his or her own lifetime. Happily, most of us in the Western world still have a sufficient measure of political freedom to determine the success of a large portion of our lives.

The relationship between the personal and the political provides one more opportunity to ask that most difficult question, "Should the individual exclusively pursue self-interest?" In regard to politics, we may ask if it is not right and just for the person to make personal sacrifices in the struggle for human liberty.

I have made sacrifices of income, personal security, and overall happiness by taking on the psychiatric and governmental establishment. But, as I stand here at the midpoint of life, I would never suggest to anyone I love that he or she make similar sacrifices. I am not sure that I would do it the same way over again. My own increasing self-love, as well as my love for my family, encourages me to take better care of myself in my current political pursuits.

Perhaps at an earlier age, my own sense of identity, and hence my own happiness, was wrapped up in taking risks for the sake of my ideals. Certainly I learned and grew a great deal. But life should begin with self-love and then grow toward love for others. In that process of growing love for life, some of us do gain satisfaction from joining in the struggle for liberty.

For those of us who can find joy and satisfaction in the fight for political liberty, such activities make sense. For those who cannot find joy in them, they are self-defeating. Each person owns himself or herself. Neither reason nor experience tells me that a person must join in the fight for human liberty. Some of the finest people I know don't give a hoot about political action, while some others devote much of their life work to the cause of liberty. Reason and experience do tell me that the fight for human liberty can be very interesting, worthwhile, and exciting. That is the best way to enter the larger struggle for human liberty: as a personally satisfying experience.

Epilogue

You Own Yourself

You own yourself; you possess yourself; you belong to yourself. You have all the rights pertaining to your use of yourself. You are your own natural resource, your own and sole source of life energy. You have complete rights to yourself.

You are your most private property. You have the right to create your own life, and you have the right to end it. Your attitudes, your thoughts, your feelings, your conduct in the face of good times and bad times — all this is your own creation. You can improve upon your life, or you can waste it. It is yours.

Never compromise the knowledge or conviction that you have the right to self-ownership. That you are in your own hands makes life interesting and worthwhile. Life is meaningful because human beings are responsible for what they do with their lives. We know we are responsible for ourselves and will judge ourselves accordingly.

If this sounds true to you, consider the conclusion you must draw from it: other people own themselves.

Combined with the principle that you own yourself, this second principle gives you sufficient basis to determine all the important rules of liberty, love, and life. It tells you that you can do anything you want with yourself as long as you respect the equal right of every other person on this earth.

Think of the glorious implications of self-ownership. No one has the right to try to make you feel helpless, weak, or small. No one has the right to impose anything upon you or to use you in any way against your will.

You in turn can do anything you want except oppose another person's self-ownership. Beyond that, your rights are limitless and perhaps infinite, for you have the right to whatever you can get from life — to do what you value, to seek out challenges that excite you, to love those people whom you truly value, and to maximize your personal freedom. However unique, unusual, personal, or idiosyncratic your ambitions, you have the right to pursue them. However selfish, nonconformist, or strange your ideals, they are yours.

You have the right to one of life's most glorious experiences — a face-to-face, loving encounter with another free human being who chooses to be with you, to share with you, and to create love with you. You have the right to choose a creative and satisfying occupation for yourself — a job or task that commands your interest and promotes your values. You have the right to join others in the promotion of human liberty if you so choose.

Too many of us walk around too much of the time living as if others own us. We feel guilt, shame, and anxiety over every conflict with another human being and are forever placating others out of these corrupt emotions. We end up hating ourselves and other persons, much as slaves must end up hating themselves and their masters as well. Just like all other slaves, we end up limiting our own love for life and hence our production and creativity, for we resent slaving for others. We rob ourselves and the world of the best we have to offer.

As slaves, we also walk through life seeking others more slavish than ourselves whom we, in turn, can own or dominate. As parents who have bent before our own domineering parents, we try to make our children bend before us. As slaves we demand help from others, whether or not the help is freely given. We want love even if the other person does not find us lovable. We want financial income even if we do not want to work. We want fame and glory without taking risks and without making great contributions. We want others to feel coerced by our own fears and our own losses. We are too afraid and too hateful to stare a free human being in the eye. We are other-determined.

The world seems to do everything in its power to take away our ownership of ourselves. The average person is surrounded by persons who want to own him or her — parents, spouse, boss, and religious and political leaders. You will have to decide whether you want to be owned. But that is easy — of course you don't. You want to do things freely and by choice. This means that you must decide if you are willing to face the consequences of fighting those who aspire to own you. It may mean leaving your marriage or leaving your job. It may also mean changing your religious or political views.

Liberating yourself may cause pain to your spouse, your friends, and your bosses. They may attempt to make you feel so guilty, ashamed, or anxious that you won't dare leave. But remember that they feel your loss much as slaveholders feel the loss of runaway or rebelling slaves. It is the slaver's ethical dilemma, not yours.

You may find that your spouse, your friend, or your boss decides to change his or her own life for the better when confronted with your determination to own yourself. You may get the dividend of helping liberate someone else. But don't compromise yourself by making your own freedom contingent upon another person's discovery of freedom. Don't mortgage self-ownership to such a hope. Take your freedom! It is your right. Then welcome and seek out others who share your belief in self-ownership.

I'm not the only other person in the world who believes in his right to own himself. You will find many others, once you have declared which side you are on. If anything, you will find it is less lonely in the world once you decide that you own yourself — for it will enable you to seek out other persons more freely and more independently.

The principle of self-ownership means we must treat all other beings with absolute respect for their rights. You literally have no claim whatsoever on the lives of others. You can only relate to them when, where, and how they want you to; otherwise, you must let them be. You must treat them with respect for their self-ownership or not at all. This is what is meant by voluntary exchange. It is exchange based upon mutual self-interest between sovereign persons.

Love itself is made more pure within the ideal of self-ownership. You may love and appreciate whomever you please, but your love can only be fulfilled through voluntary exchange. You cannot impose a relationship upon the loved person, no matter how much you need or desire your loved one. I can imagine no psychology or philosophy based upon less selfish principles of love. It is a selfish philosophy and psychology only in the best sense of the word — respect for the rights of every self or person in the universe.

The psychology and the politics of freedom are derived from the inherent right of *every* individual to exercise free will in the determination of his or her own life. The freedom-loving individual does not believe that he or she alone has been mysteriously chosen to be free. He or she believes in the right of each person to pursue self-interest and his or her own ideals.

Liberty is the context within which each individual can best develop himself or herself. Love is the liberated individual's affirmation of life. Liberty and love are the twin principles of the good and happy life.

SELECTED BIBLIOGRAPHY OF THE AUTHOR

FICTION

Breggin, Peter R. *The Crazy from the Sane.* New York: Lyle Stuart, 1971.

Breggin, Peter R. *After the Good War: A Love Story.* New York: Stein and Day, 1972; Popular Library Edition (paperback), 1972.

NONFICTION

Breggin, Peter R. "The College Student and the Mental Patient." In *College Student Companion Program, Contribution to the Social Rehabilitation of the Mentally Ill.* Rockville, Maryland: National Institute of Mental Health, 1962.

Umbarger, C.; Dalsimer, J.; Morrison, A.; and Breggin, P. *College Students in a Mental Hospital.* New York: Grune and Stratton, 1962.

Breggin, Peter R. "The Psychophysiology of Anxiety." *Journal of Nervous and Mental Diseases* 139 (1964): 558-568.

Breggin, Peter R. "Coercion of Voluntary Patients in an Open Hospital." *A.M.A. Archives of General Psychiatry* 10 (1964): 173-181.

Breggin, Peter R. "The Sedative-like Effect of Epinephrine." *A.M.A. Archives of General Psychiatry* 12 (1965): 255-259.

Breggin, Peter R. "The Borderland of Criminal Justice." *Journal of Nervous and Mental Diseases* 141 (1965): 387-394.

Breggin, Peter R. "Psychotherapy as Applied Ethics." *Psychiatry* 34 (1971): 59-75.

Breggin, Peter R. "The Return of Lobotomy and Psychosurgery." *Congressional Record*, February 24, 1972, E1602-E1612. Reprinted in *Quality of Health Care — Human Experimentation*. Hearings before Senator Edward Kennedy's Subcommittee on Health, United States Senate. Washington, D.C.: U.S. Government Printing Office, 1973.

Breggin, Peter R. "Lobotomy Is Still Bad Medicine." *Medical Opinion*, March 1972.

Breggin, Peter R. "The Politics of Therapy." *M/H (Mental Health)* 56 (1972): 9-13.

Breggin, Peter R. "The Second Wave of Psychosurgery." *M/H (Mental Health)* 57 (1973): 10-13. Reprinted in French in *La Folie II*. Edited by A. Verdiglione. Paris: Union Generale D'Editions, 1976.

Breggin, Peter R. "Therapy as Applied Utopian Politics." *Mental Health and Society* 1 (1974): 129-146.

Breggin, Peter R., and Breggin, Phyllis. "Psychiatric Oppression of Prisoners." *Psychiatric Opinion*, June 1974.

Breggin, Peter R. "Psychosurgery for Political Purposes." *Duquesne Law Review* 13 (1975): 841-862.

Breggin, Peter R. "Psychosurgery for the Control of Violence: A Critical Review." Chapter XVI in *Neural Bases of Violence and Aggression*. Edited by W. Fields and W. Sweet. St. Louis, Mo.: Warren H. Green, 1975.

Breggin, Peter R. "Psychiatry and Psychotherapy as Political Processes." *American Journal of Psychotherapy* 29 (1975): 369-382.

Breggin, Peter R. "Needed: Voluntaristic Psychiatry." *Reason*, September 1975.

Breggin, Peter R. "Why We Consent to Oppression." *Reason*, September 1977.

Breggin, Peter R. "If Psychosurgery Is Wrong in Principle . . . ?" *Psychiatric Opinion*, November/December 1977.

Breggin, Peter R. "Madness Is a Failure of Free Will; Therapy Too Often Encourages It." In *La Folie Dans La Psychanalyse*. Edited by A. Verdiglione. Paris: Payot, 1977 (in French). Reprinted in *Psychiatric Quarterly* as "A Libertarian View of Psychology and Psychiatry" (tentative title), 1980-1981, in press.

Breggin, Peter R. "The Psychiatric Holocaust." *Penthouse*, January 1979. Revised and reprinted in *Reason*, 1980, in press.

Breggin, Peter R. "A Libertarian Psychology: Self-Ownership—A Condition for Happiness." *The Humanist*, May/June 1979.

Breggin, Peter R. "Psychiatry in Retreat." *Libertarian Review*, May 1979.

Breggin, Peter R. "Liberalism and the Liberal Ethos." *Libertarian Review*, November 1979.

Breggin, Peter R. "Why Libertarians Need Humanists." *Frontlines*, November 1979.

Breggin, Peter R. *Electroshock: Its Brain-Disabling Effects*. New York: Springer, 1979.

Breggin, Peter R. "Brain-Disabling Therapies." In *The Psychosurgery Debate*. Edited by E. Valenstein. New York: W.H. Freeman, 1980.

Recorded Speeches and Workshops

Breggin, Peter R. "Libertarian Foundations for Personal Conduct," "How to Help Yourself and Others with Personal Problems," "Romantic Love, Bodily Sex and Freedom," "Raising Free and Happy Children," "Gay Love and Gay Sex," "Psychiatric Oppression," "Brain-Disabling Therapy," and other tapes on psychology and psychiatry. New York: Audio-Forum (145 East 49th Street, New York, N.Y. 10017), 1972-1980.